my own

I'll Love Ye Forever

*A Mother and Daughter's Journey
Through Long Term Care*

Sally K. Browne

ISBN 978-1540677273

Cover photo by David Browne
Cover design by Joe Burbank

Disclaimer

This book is a story about the author's mother and aunt during their "golden years." The conversations and events in the book all come from the author's memory. While the gist of the stories are true, the dialogue is not intended to be verbatim. The author has told the stories in a way that kindles the emotions and significance of what transpired. The names of people and places have been changed to protect the privacy of those involved, although similar stories are taking place across our country as you read these words.

This book is not intended as a substitute for the medical advice of physicians. The reader should always rely on the advice of his or her health care provider for any symptoms that may need medical attention.

Visit the author's website at sandwichedboomer.com

Dedication

To Mom and Aunt Delia
and to David, Michael, and Kathleen

Contents

Acknowledgements

A big thank you to my family and friends who encouraged me to tell this story—David, Michael, Kathleen, Amy Hermesch, Kim Gardner, Paula Brodkin, Ninetta and David Sevigny, Maryellen Bettis, Pamm Dwyer, Julie Poyer, Monica Godby, and Judy Kesselman. After you each read my manuscript you enthusiastically kept the fire lit under me to get the book published.

My gratitude also goes to John Browne for his time and his help with technical issues, to Brendan Linnane for his sage advice with legal questions, and to Pastor Robert Garment for writing the beautiful Foreword to my book.

Most of all, a very special thank you goes to my husband, David, for all his love and support during our "nursing home years." I could not have done it without him.

Foreword

If you are expecting a foreword written by someone famous, or someone who is the world's leading authority on the theme of this book, prepare to be disappointed. My chief credential for introducing this book is more than forty years of friendship with the author. Sally Browne and my wife were high school friends. (I met Sally and my wife the same day in the place where the three of us worked.) We went to the same college, took part in each other's weddings, celebrated together the arrival of our children, and wept together at our families' funerals. I could recommend this book based solely on my professional involvement in guiding families through endless decisions about the care of aging loved ones. Nevertheless, my highest recommendation of Sally Browne's work is based on having witnessed this narrative unfold among people I love.

This is not a novel. The characters in this book are quite real. That reality takes on even deeper meaning for me since I can hear their voices, remember their faces, sense their unspoken feelings, and smile at the memory of stories not recorded in this volume.

My purpose in stressing that intimacy of friendship is not to claim some preferred status over the reader who is about to meet this family for the first time. On the contrary, it is intended to serve as an invitation to join this extended family with me. For the duration of this unique narrative, I invite you to move into the lives of the Brownes and their extended family. Make them your family and loved ones as you take this journey with them. Experience the joys and challenges with them, for the time may well come when you embark on a similar journey with your own family.

I'll Love Ye Forever is not an exposé of nursing homes, rehab centers, or any institutional elder care in America, though it is packed with valuable information about how our health care system works. Neither does it describe a unique chain of events for just one family.

As I have worked as a pastor, a hospital chaplain, and a family counselor, I have watched the scenes in this book play out a thousand times over. The circumstances differ, but the challenges are all too predictable. Caring for an aging loved one requires navigating a labyrinth of policies, procedures, prejudices, and dangerous assumptions. Every twist and turn of events assaults the mind and heart with confusion, fear, anger, frustration, and a fatigue which threatens to exhaust one's very soul.

The story you are about to read cannot prepare you for when your family faces similar challenges. There are no pat answers in this book, but there are flashes of insight, small victories, and countless examples of courage.

Consider this a spoiler alert if you like, because there is one overriding truth that Sally Browne's story will demonstrate. In every case like this one, where we are challenged to be advocates in unfamiliar settings, there is only one tool which can bring lasting healing—the unrelenting and determined love of family. For that reason, the truth and value of this narrative is best summarized in its very title, *I'll Love Ye Forever*.

Reverend Robert Garment is an ordained minister in the Evangelical Presbyterian Church, a member of the American Association of Christian Counselors, and a Board Certified Pastoral Counselor.

Preface

Even though we've never met, I think you're a lot like me in one way or another. I'm married, raising kids, and I work full time. I've been on a journey for a while now and if you're a baby boomer, you may have already taken a similar trip with an elderly parent. If you came after the "boomer" generation, one day you will probably walk the same well-worn path that I've been on.

During the last two years that my elderly mother lived in her own home, I did my best to help her stay at home. She never wanted to go into long term care. Sadly, however, we don't always get what we want. She ended up living the last two and a half years of her life in long term care. During that time I visited her daily and was her advocate. I learned volumes during those years, and I sincerely believe that because of me she got the best care that she could have gotten. This is not a "how to" book. It is simply a mother and daughter's love story, and what I did to make the best of a not great situation.

This journey that I shared with my mother was a bittersweet experience for me, but if I could go back in time and change my destiny, I would do it all again. In my heart of hearts, I know that I made a positive difference in her life. I have no doubt that she would have done the same for me.

Chapter 1

It Wasn't in the Plans

"Matt, I'm sorry but I need to take another long lunch break today. If it's okay with you, I'd like to leave around 11:30 to get to my mother's nursing home in time for her lunch. And then after I see her, I really need to check on my aunt on my way back to the office. She's not doing well either," I explained to my boss, and then continued, "I'm sorry. I know that this has been happening a lot lately."

"Sally, don't worry about it. It's not a problem. I know that you have everything under control here. Do what you need to do and I'll see you when you get back. You know your family comes first. It's almost 11:30. Why don't you go ahead and leave now," he said.

"Thank you so much. And thanks for not making me feel guilty about work. That helps me more than you'll ever know," I said. Then I went back into my office, grabbed my purse and headed to my car.

As I drove the 20-minute drive to the Calafort nursing home I noticed how dark the sky was getting and I had a feeling that we were in for a downpour. Darn, I should've brought an umbrella with me, especially since I needed to make two stops before going back to work. The way that things had been going lately, I'd probably be soaked before I got back to the office.

When I reached Calafort, I walked down the long hall-way leading to my mother's room just as quickly as I could go. Sadly, I could hear her, long before I could see her, and before she saw me. I heard her pathetically calling my name, "Sally, Sally, Sally." I wondered how long she'd been calling for me. In her heart and soul, she knew that I was the one person who could help her, and so she called my name over and over again.

I knew that she was annoying to the staff, but I really didn't care anymore. She was the only person in that building that I worried about. I prayed that they took good care of her when I wasn't there, but unfortunately they'd given me reasons to have my doubts.

I stopped to compose myself before I turned the corner where I knew she was sitting in her wheelchair. I took a deep breath, put a big smile on my face, and walked towards her. The second she saw me she started to cry and tried to lift her arms to hug me. Pitifully she asked, "Baby, how did ye find me? Where have ye been? How did ye know where I was?"

I bent over and hugged her for a minute until she calmed down and then I squatted to be at the same level as her and said, "Mom, you never have to worry that I won't be able to find you. I always, always know where you are and I will always come to see you. I was here yesterday and I'll be here tomorrow, and the next day and the next day. I promise you, I always know where you are. You're safe here, Mom."

As many times as this scene had played out before, it never got any easier for me. There are few things sadder in life than to look into your mother's eyes and to see fear looking back at you. She couldn't help it. She didn't understand. My mother would never do anything to hurt me, not in a million years.

After a few more minutes of consoling her, I said, "Mom, I'm going to talk to your nurse for just a minute. I'll turn your chair around so you can see me, okay?"

"Sure, Baby, ye know what's best," she said.

I wished that I knew what was best. I wished that I knew what I could do to help her, but I didn't. All I could do was to use my common sense and to question all the things that didn't seem right to me that the doctors and the nurses and the CNAs (certified nursing assistants) didn't question.

"Sandi, did she eat today?" I asked her nurse.

"No, just the instant breakfast drink and a little thickened juice and thickened water," she answered.

"My God, it's closer to two months than one month, since she's eaten anything. How much longer can she stay alive like this? She's going to starve to death."

"All we can do is to keep trying. I'm not sure why, but your mother is still amazingly strong," Sandi said.

"I guess there is nothing else left to do, but to keep trying, and to keep praying," I said, and then I walked back over to Mom.

The relationship between the staff and me ran the gamut, somewhere between a strong dislike and love. There'd been far too many times that they'd missed huge issues that were important to her well-being. Other times they created problems by things that they proactively did. At the opposite end of the spectrum, they occasionally did something that was surprisingly kind and loving. It puzzled me how ineptness and brilliance could come from the same source.

"Mom, I brought my lunch today. Let's go eat our lunch together in the pretty dining room," I said.

"Whatever ye want to do, Doll," she said. She was so happy to see me.

I wheeled her down to the big dining room where the residents who still had the hope of eventually going back to their own homes dined. This hadn't been my mother's assigned dining room for a long time, but if I was there at mealtime, I'd occasionally still bring her there. It had the look of a nice restaurant, with big windows that looked outside on to a pretty garden. The residents who ate in there fed themselves and socialized with each other. They were categorized as "higher functioning."

The dining room where my mother usually ate was small and crowded. Most of the people who ate in there could no longer feed themselves and so they were fed by the CNAs. I hardly ever heard meaningful conversations going on in that room between the residents. Most of the talk in there was among the CNAs discussing what they did on the weekend, what they'd watched on TV, where they wanted to go for lunch, or other conversations of that nature. Seldom did I hear them trying to engage the residents in small talk.

"Look, Mom. I brought a salad from home for me to eat. What can I get for you?" I always brought a lunch with me because I thought that if she saw me eating, that might encourage her to eat, too.

"Baby, I'm not hungry now. I'll just watch ye eat. I'll fix a big supper for myself tonight."

I wished that I could go inside her head and figure out what in the world she was thinking. Did she think that she really was going to cook herself supper tonight? Did she think that I believed her?

"Mom, I'm going to run into the kitchen and get you some mashed potatoes. I know that you love the mashed potatoes that they make here. I'll be right back," I said, in hopes of getting her to eat something.

I hurried to the kitchen and they gave me a small dish of mashed potatoes. When I brought it back to the table and tried to feed it to her, she just clenched her lips closed and said once again that she wasn't hungry and wasn't going to eat anything. She insisted, however, that I eat my lunch because I looked like I was getting too thin.

"I'm not getting too thin at all. Actually, I think that I'm finding the weight that you're losing," I said, but she didn't see the humor in my joke.

I would have loved to have lingered over a leisurely lunch with my mother but I knew that I still needed to see her sister, my Aunt Delia, and then I had to get back to work. After I finished eating, I quickly slugged down the water in my water bottle.

She looked at me and said, "Honey, are ye sure it's okay that ye drink all that?"

"Yea, why?" I asked.

"Aren't ye going back to the office or are ye finished for the day? I don't want ye having an accident driving back," she said.

It took me a moment before I realized what she meant. "Mom, do you think that I have booze in my water bottle?"

"Well, don't ye?" she asked.

I laughed and it felt good. There wasn't much laughing going on in that place. "Ma, I promise that I won't be drinking and driving." I gave her a hug and then brought her back to where I found her nearly an hour earlier.

"I wish that I could stay longer but I really have to get back to work," I said.

"Will I see ye later today?" she asked.

"I'd love to come but when I get off work I need to go home 'cause I have a lot to do this evening," I said.

"I know that you're busy. Ye have a husband and a family. Go straight home to them when ye get off from the job," she said.

"Thanks, Mom. I love you," I said as I squeezed her hands.

"I love ye, too, Baby. God knew what He was doing when He gave ye to me," she answered.

"Ah, Mom," I said, as I leaned over and gave her another hug. "See you tomorrow."

"Safe journey," she added. That's an old Irish blessing that she often said as I was leaving her.

As I headed down the hallway I turned around one last time while she could still see me. I blew her a kiss as she waved goodbye. She looked so small sitting in her wheelchair. *When did she get so small?*

As soon as I walked out the front door I took a deep breath of the fresh non-antiseptic air. I felt bad that she was still inside that building. I wondered how much longer could I keep doing this. It was breaking my heart.

She'd been in there for over two years. I thought that when she went into Calafort for her broken hip that she'd only be there for a few months for physical therapy and rehab. I naïvely thought that eventually she'd be going back home and that she would be her old self again. I'm not sure when I sadly resigned myself to the fact that this is where she would be living out her days.

I suppose I shouldn't have been wondering how long could I continue taking care of her to the extent that I did. The better question was how much longer could my mother keep living this way. I don't mean to sound melodramatic but it was as if she were a prisoner inside the walls of the nursing home. She used to say to me, "Shoot me first. Don't ever put me in a home." I knew she didn't literally mean to shoot her; she was far too religious for that demise, but there wasn't a question in my mind how adamant she was about not going into a nursing home.

No, long term care was definitely not in the plans. I'm so very sorry that I didn't succeed in keeping her out of one. I tried my best, but in the end it became her reality. All I could do at that point in our lives was to help her make the best of it.

As I walked through the parking lot to my car, I could almost smell the rain in the air. I knew that without an umbrella I was going to get drenched before I made it back to work. I decided to swing by my house and get one since it was sort of on the way to see Delia.

When I got home, I ran in and out in less than a minute, relieved to have an umbrella in my hand. As I backed out of the driveway I started to think about all the work that I needed to get done when I got back to my office. I made a mental to-do list as I waited at the light at the end of the street. Then I started thinking about Delia. Things weren't looking so good for her at the moment, either. I had already decided not to tell my mother what had happened to Delia. I didn't see the benefit of telling her.

When the light turned green, I turned left on to the highway. I drove for about a mile, still deep in thought, before I realized that I didn't have a clue on earth where I was going. My God, I couldn't remember where Delia was. Was she still in the hospital? Was she back in her apartment? Was she in the rehab center?

I just saw her yesterday, but for the life of me I couldn't remember where that was. I visited her almost every day. Where was she yesterday? After a few more minutes, I remembered that she was in the hospital, but then I couldn't remember which hospital. There had been so many visits to hospitals over the years between my mother and father and father-in-law and Delia that for that moment they all blended together in my mind.

I started to cry. I was crying not because I didn't know where she was, but because of how bizarre this situation was. I didn't want to have an accident, so I pulled into a parking lot, and I tried to calm myself down. This sort of thing had never happened to me before and it scared me to have such a total loss of my memory. I'd always had a great memory. I was scared because my mother had dementia; my Aunt Kate in Ireland had Alzheimer's. They, too, had excellent memories once upon a time. When did it start with them? How did it start with them?

It would have been easy to dwell on those questions, but I didn't. I sat quietly for just a minute or two, and as soon as I calmed down, I remembered where Delia was. I pulled back onto the road and headed to the hospital, reassured that I didn't have dementia—I just had a hell of a lot on my plate.

I wished that I could share my plate with someone else, but there was nobody else. There was no use dwelling on that either. I just needed to make the best of the cards that I'd been dealt, and to keep on keeping on.

When I finally made it to Delia's hospital room, I only had time for a short visit.

"How's your mother?" she asked. I could see the concern in her beautiful blue eyes.

"She's a little bit better than yesterday," I fibbed.

"Has she eaten yet?" she asked.

"No, she's still only drinking the thickened liquids and the instant breakfast drink; no real food yet," I said.

"Then we can't say that she's getting better," she answered. Delia was a sharp cookie.

"They tell me that the liquids are more important for her now than food is," I told her.

"Pray for her, Sally. Did ye try potatoes on her?" she asked.

"Dee Dee, I pray for both of you every day. And, yes, I tried mashed potatoes but she said that she wasn't hungry. She told me that she'll cook her own supper later."

She slowly shook her head and said, "God help her. I feel very bad for your mother."

I probably told her more than I should have. I didn't want to worry her. She needed to concentrate on getting better herself and not to be worrying about my mother. I wished that I could have stayed with her longer, but after about 10 minutes I told her that I needed to get back to work.

As I was getting ready to leave she said to me, "Sally, take care of yourself. If ye get sick, ye won't be any good to anyone, especially to yourself. Your mother and me are old. Ye have your whole life ahead of ye. Take care of yourself." I knew that she loved me a lot.

I hugged her and told her I loved her and that I would see her tomorrow. I hoped that tomorrow I'd remember where she was.

I didn't get back to my office until nearly 3:00 and ended up working until after 6:30 trying to get caught up. I decided that I'd come in early the next day and I was thankful to have such an understanding boss.

****

The following morning, I glanced down at my watch—6:50. There was still plenty time for Dave to get the kids to where they needed to be—Kathleen to her bus stop that was about a mile from our home, and Michael to his high school before the morning bell rang. At that point, however, I was the only one waiting in the living room to give hugs and to say goodbye to everyone for the day.

That's when I heard a small commotion down the hallway.

"Kathleen, get out of the bathroom. You've been in there forever and I still have to brush my teeth. Get out NOW!" Michael sounded totally exasperated with his little sister.

"I'm almost finished and stop yelling at me. You're so mean!" Kathleen snapped back.

"I'm not mean. I need to get in there. Get out NOW," he said with little patience.

I heard the bathroom door open and quickly close again.

Kathleen had finally gotten out of the bathroom and given Michael a little time to finish getting ready for school. She walked slowly down the hallway towards me with her backpack on her back and a princess lunchbox in her hand.

"Baby, you look very pretty today," I said to my youngest as she walked up to me.

"Mom, I'm not a baby. I'm 10 years old," she said.

"I know, Honey, you really are getting to be a big girl, but you'll always be my baby. Grandma calls me 'Baby' and you know it's been forever since I've been a baby," I said.

"Yea, but that's Grandma," she answered nonchalantly.

I wasn't sure what she meant by that statement but I took it to be a good thing.

"Mom, Michael is sooo mean to me. Will you talk to him and tell him that he has to be nice to me?" she complained.

"Honey, it's really not fair that you hog the bathroom all morning and your brother hardly has any time to do what he needs to do in there. You have to be nice to him, too," I said.

Two minutes later Michael was also in the living room. "Honey, do you want me to go over your science words one more time since the test is today? It'll only take us a minute while we're waiting for Dad. One last review would be good," I said.

"No, Mom, I'm fine," he said. At 15 years old, he really didn't need my help anymore to get ready for his tests, but I still felt compelled to offer.

"What about your Spanish? Did you get that all done?" I asked.

"Mom, stop worrying. Everything's good," he said, but his words could probably have been interpreted as "Mom, please leave me alone."

That's when Kathleen piped in, "Mommy, tell him."

"Tell me what?" Michael wanted to know as Dave walked into the room.

"You guys ready to go?" Dave asked.

"I am," said Kathleen. No response from Michael, but he looked ready, too.

"Dave, I'm going to be pretty swamped at work today since I was out so long yesterday. Can you take Kathleen to her ballet class this evening? I'm not sure what time I'll be home," I said.

"No problem. Take it easy today, Honey. Everything will be okay," he said as he gave me a hug, and then added, "I love you."

"Thank you, and I love you, too," I said.

I gave Michael and Kathleen quick hugs, as they followed Dave out the door. I hollered to them as they were almost to the car, "Have a great day, guys. Michael, good luck on your test!"

Kathleen turned around and said, "Mom, tell him to be nice to me."

"Michael, be nice to your sister!" I answered back.

He looked at me but didn't have a clue what I was talking about. I knew that I needed to talk to him later and remind him that he was the older one and that he needed to have a little more patience with Kathleen. She also needed a "mom lecture" about sharing the bathroom with her brother. I loved being a mother.

As I was deep in those thoughts I heard both kids shouting, "Shotgun!" Thankfully, that was something that Dave would deal with.

I looked over at the clock on the wall. It was already after 7:00 and work started at 8:30. Since I wanted to get there early, I needed to get a move on. I walked quickly through the kitchen, the playroom, our bedroom, and into our bathroom. I was already dressed for work and pretty much ready to go, but thought that I would primp for a few minutes before going into the office. When I looked in the mirror I saw how tired I appeared. I sighed and said out loud to the reflection, "I think this is as good as it's gonna get today."

I went back to the kitchen and grabbed my lunch from the fridge and my purse off the counter. As I walked outside to my car I wondered what new challenges were in store for me. I was feeling totally overwhelmed by the responsibilities of my life and I wondered if this is what people meant when they said that they had the weight of the world on their shoulders?

I got into the car but instead of turning the key, I just sat there for a minute holding on to the steering wheel and staring straight ahead. My brain was going in so many different directions, each thought more unpleasant than the one before.

Finally, I started the engine but I continued to just sit there and think. I knew that I needed to get going, but I was once again on the verge of tears. I did the best that I could to hold them back, but my emotions weren't cooperating. I could feel my eyes welling up, and as hard as I tried not to cry, I couldn't help it. The floodgates opened. First came the tears, and then came the sobs. I knew that I was in an emotional pressure cooker but these private meltdowns were happening far too often.

Lots of thoughts filled my head as I wondered what in the name of God was happening to me? *Am I having a breakdown? How am I going to get through this? I have to get through it for their sake. And I have to do a good job. No, I have to do a great job, because there's no one else to do it. It's all on me.*

I don't know how long this meltdown lasted, probably only a few minutes, but by the time the sobs had turned into sad little whimpers and I started breathing more slowly, more calmly, I was worn out. I continued staring blankly straight ahead for a little longer with the engine running. Then I said a prayer that sounded more like a plea, "God, please give me strength. Please help me." Then I put the car in reverse, backed out of the driveway, and headed into work.

Chapter 2

Back to the Beginning

Three years earlier...

Here's how my morning started out before I ever made it to work.

I woke up about 5:30 on what would eventually turn out to be a beautiful September day. I hopped into the shower and waited for the nice warm water to drench my hair and the shower massage to do its thing on my shoulders. Even though I was sleepy, it didn't take long for me to realize that something wasn't right with this picture. We had no water. So, I woke up a tired Dave, about an hour earlier than he planned to wake up.

"Honey, wake up. We don't have any water," I said.

"What? What? What? We don't have any water?" he asked, still half asleep.

"Honey, I'm sorry but you need to get up and figure out what's going on," I said.

He dragged himself out of bed, threw on some clothes, and went outside to see what was wrong with our well water. When he came back into the house he told me that the pump wasn't working and that something was smoking. That didn't sound good to me.

"What are we going to do about showers?" I asked.

"I guess we don't take showers this morning," he answered, and was soon on his way to 7-11 to buy bottled water so that we could wash our faces, brush our teeth, and make a little breakfast.

It was now after 6:00 so I needed to wake up the two kids and tell them about the water problem.

Michael was usually easy to wake up but that morning he was particularly sleepy because of all the homework he stayed up late to do the night before. A shower would have helped to wake him up.

Kathleen got out of bed when she heard me talking to Michael and told me that she wasn't hungry for breakfast because she had a bug bite and that "it really itches."

"Baby, it's going to be a long time before you get to eat your lunch. You really need to eat some breakfast now or you're going to be starving before it's time for lunch. What would you like?" I asked.

"Nothing. My bug bite itches too much to eat," she complained, and then she headed to the bathroom.

While she was in the bathroom, I went into her bedroom to ask Delia what I could fix for her breakfast. She'd been sharing Kathleen's room with her for a couple of months because she had fallen in her apartment and hurt her arm. Dave and I thought that it wouldn't be safe for her to be on her own right then and the thought of her in a rehab facility wasn't something that any of us relished. The doctor didn't see any problems with her staying with us and he ordered a physical therapist to come to our house several times a week.

Delia was awake but still snuggled under a Barbie doll comforter when I walked into the room.

"Dee Dee, I'm sorry to tell you this, but we don't have any running water this morning. Dave went up to the store to buy some bottled water and he should be back pretty soon. I can fix you a cup of tea now because there's enough water in the kettle, but what would you like for your breakfast?" I asked.

She quietly answered, "I don't know yet."

What do you mean, you don't know yet? This isn't a restaurant. I have to get the kids ready for school and I need to get to work, was what I was thinking. But the words that cheerfully came out of my mouth were, "No problem, you think about what you'd like and I'll be back in a few minutes."

I heard the front door open as Dave walked into the house with several jugs of bottled water. The two kids had gotten dressed for school and were waiting in the kitchen, but neither of them were in a good mood. Michael wasn't happy not being able to take a shower because he wouldn't be able to slick down his curly hair, and Kathleen's bug bite was REALLY itchy.

"Michael, your hair will look just fine," I said. "Dave, please go with him into the bathroom and pour some water on his head so that he can do whatever he needs to do to fix his hair."

Kathleen looked like she was about to cry. I went over to her and gave her a big hug. "I'm sorry that your bug bite itches, Baby. I wish that I had the itch instead of you. Let's go into my bathroom and see what we can put on it so that it'll stop itching," I said. As we walked side by side to the bathroom I pulled her close to me.

After a few minutes of searching through bathroom drawers, I luckily found an anti-itch stick that almost immediately fixed the problem. I gave her another hug and a kiss.

"Thanks, Mommy. I love you," she said.

"I love you, too, Baby. Now can I fix you some breakfast?" I asked.

"Okay. What are you going to make?" she asked.

I decided that the only thing that the kids were getting for breakfast that morning was cereal and fruit and milk. That wasn't a great breakfast but it was better than nothing and would tide them over until they could eat the lunches that I had made for them the night before. While the two of them sat at the kitchen counter and ate their breakfast, I got myself ready for work.

Then I checked on Delia again to see if she'd decided what she'd like for her breakfast.

"A cup of tea and some cream of rice cereal would be lovely, but please don't make the cereal too thick," she said.

"No problem. I'll make you some toast, too," I said. "It'll be ready in a few minutes and then I need to go to work."

As I was fixing her breakfast the house phone rang and Dave answered it in the kitchen. It was obvious that he was talking with my mother.

"I'm sorry, Mom, that you don't feel well," he said.

There was more talking going on from my mother's side of the phone than there was from Dave's. There was only the occasional "okay" from him. The call ended with him saying, "I love you, too."

I was a little worried as I asked, "Is everything okay?"

"Well the gist of it is that your mother says that she's downtown at Sally's house and doesn't feel well, and wanted me to pick her up and bring her home."

I just stood there for a minute wondering what was happening to my mother. What was she thinking? Dave hugged me as Michael and Kathleen looked at us.

"I guess I'll be stopping at Grandma's house on my way into work this morning," I said.

I turned to the kids and said, "Guys, your lunches are by the front door. Go get your backpacks and finish getting ready. Dad'll be ready to leave in a few minutes."

By that time Delia was waiting patiently in the dining room for her breakfast which I brought to her.

"I hope that your breakfast is okay. Take a bite of the cream of rice and let me know if it's alright," I said. "Oh yea, I left a sandwich for you in the fridge for your lunch, but help yourself to anything else that you'd like."

"Sally, ye worry too much about everyone. Ye didn't have to fix me anything this morning. I could have made myself a slice of toast and that would've been plenty for me," she said as she started eating her breakfast.

"You're sweet, Dee Dee, but you need to eat well and stay strong so that you'll be able to get the most that you can get out of your physical therapy. That's what'll get you back to your apartment. We'd love for you to stay here with us, but I know that you want to go back to your own home."

Our conversation was interrupted when Dave and the kids walked into the dining room. They wanted to say good-bye before they left for the day. Michael and Kathleen gave quick hugs to Delia and to me and then raced out the door, each yelling, "Shotgun!"

"Delia, I hope that you have a good day today. I'll see you tonight," Dave said as he patted her shoulder.

"I hope that ye have a good day, too," she answered.

"I'll walk outside with you," I said to Dave.

"I'll be back in a few minutes, Dee Dee," I said over my shoulder as I walked towards the door with Dave.

As soon as we walked out onto the porch, I saw that Kathleen was riding "shotgun."

"Do you think that he lets her win?" I asked.

He smiled at me and said, "Maybe."

"Dave, I don't know how I can pick up Kathleen at 2:00 and Michael at 3:30. I can't go to lunch that late today. I know that you have two meetings this afternoon. What're we gonna do?" I asked.

"I don't know, Sal. I can't get out of the meetings," he said.

"I know that you can't. I guess that I'll call Eileen again. Maybe Kathleen and Michael can walk over to her house when they finish with school. I don't know what we'd do without her, but I feel bad that I can't reciprocate with her kids very often these days," I said.

"Don't worry. There'll be plenty time for paybacks down the road," he said, and then he gave me a quick goodbye hug. I waited on the front porch and waved goodbye as Dave's car backed out of the driveway.

By the time I got back into the dining room, Delia had finished eating her breakfast and was putting her dishes on the seat of her walker to bring them into the kitchen.

"Dee Dee, you know that I would've taken your dishes into the kitchen. You really don't need to do that sort of thing," I said.

"Please don't make an invalid out of me. The more ye do for me, the less I'll be able to do for myself. If ye keep it up I won't be able to manage when I get back to my own home. I appreciate that ye do so much, but please let me do the things that I'm still able to do," she said with the wisdom of age.

"I love you, Dee Dee, and I'm so proud of you. I get it what you're saying and you're absolutely right. I just like helping you," I said.

I decided not to tell her about Mom's odd phone call. Why worry her? As I got ready to leave the house, I told her to call me during the day if she needed anything or if she just wanted to talk for a few minutes. I also wished her good luck with her physical therapy that she'd be having in the afternoon.

****

My mother and aunt were on my mind as I drove to my mother's house. Dave always joked that their birth certificates must be wrong because they both looked much younger than they actually were. At 88 years old, my mother still looked naturally pretty. She was lucky that she still had all but one of her own teeth, and that missing one was replaced many decades earlier. Her teeth were straight and not very yellowed. Her wavy jet black hair, dark eyes and olive skin made her look more Spanish than Irish. That probably was a throwback to the Spanish Invasion of Ireland hundreds of years ago.

Delia was 91 years old, and it was still obvious that she was 100% Irish. She had deep blue eyes and fair skin. However, the color of her hair was more difficult to determine since grey hair had moved in with her wavy auburn locks.

Both sisters used to be about 5'4" but old age and gravity had robbed each of them of a few of their inches. I doubted that either one of them was still much over five feet tall. I would describe my mother as a little pudgy at 140 pounds. Delia looked frail and fragile at 100 pounds. Neither of them had lost their beautiful Irish brogues.

Even at their advanced ages, however, they were both incredibly independent. My mother was 41 when she married my father. Delia never married. Every now and then I cringed at the thought of them ever losing their independence by having to live in an assisted living facility, or worse yet, long term care. It would not only kill their spirits, it would kill them. The older they got, the more often I'd think about my mother saying, "Shoot me first. Don't ever put me in a home."

The sisters grew up in Ireland during the War of Independence with England. That war was immediately followed by Ireland's Civil War. I think that living through the oppression they encountered during their early years contributed to the love of their independence they achieved when they came to America. Delia came first, followed by my mother a few years later. They were both 17 years old when they landed by boat on American soil. Mom arrived shortly before the stock market crashed in 1929. Gaelic was their native language, and so neither of them could speak much English.

Thinking about the two of them made the 10-minute drive fly by and it didn't take long before I was pulling into my mother's driveway. I was nervous as I got out of my car and walked up to her front porch. This confusion that I was seeing in her lately had come on slowly, and it really threw me for a loop. My mother never used to behave this way.

As I unlocked the front door and walked inside I tried to be as chipper as possible. "Mom, I'm here," I announced.

She walked out of the kitchen slowly and said, "Baby, I don't feel very good. I've been here long enough and I'd like for ye to take me home. Will ye take me home?"

I hugged her and kept my arms around her much longer than usual. I thought that it was important that we both stayed calm. I held her hands and slowly said, "Mom, look around you. This is your home. This is where you and Dad lived for over 30 years. This is where you raised me. This is where you used to play with Michael and Kathleen when they were just little tykes. Do you remember any of that?"

I could tell that she was trying hard to remember, but couldn't, so she said, "If ye say it's so, then I believe ye. So ye want me to stay here a little longer?"

"Mom, do YOU want to stay here?" I asked.

"I guess I can stay here for a while. It looks like a nice little house. It looks clean. I'll stay here if that's what ye think I should do," she said.

"I think it would be just fine for you to stay here in your house," I said as I gave her another hug for reassurance.

Then I added, "Dave told me that you didn't feel too well this morning. What's the matter?"

"Ah musha, I'm feeling a little better now. I always feel good when I see ye. Are ye off from the job today?" she asked.

"I wish that I was off and that I could spend the day with you but I have to go to work now, if you think that you'll be okay. I'll stop by and see you on my way home tonight and I'll fix supper for you. Will you be okay until this evening?" I asked.

"Aw sure, I'll be just fine till then," she said.

"Okay, call me at work if you need anything. Do you want to walk outside with me?" I asked.

"Of course I do," she said as she held my hand and walked outside to the front porch with me. We gave each other another hug.

"I love you, Mom. I'll see you tonight," I told her as I got into my car.

"Safe journey, Baby," I heard her say as I backed down her driveway.

For as long as I could remember, my mother would always stand on the front porch and wave goodbye to me, when I left her house. When my dad was alive, the two of them would stand side by side, waving goodbye. That's a sight I still missed seeing.

On my drive to work my mother remained on my mind. I wasn't sure if I was more relieved that she seemed pretty okay when I left her, or if I was more worried about the state that I found her in. This was an uneasy time for us all, and I didn't know where it was leading.

It troubled me a lot that she was often confused and tremendously lonely, but thankfully I always felt that she was safe. I wasn't worried that she would wander away, and she had always been conscientious about double checking that the stove was turned off.

I was distressed, however, about this new issue with her wanting to "go home" even when she was in her own home. I wasn't sure where "home" was to her. For as far back as I could remember, whenever she spoke about Ireland she always referred to it as home, but it was perfectly clear that's what she meant. She would say something like "I'd love to go back home and see everyone. I think that would be a nice vacation. What do ye think?"

It was different now when she talked about going home. Did she mean Ireland? Or another home she may have once lived in? Or did she maybe think that she lived with me in my home? It was a puzzle to me and I wasn't having much success in figuring it out, even though she was giving me ample opportunities to come up with an answer.

Chapter 3

Truer Words Were Never Spoken

I'd love to be able to say that I could relax on the weekends and not worry about my mother, but unfortunately that's not how it was. I'd love to be able to say that my brother or my sister would help out on the weekends, but Mom had her only baby when she was 42. This responsibility was mine alone.

Nope, the weekends weren't any different than the weekdays. I still made a point of spending a few hours both days with her and I usually brought one or both of the kids with me. She doted over them and I told them that they were like medicine for their grandma. She was always in a good mood when they came to visit. The Saturday that I'm about to tell you about was an eventful day. I just didn't realize how much so at the time.

While Kathleen played outside, Mom cooked lunch, and I filled a seven-day pill box with her pills for the week. This was a new bright idea that I had. I thought that it would give me a clue whether she took her pills each day. I wanted to know if she was still capable of this simple level of self-care.

As my mother and I chitchatted, I heard the front door open and Kathleen running through the house. She ran into the kitchen holding a small grey kitten. I had recently been noticing a lot of stray cats in the neighborhood and I was worried that they would get run over.

"Mommy, Grandma, look what I found. Can I keep it? Can I? Pleeeeease?" she asked with such hopefulness. "I found it in Grandma's azalea bushes. I promise I'll take good care of it."

"I'm sorry, Sweetie, but there's no way on earth that we're getting another kitten now," I said.

I'm a pushover but I knew that I couldn't handle one more thing on my plate. Two youngsters and two oldsters, and one kitten was more than enough for me for the time being. There was no way that I was going to get a second kitten.

Kathleen looked down at the floor in disappointment as she petted the young cat. Being the resourceful child that she was, she quickly went to Plan B.

"Grandma, would you like to keep it?" she asked slowly. She knew that if Grandma kept it, it was almost as good as getting to bring it back to our house. She knew that she'd have something else to play with whenever she visited her grandmother.

"Honey, I think I'm too old to take care of a cat. I have enough to do just taking care of myself." But almost before those words were out of her mouth, she said, "Let me think about it for a while. It's a big responsibility. Your mom and I need to talk about it."

Then she turned to me and asked, "What do ye think? I'd love to have something else in this house besides myself that's alive."

Over the next few hours we talked about the pros and cons of keeping the kitten. When we weren't talking about it, I could tell that my mother was thinking about it. It was a big decision to make, over such a little kitten.

"What should I do, Sally? What would ye do?" she asked.

I'd been thinking about those questions all afternoon. I hoped that the answer that I was about to give her was good advice.

"Here's what I think. If you're able to take care of it, I think that it probably would be good for you. When I was growing up, we always had a dog or a cat or a rabbit or a bird. Remember, once upon a time, we even had a couple of ducks and a rooster. If you keep the kitten, it would give you something else to focus on, other than just waiting for me to come over. Do you think that you'll remember to feed it each day?" I asked.

"I think so," she answered.

I could tell that she was close to making a decision.

"Baby, I hope that I won't be sorry for doing it, but I'm going to keep it," she said.

I was quiet for just a moment, but then I walked over to her and gave her a hug. "Congratulations on your fur baby," I said.

"Thank ye, Sally. Will ye do me a big favor and run up to the store and get some food for it?" she asked.

"Of course, I will. I'll buy a litter box and some litter, too," I said.

"While you're at the store, I'll look in the garage for a nice box for its bed, and I'll put an old towel in it so that it'll be comfortable. I think that I'll put the bed over there in the corner. What do ye think?" she asked.

"Perfect, Mom," I said.

Then I shared the good news with Kathleen. "Kathleen, Grandma is going to keep the kitten," I said, loud enough for her to hear in the next room.

She came running into the kitchen. "Grandma, thank you! Thank you! I'll help you take care of her." She was still carrying the kitten around with her. She was smiling from ear to ear as she gave her grandmother a big hug with the poor kitten sandwiched between them.

"What'll we call it? I don't even know if it's a little girl or a little boy," my mother said.

"I know. Let's call it Pepper," Kathleen piped in.

"I guess that'll work whether it's a boy or a girl," my mother answered.

"Mom, I'll make an appointment with the vet for next Saturday so that we can make sure it's healthy and get it its shots."

"Thank you, Baby," she said, and then she headed into the garage in search of a bed for Pepper.

If this had been a few years earlier, I would have been thrilled with her decision to get a pet. At this point, however, I didn't know if it would be a very good thing for my mother, or a decision that I would l regret for a long, long time. Time would tell.

Pepper and my mother bonded well, and the little kitten was good company for her. Sadly, however, my mother's dementia continued to progress. Remember my great pill box idea? It didn't work out the way that I had hoped it would. I'm not certain where the pills went, but I suspect that they were probably thrown away. My mother creatively used the box for another purpose. Pennies, nickels, dimes, and quarters were neatly stacked in the seven compartments.

"Great idea!" I told her. There was absolutely no reason in arguing, explaining, or getting frustrated. She was proud of her little invention. Why not make her feel good about it? Luckily, she only had one or two prescriptions at that time, and I would make sure that she took them.

****

As the months went by, the days that she was confused when I stopped by after work were occurring more often. Sometimes she would greet me happily when I arrived, a suitcase packed near the front door. She would hug me and tell me that she was all ready to go home. She'd be full of energy, her eyes full of excitement, as if she was about to go on a fun trip.

Other times she was distraught and would say that she wasn't feeling well, but that she would feel better once she got home. I would always hug her and tell her I loved her and then would explain patiently that she was in her own home where she'd lived for decades. Every now and then I would ask her where she thought she was. She would think for a minute or so, and then embarrassingly say, "I don't know, Baby."

At that point I would put my arm around her and slowly and patiently recite a litany of memories that might help her remember where she was.

"Mom, let's sit on the couch for a few minutes." I would hold her hand and point to things that I hoped would trigger a memory. If I pointed to the dining room I might say, "Think about all those great turkey dinners that you cooked for the holidays that we ate at that table." I would then pause for a moment to give her a chance to recollect, and then I'd go on, "Think about all those times that you sat at the dining room table coloring with Michael and Kathleen. Think about putting jigsaw puzzles together with them." Another pause, and then, "Mom, I remember many times I would come for a visit on my lunch hour and I would find you and Kathleen playing with Barbie dolls right here on the living room floor. Do you remember those good times?" I asked hopefully.

Sometimes she would say that she remembered everything. Other times I knew that she had difficulty remembering any of them. When she said that she remembered, I hoped that she was being sincere and that she wasn't just saying that she remembered for my benefit. I was afraid that she was losing the warm fuzzy feelings that we get from happy memories.

I knew that she was aware that her memory was failing because she would occasionally ask me why she couldn't remember things. I really didn't have a great answer other than to say that sometimes that happens to people as they got older. I told her that it might help her memory if she kept her mind busy.

I suggested that she read more than just the daily newspaper. I suggested that she write letters to her family in Ireland more often. I suggested that she join a senior citizen club. I even reminded her that Delia did those things and that her memory was just fine. I thought that a little sibling rivalry might inspire her, but it didn't.

One day while we were sitting at her kitchen table enjoying a cup of tea and a slice of coffee cake, she told me that there was a beautiful letter in the newspaper in an Advice Column. She handed the paper to me so that I could read it, too. It was a letter from a grown son explaining that some of his friends would ask him why he visited his elderly father so often. His dad lived in a nursing home as the result of a stroke. His friends told him that his father was so bad off that he probably didn't even know whether he visited him or not. He didn't understand why his friends would have that sort of conversation with him.

He continued his letter by saying that he told his friends that he talked to his dad as if he understood everything that he said. He said that every now and then his father turned his head and looked into his eyes. The son told his friends that it was during those times that he totally believed that his father knew who he was and that he was there with him. That was why he visited his dad so often.

It was a heartwarming article but I'll never know for sure why my mother showed it to me, but it's something that

I'll always remember. Did she think that was going to be our destiny?

****

Thank God that Delia was doing much better at that point and was able to go back to her own apartment. I know that she appreciated the months that she lived with us while she was recuperating but Miss Independence was ready to go home. She and I were both thankful that her doctor continued her physical therapy when she returned to her apartment.

She had never married and was the definition of independence. She had a huge circle of friends of all ages that visited her often. She belonged to a senior citizen organization that she went to a few times a week, she exercised daily, she did volunteer work, and she never neglected her prayers. Even though she was in her 90s she had an incredibly good memory and she would sometimes even remind me to do things. I stopped by her apartment several times during the work week after I left my mother's house. On the days that I didn't see her, I called her. I honestly wasn't worried about her for the moment. Thank God for small favors.

Michael and Kathleen were both busy with kids' stuff— ballet, piano, Brownies, and basketball for Kathleen, and track, piano, altar serving, and school plays for Michael. We often brought Mom and Delia to as many of the kids' events as possible. I think that it was as beneficial for the youngsters as it was for the oldsters.

Even though my mother was confused sometimes, up to that point she had never given me any reason to think that she wasn't safe in her home. That level of complacency on my part changed one evening when I was visiting her and she told me about her day. She told me that she had been doing yard work in the front yard when a couple of "very nice men" started talking to her while she was pulling weeds.

They asked if she needed the inside of her house painted. She told them that it could probably use a fresh coat of paint and invited them inside her house to look for themselves. When she told me that story I immediately had visions of walking into her house and finding her dead in a pool of her own blood.

"Mom," I said sternly, "you have to promise me that you will never let any stranger inside your house again. They could have done terrible things to you. It's not like the good old days when you could trust just about everyone. It's not like that anymore. If you think that there's work that needs to be done anywhere in your house, let me know and I'll make sure that it gets done. Please promise me that you'll never let a stranger into your house again. I love you so much and I would never want anyone to hurt you. Promise me, Mom."

She looked like she was about to cry but said, "I promise." I later wondered how long she would remember her promise.

I stayed with her longer than usual that evening. I wanted to make sure that I hadn't scared her too much and that she would be able to sleep later on. I wasn't so sure that I was going to be able to sleep.

Throughout that visit I reminded her several times that she had a doctor's appointment the next day. "Mom, you have a check-up with Dr. Diarmuid tomorrow. I'm going to be here around 8:00 in the morning so you need to get ready early. I'll put a big note on your refrigerator and another one on the medicine cabinet in your bathroom to remind you. Okay?" I asked.

"Whatever ye want to do is fine. Tell me something," she said. "What would I do without ye?"

"You probably wouldn't have someone annoying you all the time, the way that I annoy you," I joked.

"Don't be funny. I need ye to tell me the things ye tell me," she said. And then after a short pause, she added, "I hate seeing ye leave, but please go on home now to Dave and the kids. Ye must be starved to death."

"I'm in no rush to leave quickly tonight. I want to heat up a little dinner for you and I'll sit with you while you eat. I know it's no fun always eating by yourself," I said.

After I fixed her supper and she ate it, she walked me outside to my car.

"Mom, remember to lock all your doors after I leave. I love you. See you in the morning," I said.

She gave me a hug and said, "I love ye, too, my baby. Safe home."

As I drove away I smiled and thought about what she had just said. I guess no matter how old we are, we'll always be our mothers' babies.

When I got home Dave had our supper cooked. I was thankful that he helped out so much. The evening went by quickly as I helped the kids with their homework and did our nighttime routine. When they were ready to go to bed, I gave them each a kiss, and told them both, "I love you most."

I got up early the next morning and drove to Mom's house. It seemed like it had only been a few hours since I was backing out of her driveway, but there I was again unlocking her front door to take her to her doctor's appointment. I hoped that she was almost ready to go.

"Hiya, Mom, I'm here," I called out as I walked into the house. "I picked up your newspaper from the driveway for you."

Surprisingly, she was all ready to go.

"Honey, I don't feel very good. I think that we should change this to another day," she said.

"I'm sorry you don't feel well, but if you're sick, the doctor is exactly where we should be going this morning. What's the matter?" I asked.

"The pain in my leg and my hand is terrible. It's never been so bad. And it's hard to breathe," she said.

"Have you taken your puffer?" I asked.

Both Delia and my mother called their inhalers, their puffers. I long ago stopped trying to correct them.

"I took it when I first woke up but I'll take it again before we go to the doctor," she answered.

"Mom, your hand and leg are probably hurting because of your arthritis. Have you taken anything for the pain today?" I asked.

"Not yet, but I think that I should," she said.

I brought some water and a couple acetaminophens.

"Thank ye, Honey. Ye know that I don't like taking them, unless I really need them. If I take them too often, they won't do me any good in another 10 years," she said.

In 10 years, she'll be 98 years old. Dear God, will I still be doing this, every day, for another 10 years?

"You're smart, Mom, to only take them when you need them. I don't know if you can build up a tolerance to them, but I know that if you take them too often that it could mess up your liver," I said.

A few minutes later we were on the way to her doctor's appointment.

We arrived at Dr. Diarmuid's office right on time and he took us on time which I appreciated since I had to go to work after the appointment. He did a thorough checkup and gave her a good bill of health. During the appointment he asked her questions that she answered surprisingly well. She also flirted a little bit with him and told him that she was happy to have such a handsome doctor.

After the exam was over, they visited for a few minutes. He knew that she often went to Ireland and asked if she had an Irish vacation planned. She told him, "Not yet." He told her that he and his family were planning a vacation the following summer to Germany, and that he'd be out of the office for two weeks. She told him that she hoped that he would have a great time. I was a little surprised, and extremely impressed, how articulate my mother was while she was talking to the doctor.

While she was getting dressed after the exam, I had the opportunity to talk to him outside the room that she was in. He was aware of her dementia, but if he hadn't already known it, I don't think that he would have noticed it during that examination. I asked him why some days she acted like my mother before the dementia and other days she was a totally different person who didn't even know where she was.

He said that since the appointment was early in the morning her brain was rested. He also said that she was concentrating on answering his questions correctly. He said later that afternoon or into the evening, it might be more obvious that she had dementia. He called it "sundowning."

"You know what I worry about?" I asked him.

I didn't give him a chance to answer. "As confused as she is sometimes, I worry that she'll end up having to leave her home. As much as I'd love for her to live with us, she wouldn't be safe in my house whenever she'd be by herself, so that's not an option. And, I sincerely don't think that she'd be able to adjust to assisted living. And God forbid, the thought of her in long term care makes me cringe," I said.

His demeanor became serious and he said, "You're absolutely right. There's no place like your own home. Elderly people often get confused when they're uprooted from everything that's familiar to them. My father was recently in Calafort for rehab after he had surgery. My cousin and I visited him every day. We're both doctors and it was still hard on him. Keep your mother in her own home as long as you can, and you feel that she's safe," he answered wisely.

"That's what my plan is. I may need your help in keeping my plan. You're great with my mother. Thank you, Doctor. I really mean that," I said.

"My pleasure. Since my father is elderly, too, I appreciate what you're dealing with. I'm having some of the same issues with him," he said. "I'm going to write a prescription for donepezil for your mother. Let's see if it helps with the dementia. Maybe we can slow down the progression of her memory loss. I think it's worth a try," he said.

"Thank you. I'll try just about anything if it helps her memory," I said.

On the drive home we were both relieved that her doctor's appointment was over, and that the doctor said that she was healthy. Mom had gone to Dr. Diarmuid for several years and I felt fortunate to have him as her doctor. Granted, he had only seen her for regular checkups and non-emergency ailments like bad colds and bronchitis and flus, but we always left his office knowing that she was in good hands. I knew that at her age it was only a matter of time before she would need him for far more serious issues. I felt like he was her safety net and that she had a great doctor in him.

****

The holidays were rapidly approaching which put everyone in a good mood, even though it made for an even busier schedule. We took my mother with us to watch the kids in the Christmas pageant at their school. She couldn't have been happier when she saw them on the stage. She was so proud of her grandchildren. A few weeks later Delia and Mom drove with us to look at Christmas lights. They both were glad to have such a festive diversion in their routine lives. I even took my mother Christmas shopping with me one day and I was seriously surprised at how much energy she had. I was proud of her because she could run circles around many of my friends' mothers who were decades younger.

One thing that I'll always remember from that Christmas season happened on Christmas night at our house. After my mother helped me do the dishes, I asked if she wanted to go for a walk to look at the lights in my neighborhood. Since Delia was using a walker at that time, the thought of a walk, in the dark, on a cold December night, wasn't too appealing to her. She wanted to stay inside by the inviting fire that was burning in the hearth and listen to Christmas music. However, to my surprise, my mother said, "Yes." So, we bundled up and ventured outside for a walk that will always be happily branded in my memory.

I liked smelling the smoke wafting from my neighbors' chimneys while we walked hand in hand slowly up the street. The sky was particularly dark that night and we each pointed out the twinkling stars high above and the blinking Christmas lights on the houses. We commented on the decorations that juxtaposed holy manger scenes with jolly Santa Clauses.

As we made our way up the street Mom noticed that most of the driveways were filled with cars. "It's lovely to see the houses filled with company," she said.

When we reached the top of the street I asked her if she wanted to go back to my house. She serenely answered, "Not yet. Let's just keep walking and enjoy this night because we don't know where we'll be next year at this time." Truer words were never spoken.

Chapter 4

Unwashed Dishes

Here's a great bit of advice. Don't ever say "I can't handle one more thing." Because guess what? You can.

A few days after Christmas I went to the dermatologist because of a teeny tiny patch of dry skin on my shin that wouldn't go away. In no way did it look like a mole, but before I knew it the doctor was taking a biopsy of my leg. I had had many biopsies throughout the years because I have a lot of moles, but the results were always that they were benign.

This time the news was different, and it wasn't good. The doctor called me when he got the results to say that I had a melanoma and that I needed to have a wide incision surgery. I knew that I'd been given a possible death sentence because I had two relatives who were only in their 30s when they died from a melanoma.

As difficult as it would be for me to do it, I knew that I had to put myself first while I dealt smartly with this dangerous cancer. I didn't know how I would be able to take care of my mother and Delia while I recuperated after the surgery, but I prayed that God would help me.

Deep in the recesses of my memory I remembered something that my mother used to tell me whenever I would say that I didn't think that I could do something. She would convince me that "where there's a will, there's a way." I knew that I would have to keep that in mind for the next month or so.

There was no easy way to tell my mother and Delia that I had cancer, so I took the chicken way out and didn't tell them about the melanoma. Luckily, since I had had many biopsies in the past, the groundwork had already been laid for my little white lie. I told them both that I was going to have surgery to have a mole removed and that the surgeon had already told me that the surgery was going to be a little more uncomfortable than usual and that I wouldn't be able to drive for about a week. They bought the story.

A little uncomfortable? The surgery hurt like hell. Just moving my toes hurt my leg. I also needed to be careful that the long, deep and wide incision, which was held in place with staples and stitches, wouldn't open up. As difficult as it was for me to slow down, I had to be diligent about not walking too much or driving at all for the week after the surgery.

I called my mother and Delia daily and pretended that I felt fine. I reminded them, however, that I couldn't visit them because I was following the doctor's instructions. A week and a half after the surgery, I finally felt well enough to start visiting my mother every day, and Delia every other day. I still wasn't walking normally but when they could see me walk, I did the best that I could do so that they wouldn't see my discomfort.

Two weeks after the surgery, I had the last of the stitches taken out of my leg and that same night Michael was in a school play. I was so proud to see him on the stage, having fun, and doing a great job. While it wasn't always easy raising the kids and taking care of my mother and my aunt, all at the same time, it was a huge blessing for me to have the joy of the children to balance the occasional sadness of old age.

It took nearly a month before I could stop pretending that I felt fine, and that I really was fine. That's when I went back to work. The rest of the school year zipped by and before I knew it I was putting the end of the school year events on my calendar at home, as well as on Mom's and Delia's calendars. There was the ballet recital, the piano recital, and Kathleen's First Holy Communion.

Kathleen's First Communion was a big day that we had all looked forward to for a long time. Since I didn't want to take any chances on anything going wrong on this special day for her, I invited my mother to spend the weekend at our house, and I told her that I'd check on Pepper. I knew that she would enjoy our company and it would be a nice change for her to be away from her house. She had a great time staying with us that weekend and she stayed busy most of the time. She made Irish soda bread with Kathleen and she even washed some of my windows.

I know that I should be embarrassed to admit that she washed my windows, but I'm really not. It's not that the windows needed washing, it's that my mother couldn't do enough to help me. I felt the same about her. No matter how much I did for her, I always wanted to do more.

She also took time to sweep around the pool and to spend time with Kathleen on the dock of our lake, feeding the fish. She never learned to swim so the pool and the lake were the two reasons that she could never live safely with us.

The First Communion turned out beautifully and I was happy that my mother and Delia were both a part of that important and joyful experience. I still smile when I look at the pictures that we took and the happy memories we made on that day in May before things were forever changed.

Mom went back to her house Sunday night and things were back to the usual routine again on Monday.

When summer rolled around Michael went to various sports camps. We enrolled Kathleen in a couple of camps later in the summer, but for the first month three other moms and I did "mom camp." We each took a week and during that week we put on the camp for the four girls. It saved a lot of money and it gave us the chance to spend time with our daughters and their friends.

During my week we went to a museum, parks, the library, a scenic boat tour, swimming at my house, and did a lot of arts and crafts. It was wonderful to have this opportunity, but I was always concerned that if something came up with my mother during the week that I had the four girls, that I'd be up the creek. Thank God, there were no emergencies.

Being sandwiched between the oldster and the youngster generations took some planning in order to make sure that both sides got the most of me and the best of me. I never wanted my children to miss out on anything because I was taking care of my mother or my aunt. And I never would neglect Mom or Delia because I was too tired or wasn't in the mood. I always chaperoned the kids' field trips and I never missed any of the many activities that they participated in. I would just plan my visits to my mother and Delia around the kids' stuff. Was it easy? Not always. Was it worth it? Not a doubt in my mind!

****

Dave and I made plans to take the kids to a water park on Saturday, July 7th. I didn't feel comfortable not seeing my mother for an entire day, but I convinced myself that I needed a break. I was also a little nervous that it was on July 6th that I was telling her that I wasn't going to see her the following day. My dad passed away many years earlier on July 6th, and I was always happy when that day was behind me and everyone was safe and sound.

My mother seemed a little surprised, and not particularly happy, when I first told her that I wouldn't see her again until Sunday. When I explained what we were planning to do, however, she acted like my good old mom.

"Honey, you're with me all the time. Ye deserve a day off. Don't worry about me. I'll be fine. I have the little cat with me. She's been good company. And don't ye know that Jesus is always with me?" she said.

"Mom, thank you. Thank you for not making me feel guilty. The fact that you even said that to me will help me have an even better time with Dave and the kids. I love you, Ma," I said.

"I love ye, too, Baby," she said.

I had brought her a supper that I knew that she'd like— meatloaf, mashed potatoes and peas, and even some coffee cake for desert. I stayed with her that Friday night for a couple of hours and didn't even think about leaving until she finished eating.

When I asked her if I could wash the dishes before I left, she said, "No, that'll give me something to do while I'm waiting for something good to come on the TV."

While we were sitting in the kitchen, I noticed the kitten run through the dining room. She was probably full grown by then but still looked small. A few minutes later I saw her zipping through the dining room again.

"How do you like having a cat?" I asked.

"It's good to have some life around me. She's a nice little cat," she said.

"Ma, you remember that I won't be over here tomorrow, right?" I needed to repeat my plans a few times so that she'd remember. I didn't want her to be worried when she wouldn't hear from me the next day.

"Remind me what will ye be doing?" she asked.

"Dave and I are taking the kids to a water park. We'll be getting there in the morning and we won't get home until tomorrow evening. We'll probably go out to dinner on the way home. It'll sort of be like a vacation day for me. I really need a day off with just Dave and the kids," I said, with as much patience as I had in me.

"I'm sorry, Baby, I forgot that ye just told me that. I want ye to have a good time. Is there anything that I can do for ye?" she asked.

"The only thing that you can do for me is to take care of yourself tomorrow, and to be happy. Are you happy, Mom?" I asked.

"Ah musha, what's happy when you're my age? Ye and Dave and the kids is what makes me happy," she answered.

"That's such a nice thing to say. You make us happy, too," I said.

We talked a little bit longer and then I said, "I'd love to stay longer, but I think that I need to be heading home now. Remember, that you won't be hearing from me tomorrow at all, but I'll come over here on Sunday morning, okay?"

"Sure, that's fine," she said.

"You sure that you don't want me to do the dishes before I leave?" I asked.

"No, Baby. I'll do them as soon as you're gone. Thanks for bringing me the delicious dinner. You're too good to me. Have fun tomorrow and tell the kids to be careful," she said.

She walked me out to the front porch and hugged me goodbye like she had done thousands of times before. That image of her standing on her front porch, waving goodbye, will be forever with me.

"Safe home," I heard her say as I backed out of her driveway.

The next morning we all got up early, ate a quick breakfast, and headed to the park. It had been a long time since I spent a day without seeing either my mother or Delia. Oh my gosh, it was wonderful! I felt like a free woman! Freedom!!!

That feeling was short-lived, however, because it didn't take long before the guilt kicked in. When it came to feeling guilty, I was doomed. My father was Jewish and my mother was a staunch Irish Catholic. I definitely had the guilt gene. The funny thing is that neither one of my parents ever did or said anything to make me feel guilty. I think I put the guilt on myself.

That's when my inner voice gave me a pep talk. *You're being ridiculous. It's not like you're taking a two-week vacation—it's just one day. If you don't start doing this sort of thing more often, you're going to resent them, or worse yet, you're going to have a breakdown.* I listened to that voice, and I was glad that I did.

Throughout the day Dave and I had as much fun as the kids did. We slid down fast water slides, tubed on a lazy river, zipped through winding tunnels, and relaxed in a wave pool. The hours flew by, and as much as I didn't want the fun and freedom to be over, I knew when it was time for us to leave. Dave and I agreed that we needed to plan more days like that one while the kids were still on summer vacation; it was good for all of us. As the four of us walked to our car, I pictured my mother fixing her supper. I hoped that she had had a nice day, too.

On the way home we stopped for pizza. It was a great ending to a great day. By the time we got home our bellies were full and we were all pooped from the long day in the sun. I knew that it wouldn't be long before we'd all be in bed, and drifting off to sleep.

As I was about to fall into bed after one of the most carefree days I had had in ages, I noticed that the answering machine next to the bed had six messages. That was a lot for one day. I pressed the button and listened to the first one. It was from St. Blaise Hospital and the voice said that she was calling in reference to my mother and to please call them as soon as possible. I figured that must have been about her health insurance or the bill for a recent mammogram that she had, although I thought that it was a little odd that they'd be calling on a Saturday. I pressed the button again and the next caller said that she was a nurse in the emergency room of St. Blaise. She, too, was calling in reference to my mother and said to please call right away. My heart sank as I listened to the next four messages. I listened to them all to see if they would give me any additional information. They didn't.

Dave was brushing his teeth in the bathroom. I banged on the door. "Dave, I need you. Please come out. Hurry, please hurry. My mother is in the hospital."

I must have sounded pretty upset because he came right out. "What's the matter with your mother? What happened?" he asked.

"I don't know. There're six messages from St. Blaise Hospital. I don't know what's going on. Please call the hospital for me. I'm too afraid to make the call," I said.

Dave hurried to the phone and called the same number they had left on each of the messages. He was on hold for a couple of minutes before a nurse spoke with him. She told him that my mother had fallen in her home and was brought to the emergency room in an ambulance. She told him that a surgeon had already seen her earlier in the day, but that he needed to speak with us before doing anything.

Wild horses couldn't have kept me from going to the hospital right away. The kids were still awake and so we told them that Grandma was in the hospital and that she would be fine, but that we needed to see her. They asked if they could come with us and we told them, "Maybe tomorrow."

There were so many unanswered questions. How did she fall? Where? Who found her? Who called an ambulance? Will she be okay?

As we speeded down the highway to the hospital, my heart was pounding. *Why didn't I check on her before we left for the park? Why did we stop for pizza? Why wasn't I with her?*

It was the longest 15-minute drive I think I ever had, but once we got to the hospital we found out what room she was in and hurried to it.

When we arrived at her room, she was sleeping soundly. She actually looked peaceful and didn't look like she was in pain. I kissed her forehead and whispered to her that I loved her. Dave patted her shoulder and told her to sleep tight. Then we went in search of her nurse.

We waited a few minutes at the nurses' station before her nurse had time to talk with us. She told us that my mother was brought to the hospital in an ambulance. She didn't know any of the details of the fall or who called the ambulance. She said that she was resting comfortably now because she had been given medication for the pain and for her anxiety. She said that she would probably sleep throughout the night.

The nurse told us that the surgeon was actually still on the floor talking to another family and that we needed to speak with him before we left. We said that we would defi-nitely wait for him. Dave stood out by the nurses' station and I went back into my mother's room. I just stood over her bed and watched her sleep. I wondered what hell she'd been through without me being by her side to help her. The guilt had returned.

After a few minutes, Dave stuck his head into the room and said, "Honey, the doctor is waiting down the hall for us. You have to come now."

I kissed my mother's forehead again and followed Dave down the hallway.

The surgeon's name was Dr. Robinson. He seemed nice but very matter of fact. He told us the same information that the nurse had told us—that my mother had fallen inside her house and was brought to the hospital in an ambulance. He said that she was extremely dehydrated when she got to the hospital and that they were addressing that issue, also. That was all he knew about the circumstances of what happened. I wanted more details. I needed to know all the details.

"We took x-rays when she got here this afternoon. Her hip is broken; a better way to describe it is that it's shattered. You need to decide if you want her to have surgery to fix it. If not, we'll just—"

Dave interrupted, "What do you mean by IF we want to fix it? Of course, we want to fix her hip. Why would anyone not want to fix it? Would she be able to walk again without surgery?"

I'm not sure if the doctor was prepared for all those questions to be thrown at him all at once.

"No, she wouldn't be able to walk again without surgery. It's important that you understand that this is major surgery and that we'll be using general anesthesia. There are increased risks for a woman her age having this type of surgery. Some families decide that they don't want to put their mom or their dad through that ordeal."

"Doctor, I know that my mother is 88 years old but you don't know her. She's not the typical 88-year-old. Not long ago she was at our house on a step ladder washing my windows. Two years ago she was in Ireland with me and our kids and she was able to keep up with us just fine and we did a ton of walking. It would kill her if she wasn't able to walk again," I said, trying to get him to understand a little bit about my mother. I didn't want him to see her as the "cookie cut" 88-year-old. "Dave, don't you agree it would kill her if she couldn't walk?"

"I can't imagine your mother in a wheelchair for the rest of her life. She wouldn't want to live like that," Dave said as he looked at me, and then at the doctor.

"Okay, it sounds like you want the surgery," the doctor said.

"There's no question about it. Yes, we want you to fix her hip," I said as I glanced at Dave for reassurance that I was making the right decision.

"Okay, we'll schedule it for tomorrow morning. She'll be in the hospital for a few days and then we'll transport her to a rehab facility. She'll probably need a few months of physical therapy before she'll be able to go back home. Do you know what facility you want us to try to get her into?"

"There's a place called Calafort. Please try to get her in there, Doctor, if possible," I said.

A few years earlier Dave's dad also fell in his house and broke his hip. Dave and Michael found him lying on his kitchen floor. They called 911, and then he was rushed by ambulance to the hospital where he had surgery. He, too, was going to go into a rehab for physical therapy and would then go back to his own home. Dave looked at a bunch of facilities and he thought that Calafort was by far the best. In the end, however, his dad had all sorts of complications and setbacks and never made it out of the hospital. He spent a roller coaster month in the hospital, but then passed away.

I also remembered that Dr. Diarmuid said that his father had been in Calafort, so I felt comfortable saying that's where I wanted my mother to go for her rehab.

"Ok, give us a few minutes to get the consent papers ready for you to sign for her surgery and then we'll see what we can do about getting her into Calafort," the doctor said.

While Dave waited at the nurses' station I went back into my mother's room. I stood over her bed again and just watched her sleep. I didn't want to risk waking her. I wanted her to be well-rested for the morning.

Dave came to the doorway and said quietly, "C'mon out here. The nurse is waiting for you to sign the papers and then we can go home."

I looked back at my mother and whispered, "Goodnight, Mom. See you in the morning."

I signed the papers and hoped that I had made the right decision. As Dave and I slowly walked down the hallway towards the elevator I spotted the doctor coming in our direction. I walked up to him and asked, "Doctor, my mother will come through this okay, won't she?"

"She should, but understand that this type of fall is often a life changing event in elderly people. Sometimes they never get back to how they were before the fall," he said, and then added, "Your mother has been resting most of the day. You and your husband should go home and get a good night's sleep, too."

Life changing event—I didn't like the sound of those three words.

"Thanks, Doctor, we're leaving now. I'll see you in the morning," I said.

Dave and I didn't say much as we walked to the car with our arms around each other's waists.

"She'll be okay, Honey. Your mother is strong," he said.

"I wish the doctor didn't say what he said about how this could be a life changing event. I didn't like hearing that. I don't want... I don't need any more changes," I told him.

Dave tried to say what he could to make me feel better. "Nobody knows your mother the way we know her. She'll come through this just fine. Remember not that many years ago on Christmas Eve when we thought that she was having a heart attack? We waited at the hospital most of the day. The doctor did a heart cath and when he came out to the waiting room he told us that she had no blockages and that her heart was like a teenager's. Keep that in mind," he reminded me.

"Oh yea. I forgot about that," I said.

How could I forget? I guess that there'd been so many things that'd happened with my mother and Delia over the years that it was hard to remember them all.

Dave looked as tired as I felt. "Honey, you don't need to come tomorrow," I said. "The surgery is early in the morning. I'll be fine by myself. I'll call you if I need to talk."

He interrupted me. "No, I'm going to go with you. You don't need to be by yourself," he said firmly.

"Listen to me, Dave. I'll be fine. I know that the kids will be worried about Grandma, so please stay home with them. I don't want to take them to the hospital. Stay home, sleep in, fix a nice breakfast for everyone, and I'll be home as soon as I can. After the surgery is over and I know that she's okay, I'll need to stop by Delia's and let her know what's going on. That's really not something that I look forward to doing."

Those words made me think of all the other times in the last few years that I was the bearer of bad news for Delia and my mother. I was the one who told them when they lost a brother or a sister. My mother was always the emotional one who broke down and cried. Delia was the strong one with the stiff upper lip. I don't remember ever seeing her cry. She was the one who consoled me, rather than me being the consoler. There had been eight children in their family. Now only Mom, Delia, and their sister, Mag, in Ireland were left.

"Okay, now that I told you that I want you to sleep in, in the morning, I want to ask you to do something for me. I want to go to my mother's house now. Let's see if we can figure out what happened," I urged.

"C'mon, Honey, let's call it a day. It's after 10 at night. It's been a long day and you'll be getting up early in the morning," he said.

"I want to go now. I won't be able to sleep otherwise. I'm exhausted, too, but I really want to go there tonight. Please go there with me. It's on the way home and we'll only be there for a few minutes." I was on the verge of tears.

He knew the stress that I'd been under for the last few years as my mother and Delia needed more of my time and more help.

"Okay, we'll stop by there if that'll make you feel better," he said.

"Thank you," I quietly said.

We drove in silence to my mother's house. I was thinking about other drives that I had made to her house because I was worried about her. Sometimes when she didn't answer her phone for a while, I would wonder if she was in her backyard hanging up laundry on her clothesline, or doing yardwork, or if she had fallen on the floor inside her house and couldn't get up. After three or four attempts to reach her, I'd drive to her house to make sure that she was okay. Yes, it'd been a stressful few years.

When we pulled into her driveway I immediately noticed how dark her house looked, and I didn't like that sight. I walked up to the porch and opened the storm door. Then I unlocked the front door and slowly opened it. It was pitch dark inside the house. I screamed as something brushed by my leg.

"Oh, crap. The cat got out. There's no way we're gonna be able to get her back inside tonight. I'll worry about her tomorrow," I said.

"She'll be fine," Dave said calmly.

It was so dark inside the house that I had to feel my way to the lamp. The furniture that I was touching to help me find the lamp seemed out of place. When I turned the light on I saw that the chair and coffee table were feet away from where they were supposed to be. One of her house slippers was lying by the front door. I didn't see the other one. The throw rug that was usually by the front door was far away from it. It was obvious that something had happened there. Had those men who wanted to paint the inside of her house returned?

I turned on the light in the dining room. The buffet table was disheveled and there were stacks of her bills and old Christmas cards strewn across it.

"What the hell could have happened here? I don't get it," I said anxiously.

"I don't get it either," Dave said as he walked into the kitchen and turned on the light in there. I followed right behind him.

"Oh my God, these are the dishes that were on the table last night when I was here. Her tea cup is still half full. She would never leave her dishes unwashed. What happened to her?" I looked into his eyes as tears ran down my face.

He hugged me and said, "I don't know, Honey, I really don't know."

We walked into the bedrooms and bathrooms. Nothing seemed out of place in there.

"Sal, let's call it a day and go home. We're both exhausted and we're not going to find out anything tonight. Let's get her through the surgery first, and then we'll try to figure out what happened," he said.

As we got to the front door I turned around and scanned the living and dining rooms one more time. I was still looking for a clue about what happened. There were no clues.

"Thanks for coming with me. I know that I don't know any more now than I did before we came, but it was something that I had to do," I said as I started to cry again.

"It's okay, Honey. I know you want to know what happened. I do, too. Don't worry, we'll find out," he said.

"I hope so," was about all I could say.

It was a quiet drive home as we both focused on our own thoughts.

Chapter 5

Lucky to Have Her

When I first woke up the following morning I thought that I had had a terrible dream. Then I remembered what had happened, and that there was no dream. I got up and quickly dressed. There wasn't time to take a shower. I was back at the hospital at 7:30 but I was too late to see my mother before her surgery.

Her nurse told me that she was still on medication to keep her calm and that she was peaceful when they brought her downstairs to wait for her surgery. For my own sanity, I had to believe her. The nurse told me that the doctor would come out and talk to me when the surgery was over, and then she told me where the surgical waiting room was located. She said that it would be at least a couple of hours.

I was really nervous so I walked around for a while outside the hospital to try to use up some of my nervous energy. Then I went to the cafeteria and bought a cup of coffee. It didn't taste very good, but just holding the warm cup for a few minutes soothed me. Then I walked some more. I was way too antsy just to sit and wait.

I needed to talk to someone but I didn't want to call Dave in case he was still asleep. I called two of my cousins who lived in NY to tell them what had happened. They both lived with us when they came to America from Ireland many years earlier, when they were still teenagers. Both of their husbands said that they were at church. So, I walked around some more.

The time was going by excruciatingly slow. I wanted the surgery to be over and for the doctor to come out and say that everything was fine. There was a small chapel in the hospital. I went there and I prayed. I prayed that the surgery was going well; I prayed that she wouldn't be in pain; I prayed that she would be able to walk again; and I prayed for strength and wisdom for me so that I could help her get through this ordeal and to get her back to the way she used to be. I wanted my mother back the way she was before the dementia. I had a heavy heart because I knew that was one prayer that wasn't going to be answered.

I looked at my watch and decided I better go to the waiting room. I had been at the hospital for about an hour and a half at that point. I didn't know how long I would have to wait for the doctor but I didn't want to risk missing him.

It was about another hour and a half before he came into the waiting room. He looked tired and grim and I feared the worst by the look on his face. I stood up and walked across the room to meet him.

He said, "Your mother came through the surgery just fine. There weren't any complications, but—"

"Thank you. Thank you for that great news. Doctor, from the look on your face I was sure that you had bad news for me. I can't begin to tell you how relieved I am. Thank you," I said.

He continued with what he was trying to say before I had rudely interrupted, "She's in the recovery room now but she'll probably be groggy most of the day. If she does well today and tomorrow, I'll release her on Tuesday or Wednesday to go to the rehab facility. Then a lot of her recovery will be up to her. She has a lot of hard work ahead of her to get back on her feet again. It's not going to be easy, but after talking to you and your husband last night, I think that it's something that your mother is capable of doing," he said.

"She can do it. I know that she can," I said with confidence.

I sensed that he needed to leave but I had one more question for him.

"Do you think that she fell because her leg broke, or do you think that it broke because she fell?" I asked.

"It wasn't a clean break. Her hip was badly shattered. That tells me that it broke when she hit the floor. That leg will always be shorter than her other leg. She'll need to wear a shoe on that foot that's built up so that both her legs will be the same length when she walks. They'll explain all that to you and to her in the rehab. They'll also be taking out the stitches, but I'm going to want to see her again for a follow-up visit. I want to make sure that everything is healing well. Just call my office and set up an appointment to come in," he said.

"Okay," I answered.

"Do you have any other questions for me?" he asked.

"No, not that I can think of right now, but I probably will later," I said.

"Don't worry. If you think of anything, call my office and they'll let me know," he said.

"Thanks, again, Doctor," I said.

He nodded and smiled, and then we both turned to leave.

He got my attention when I heard him say, "Sally, your mother is lucky to have you. A lot of my elderly patients don't have this kind of support."

I turned back and said, "Thanks for saying that. She is lucky to have me, but then again, I'm lucky to have her."

I figured that my mother was doing well for the moment and that it would probably be hours before she would even realize whether I was there or not. I took the opportunity to drive over to Delia's apartment to let her know what was going on. When I arrived I knocked on her door and then let myself in.

"Hi, Dee Dee," I called cheerfully.

She slowly walked out of her bedroom and into the living room. I saw the front of her walker before I saw her.

"How're ye?" She asked with a smile in her voice. "Did ye have a good time yesterday?" Then she looked into my eyes.

"What's the matter with ye? Who's dead? Are the kids alright? What's the matter with ye, Sally?" she asked fretfully.

"Everybody is fine, but sit down for a minute. We need to talk," I said.

She sat down on her couch, and then made the sign of the cross. "Tell me what happened," she said.

"Mom fell," I said slowly. "She broke her hip and she had surgery this morning. The surgeon said that she came through the operation fine and he thought that she's going to be okay. She'll be in the hospital for a few more days and then she's going to have to go to a rehab for a while."

Delia had the same questions that I had. "When did she fall? What made her fall?"

"I don't know. When we got home last night there were messages that the hospital had been leaving most of the day asking that I call them and saying that she was in the hospital. I don't know how she fell or who found her. I really don't know much of anything."

"Do ye want a cup of tea?" she asked. "That might brace ye up."

"No, I really don't want anything right now, other than to go home. I'm exhausted but I wanted to stop by your apartment so that I could tell you in person what happened. I still need to check on Mom's cat, too, on my way home. Are you okay, Delia?"

"Ah, sure I'm okay. Are ye okay, Sally? You're the one running around taking care of everyone. Be a good girl and go home now and get some rest. Let David do the work to-day," she said.

"Dee Dee, I don't know what I'd do without you. Thank you. I'll call you later." We hugged each other goodbye and I drove home.

When I got home Dave was working in his home office. I filled him in on everything that had happened at the hospital and then he gave me the big news. He received a call earlier in the day from a man who said that he was in my mother's neighborhood yesterday morning. He told Dave that he seldom worked on the weekend but his wife and children were out of town, visiting her parents, so he took the opportunity to work his second job as a door to door salesman.

When he got to Mom's house the front door was ajar and he heard moans and crying from right inside the door. He let himself in and found her on the floor. It was obvious that she was hurt and that she wasn't able to get up. She begged him to get her a drink. He went to the kitchen and brought her a glass of water, and then he helped her sit up a little bit so that she could drink.

Then he asked her who he could call. She gave him my name but she couldn't remember my phone number. He went to the buffet in the dining room next to her telephone and looked to see if he could find my phone number, but couldn't. Then he looked through old mail. He found an old Christmas card from Harold Claremorris, our neighbor from years earlier in New Jersey. He called directory assistance and got Harold's home phone number. He called Harold and when he asked him if he remembered my mother, Harold said, "I haven't talked to Barbara in ages. How the hell is she?" So, unfortunately, Harold wasn't any help in providing my phone number.

He left her on the floor because he was afraid to move her, and then he quickly went to her neighbor's house that was situated to the left side of her house. He could hear people talking inside the home but nobody would answer the doorbell. He didn't want to waste any time so he then ran to the house that was to the right of Mom's house.

He had already been to that house earlier, before going to my mother's house. Nobody was home then, and still nobody was home. He knew that he needed to do something to help my mother so he went back to her house and he called 911.

What's his name, Dave?" I asked.

"Honey, I'm sorry, he told me his name when I answered the phone, but I didn't write it down. We talked for a good while before we said goodbye but I didn't think to ask his name again before we hung up. I'm not even sure how he got our number," he said.

"You don't remember his name? David, he saved my mother's life. I really want to talk to him and to thank him. I want to meet him," I said.

Things all started falling into place and it made me sad to think of what my mother probably went through.

"I think I figured out what happened," I said. "She walked me outside when I left on Friday night. As soon as I left she went inside and immediately fell and couldn't get up. It makes me sick to think that she was on that hard wood floor all night, and I'm sure that it must have been stifling hot. You know how incredibly warm she always keeps the house. I'm not sure why she didn't die from dehydration."

I was on a roll and didn't give Dave a chance to say anything.

"I can't get this vision out of my mind. The house was dark and hot and she had to have been in a lot of pain, the way the doctor described her hip. She probably cried from the pain and cried for help but there was no one there to hear her or to comfort her. Oh my God, David, I feel horrible to think how scared she must have felt as the hours went by. It must have felt like forever. I know that's exactly what happened, otherwise she would have gone into the kitchen, finished her cup of tea, and then washed her dishes."

"You can't beat yourself up over this. It's not your fault. Things happen. You can't be with your mother, or Delia for that matter, around the clock. You do more than any other daughter or niece that I know. Go easy on yourself. It's not your fault. Your mother isn't blaming you, so don't blame yourself," he said.

If I thought about it rationally I would realize that he was right, but I wasn't being rational.

"Easy for you to say," I answered.

"Honey, let me fix you some lunch. What do you want?" he asked.

"I don't care; whatever you want to fix me is fine. No, I do know what I want. Do you mind making me a peanut butter and jam sandwich, with the crunchy peanut butter?" I requested.

"And a glass of milk?" he offered.

"Yes, please." I sat at the kitchen counter and watched him make my sandwich as I went over the entire scenario again and again in my mind. Then I remembered and said, "Friday was July 6th. She fell on July 6th. Remember I told you how July 6th always creeps me out. I don't care if you think that I'm weird, but I don't ever want to travel on July 6th. I hate that day."

I'm sure that he thought that I was being silly, but he lovingly said, "If you don't want to travel on July 6th, I promise we won't ever do that."

I finished eating the sandwich and then told him that I was going back to the hospital.

"I'm not going to stay long but I need to see her. I'm really, really tired so I'm only going to make this one trip back to the hospital today and then I'm coming home and staying home. I know that I sound like a little kid, but tell me that she'll be okay," I said, looking for some hope that things would turn out all right.

"Your mother is a strong woman. She'll be fine. Old people break their hips all the time. They have surgery and get therapy and go back to their old lives again," he said, trying to make me feel better.

"Look what happened with your dad," I said, being the devil's advocate.

"The difference between my father and your mother is that my father stayed in the hospital for a month. Your mother's doctor said that she'll be out in a couple of days. If we got Dad out right away he'd probably still be with us now. The hospital made mistakes with my father. We know what to watch for this time with your mom, right?"

"I hope so," I sighed.

Dave asked if I wanted him to go back to the hospital with me. I told him that I wasn't going to stay long and that I'd be fine by myself. I needed the time by myself to digest all the thoughts that were floating around in my head.

When I got back to the hospital my mother was still fast asleep. She didn't look as peaceful as I found her the night before, however. I guess that the last two days were catching up with her. Her nurse told me that earlier she had been awake for a few hours but the pain meds were helping her sleep now. The nurse also told me that Mom had asked a few times where I was.

She told her that Dave and I were there the night before and that I was at the hospital during her surgery. It gave her comfort knowing that I knew. Before I left for the day, I kissed her cheek, told her that I loved her, and that I'd see her tomorrow. I went home and veg'd out the rest of the day.

That was the beginning of the next chapter in my mother's life, and, therefore, also in mine.

Chapter 6

No Easy Transition

I was back at the hospital early the next day. When I arrived at my mother's room there were a couple of nurses in the room with her. Since she hadn't seen me in a few days I figured it was best not to go into the room until the nurses finished what they needed to do. I wanted her to focus on what they were instructing her to do, and not on me.

I wasn't bored waiting outside her room. There was a lot more hustle and bustle going on that day than I'd noticed over the weekend. More people were being transported on gurneys and in wheelchairs than I'd seen the last few days. It seemed like there was more chitchat going on at the nurses' station, more laughter in the hallways, more people hurrying to their various destinations.

As I stared down the long hallway I noticed a man walking by himself with a definite destination and purpose on his mind. I'm not sure why, but in my mind's eye he was spotlighted. I no longer noticed all the other people walking and talking. I only saw him. It was as if I knew him and that he knew me. In fact, when he got closer, he walked up to me and said, "You must be Sally. How's your mother?"

I didn't have a clue who he was. For a moment, I thought maybe he was there to talk with me about getting her into a rehab.

"I'm Sally, but I apologize, I'm not sure who you are," I said.

"I'm the person who found your mother on Saturday. I only have a little spare time today, but I wanted to stop by to see how she's doing. I hoped that I would see you here, too."

"Oh my God, thank you. There are no words to thank you enough for your kindness to my mother. I don't know if you realize that you saved her life. If you hadn't come by her house when you did, or if you hadn't come into the house and helped her, she would have died. It was very brave for you to walk into a stranger's house. Thank you from the bottom of my heart." There were tears in my eyes.

At that point the nurses came out of my mother's room. When I asked how she was doing they said that she was a little anxious during the night but was doing okay that morning.

I turned to the man and said, "This will be the first time that I'll get to talk with her since Friday night. Please come in with me so that she can meet you. I know that she would like that."

"I'd love to see her," he said.

As soon as she saw me she slowly stretched her arms up to hug me. She looked weak and I thought that she was going to cry when she saw me.

"Baby, did they tell ye what happened to me?" Without waiting for an answer, she said, "They told me that I fell in my house and broke my leg. I'm awful sick, Sally. Can ye get me something for the pain?"

"Mom, are you in a lot of pain?" I asked.

She looked at the man standing next to me and asked, "Are ye my doctor? Please give me something for the pain."

"No, he's not the doctor. He's the man who found you on the floor inside your front door. He called the ambulance to bring you to the hospital. He's here now because he wanted to meet you, Mom."

"But how in the name of God did I fall?" she asked. "I'm always so careful."

This stranger who saved my mother's life came closer to her bed and said, "Hello, Barbara. It's a pleasure meeting you. You sure look like you're feeling much better today than when we met on Saturday. Do you remember me bringing you water? You were very thirsty."

"I remember thinking that you were an angel bringing me a drink. I was so dry. I was never so thirsty in my life. I thought I was nearly dead," she said, still speaking quietly and slowly.

"I guess God put me there for you at the right time," he said as he squeezed her hand.

My mother looked exhausted, but asked him, "What can we do to thank ye?"

"Nothing, other than to get better soon," was his sweet answer to her.

"Thank ye. God will be good to ye. I'll give ye a little something when I get out of this place, and I'm back home again," she said as she was about to drift off to sleep.

He smiled at her and said, "God has been good to me." Then he turned to me and said, "I'll wait outside the room for you so that you can visit with your mother by yourself."

"I'll only be in here for a few minutes and then you and I can talk. She looks really sleepy," I said.

As soon as he walked out of the room, I sat on the bed next to her and stroked her forehead and gently ran my fingers through her hair. I watched as her eyes slowly closed. Then I spent a minute or two looking around the room to see if there was anything that I needed to bring to her for the couple of days that she still had left in the hospital. It looked like she had everything she needed until she went to the rehab center—hairbrush, toothbrush, hospital gown.

"I'll see you tomorrow, Mom," I whispered, and then went outside the room to thank the man again, and to talk with him for a few minutes. I also needed to get his name. I couldn't remember if he told me what it was.

I didn't see him standing outside the room but I figured he probably had gone to the restroom. I waited for a while, but when he didn't return I asked one of the nurses if she'd seen him or knew where he went. She said that she'd been busy and hadn't noticed the man that I was describing. Another nurse gave me the same answer.

I wished that he had waited outside my mother's room, but I didn't think that I would have any problems finding him. I went to the cafeteria to see if maybe that's where he had gone, but no luck there either. So, I went back upstairs to my mother's room and waited patiently for a good while for him to return, but he never did.

I never saw him again. I don't know his name. I don't know how to contact him. All I know about him is that he's the stranger who saved my mother's life. I've often wondered why he didn't wait for me. I've wondered why he needed to leave so quickly. He will always be in my prayers.

My boss was very understanding when I called him from the hospital to tell him what had happened with my mother over the weekend. I told him that the doctor anticipated that she would be in the hospital for a few more days. I told him that I wanted to take off until she was in the rehab so that I could help with her transition. He said that that would be fine.

I wondered if she even knew what a rehab facility was. I didn't think that she'd ever been inside of one. I hoped that this would be an easy transition for her and that she would take physical therapy seriously so that she could get the most good out of it. The surgeon had said that a lot of her recovery would depend on her, and that she would need to work hard. I knew that she needed to hit the ground running, no pun intended.

When it's all said and done, we can hope for things all that we want, but that doesn't mean that we'll get what we're hoping for. There was no easy transition for my mother, or for me. This transition was the beginning of the toughest part of her life, and the toughest job of my life.

****

She arrived at Calafort in an ambulance, and her first few days were what I expected. She met the facility's doctor, the nurses, and the CNAs that were assigned to her. She met the physical therapists and was shown the physical therapy gym. Those first days were almost an extension of the hospital. The rehab staff were trying to get her a little stronger than when she first arrived.

Of course there were lots of forms to sign, which she asked me to take care of. There were forms for a living will, Power of Attorney, and Do Not Resuscitate. There was a booklet that explained the policies of the facility and an explanation of what Medicare would cover and what my mother's Blue Cross insurance would cover. She wouldn't have to pay anything for the first 20 days; days 21 through 100 there was a co-insurance rate; and after the 100th day she would be totally responsible for all payments to Calafort. I figured that my mother would be home long before the 100 days would be up. Boy, was I ever wrong.

In less than a week she wanted to leave the rehab and to go home, but she wasn't being cooperative about her physical therapy. I kept explaining to her that she had to be able to walk on her own before she would be able to go home. She told me that she could walk.

"Okay, Mom, let's go to the gym and show me that you can walk. I'd really like to see you walk," I said.

"Sally, leave me alone. You're bothering me as much as the rest of them here. I'll walk when I need to walk," she said impatiently.

"Mom, the longer you wait before you try to walk, the harder it's going to be to walk. If you keep putting it off, I'm afraid that you won't be able to walk." The 100 days were counting down in my brain. She needed to make the most of those days that her insurance was covering.

"Stop it, Sally." She obviously was irritated with me. She was quiet for a minute and then she asked, "How're the kids?"

"The kids are fine," I answered curtly, without giving any details.

"Honey, don't be angry with me," she paused, and then quietly added, "I'll try to walk tomorrow."

"It would really mean a lot to me if you would do that," I said. Then I sort of sighed and told her that I was tired and needed to go home.

"Baby, I'm sorry that I'm so much trouble for ye. Ye shouldn't be tied down with two old ladies. It's not right. Ye have a life of your own. Go on home now," she said.

"Please don't ever think that you're any trouble to me because you're not. I'm just nagging you so that you'll be able to walk again and so that you can go home," I persuaded.

"Baby, we'll talk about it more tomorrow," she said.

I hugged her and told her I loved her.

On the drive home I thought about what she said to me, "We'll talk about it tomorrow."

There's nothing to talk about. Just do the physical therapy, Mom; that's all you need to do.

I woke up early the next morning and decided to stop by the rehab on the way to my office. I wanted to give her some encouragement to start her day. What I saw troubled me a lot and I needed encouragement by the time I left there. As

I got closer to her room, I heard her hollering, "No! No! No! Put me down!"

I ran into her room. She was in the bathroom with two CNAs who were trying to get her out of her wheelchair and on to the toilet. My mother was a strong woman and she was resisting with all her might.

"Mom, Mom, settle down," I said. "They're trying to help you to go to the bathroom."

"Tell them to leave me alone. I don't want to sit on the toilet now," she snapped.

They had managed to get her on the toilet in the midst of all the commotion. When I motioned for the CNAs to step out of the crowded bathroom, they took the wheelchair with them. My mother was visibly upset.

"Mom, I'm here with you. You're safe. Sit here for just a minute. Try to make a tinkle in the toilet," I said.

I stood close to her so that she wouldn't fall off the seat. I could hear the CNAs outside the door whispering. I wasn't sure if they were whispering about my mother or if I was being overly sensitive. Then I heard a big pee in the toilet.

"Good job, Mom," I said, sounding much like I did when Michael and Kathleen were toddlers and I was potty training them.

"Does it hurt your leg when you sit on the hard toilet seat?" I asked.

"Nothing hurts, but those women are going to drop me. I'm afraid that they're going to drop me," she said, sounding annoyed.

"I'll talk to them and ask them to be very careful when they're helping you in the bathroom, but you have to trust them. You have to start using the toilet or else..."

I stopped myself in mid-sentence. I couldn't say the words I was about to say to my mother. I couldn't tell her that each of the CNAs had several other patients that they were working with and that they would only put up with so many of these incidents with her before they stopped bringing her to the bathroom. It would be much easier for them to put a diaper on her.

They had far too many people that they were taking care of who wanted to be taken to the bathroom to waste their time on my mother if this was how she was going to behave. Before her fall she was totally continent, but things were rapidly changing. She came into Calafort with a catheter from the hospital. It had obviously been removed and she was now in the stage where they were "training her" to use the toilet again.

She was on a schedule when they thought that she needed to "be toileted." They took her to the bathroom whether she said she needed to go or not. I remembered a Saturday afternoon, weeks earlier, when she and I were at the Mall for hours. I was the one who had to use the bathroom, not my mother. I told her that she had a bionic bladder.

"Mom, it looks like you're finished using the bathroom for now. I'm going to ask the aides to come back in here and help you get back into your chair. I'm afraid to help you myself. I don't want you to fall and they know the best way to do it. Don't be afraid. I'll be standing right here and I'll be watching them."

"Please stay here with me for a little while," she said.

"Don't worry, I will," I answered.

I motioned for them to come back in and to please take her off the toilet.

Getting her off the toilet was a much calmer scene then getting her on the toilet, although she said a couple of times, "Be careful with me, I don't want to fall."

"Barbara, we won't drop you. We'll take good care of you," one of them said with a thick Spanish accent.

After she was safely back into her wheelchair, and they were encouraging her to brush her teeth, I waited in the hallway outside her bedroom. While I was waiting, I called my office to say that I'd be about half an hour late. I was salaried so I wasn't concerned about clocking in, but I was concerned about all the work that needed to be done. I never wanted to let my boss, my co-workers, or my office down. I planned to stay late that evening.

From the talk that was coming from her room, I could tell that the CNAs were finished doing their job with her for the moment. I continued to wait for them outside the room so that I could speak with them for a few minutes, without my mother hearing the conversation.

"Ladies, I know that you have an extremely hard job and I really appreciate all that you do for my mother." I emphasized the word extremely.

"Since you don't know her at all, I'd like to tell you a few things about her that I think are important for you to know. If you knew her a little bit, it might make it easier for you to help her and to do your job," I said.

"Yes, we would like to know about your mother," one of them said.

"Thank you. First of all, it's important to know that she lived totally on her own until she fell, and the plan is for her to be able to go back to her own home again. That's really important to keep in mind," I said.

"That's wonderful that she was able to live by herself," the same CNA answered.

"Please be patient with her. If you're patient, it will be much easier for you and for her. Keep in mind that at 88 years old, she has her own way of doing things, but I'm certain that if you're patient, you won't have any problems," I said.

Both ladies were nodding at me.

"I'm sure that you've noticed that my mother is very hard of hearing. To get her to hear you, all you need to do is to stand in front of her so she can see you speaking, and then speak slowly and clearly. Talking loudly to her won't help at all. Please treat her the way you would want your mother or your grandmother to be treated. Someday you might be in the same position that I'm in now," I told them.

"We'll take good care of your mom. Don't worry," one of them answered.

"Thank you. I really appreciate your help and your kindness. You'll be seeing me here often. My mother always took good care of me. Now it's my turn to take good care of her," I said.

I wondered how many times in the past they'd heard that same speech from other family members.

On that note, I went back into her room. She looked much better than when I found her earlier. Her hair and teeth had been brushed and she was dressed in one of the outfits that I had brought from her house.

"Mom, I talked to the two aides that took you to the bathroom before. They promised that they'll be very careful with you. You have to trust them. It's their job to help you get better so that you can go back home."

"Where am I, Sally? What sort of place is this?" she asked.

"It's a rehab center. It's not a hospital but it's pretty close to it. There are doctors and nurses who work here. All the people who work here are trying to get you stronger, and better, and able to walk again so that you can go back home."

I tried to put it in the most basic terms.

"But you have to do your part. You have to help them to help you. I know that you like to do things when and how you want to do them, but for the time being, Mom, please cooperate with them. And please, please do a good job today in physical therapy. It's really important."

"We'll see how I feel later. I'm sick, Sally. Do ye think that I would be sitting around all day if I wasn't sick? I don't want to push myself too much," she said.

"Please try to walk today. You promised me that you would try." I didn't know what else to say. I was getting extremely frustrated but I knew my mother well, and showing her that I was frustrated wouldn't make her walk. It would only upset her.

"Mom, I brought you a supper for tonight. I'll leave it with the nurse and they'll heat it up for you this evening. It's baby back ribs, mashed potatoes, and beans. That's what we had last night and I thought it was pretty good. How did you like the chicken that I brought for you yesterday?"

"It was delicious, Baby. Thank ye," she said.

"You're welcome. Give me some ideas for other meals that you'd like me to bring. Salmon? Lamb chops? Just let me know. You need to keep your energy up so that you'll do good walking," I said, always trying to mention "walking."

"Honey, anything that you bring me is delicious. Don't worry so much about me," she said, and then added, "I hate to see ye leave but go to work now or you'll be late."

"Mom, I love you. If I don't see you this evening, I'll see you tomorrow. Do a good job in physical therapy," I told her as I hugged her goodbye.

I thought about her throughout the day, and I hoped that she had put in some effort to walk. Since I wasn't planning to visit her a second time that day, I wouldn't know until the next day if she had even given it a try. I had been so busy with my mother that I hadn't had time to see Delia for a few days, so I made a point of stopping by her apartment that evening on my way home from work.

I knocked on her door, unlocked it, and walked in. "Hello, Sally. How're ye?" she asked as she looked up from her supper. She was eating sardines, boiled potatoes and beets. It didn't look too appealing to me but she seemed to like it.

"Do ye want something to eat?" she asked.

"Thanks for asking but I'll eat when I get home. Dave probably has our supper almost ready. I haven't seen you for a few days so I wanted to stop by and see how you're doing. How do you feel?" I asked.

"I'm alright. Tell me about your mother. Did she walk today?" she asked.

"I don't know. I really hope so because she hasn't been cooperating much at all with them as far as her physical therapy. I'm getting really frustrated with her, but I have no idea what to do. If she doesn't start doing what they want her to do, they're going to give up on her. She keeps telling me that she'll walk tomorrow, but that tomorrow hasn't happened yet. She just doesn't get the urgency of what's happening with her."

I must have sounded like a child when I said, "She's your sister. You know her as well as I do, probably better than me in some ways. What can I, what should I do?"

She sat quietly for a moment, but it was obvious that she was thinking about the tough situation that we were in.

"I have no one to take me there or I would go and stay the day with her and go to the therapy with her. Do ye think that would help?" she asked.

"I think that's a really great idea, but I don't see how I can take you there during the week. I can't push it any more than I'm already pushing it at work. They've been so good to me letting me take all the time off that I've taken. I don't see how I can take a long enough lunch break to come pick you up, drive to the rehab for her therapy, and then bring you back here again."

"I know that ye can't do it," she said.

We both sat silent for a moment.

"I'm pretty sure that she has physical therapy scheduled for Saturday. Would you like to go with me then?" I asked.

"Of course I would," she answered without any hesitation.

I got up and went over to her and gave her one of the biggest hugs I'd ever given anyone. She was my aunt, my godmother, and my rock. She must have known that the stress was getting to me.

She held me and said, "Your mother will be okay."

A few minutes later, we said goodnight to each other and I went on home. Shortly after I arrived home Dave was putting the supper on the table, and I was able to relax for a few hours before I had to do it all again the next day. Thank you, Dave.

****

Even though I was still seeing my mother every day, just like I did when she lived in her home, it had become a totally different experience. I was no longer doing what I used to do for her, but I was making sure that her new caregivers were doing what needed to be done.

I firmly believed that the patients whose friends and family visited often, got far better care than those who were left on their own, or who seldom had visitors. I came at different times of the day, depending on what was going on at work, or depending on what was going on with the kids' activities. It was a balancing act where I was trying to please everyone and to take care of all my responsibilities.

One evening when I stopped by for a quick visit on the way home from work, I was shocked by what I saw. It had been a stressful day at work and I would have done anything to be able to go straight home. I had planned to make that night's visit a short one.

What I saw when I entered her room made my jaw drop and my heart sink. My mother was lying on the bed and a woman that I'd never seen before was putting a diaper on her. My mother was calm and not objecting in the least. Without saying a word, I backed out of the room and found her nurse.

I was obviously upset. "What in the world is going on in that room with my mother? A diaper? Who is that woman who's putting a diaper on my mother? What is the matter with you people?" I snapped.

"Calm down, Sally," she said.

"Calm down? I keep reminding everyone that weeks ago she was living in her own home, cooking her own food, and going to the bathroom when she needed to go to the bathroom. She was totally continent. There were no diapers in her life. Are you hearing what I'm saying?" I asked, totally exasperated.

It's hard to describe the frustration and the anger that I was feeling.

She calmly responded, "Our number one concern is your mother's safety. I know that you were here when the two Marias were trying to put her on the toilet. That's how it's been every time we've tried toileting her. The CNAs are all careful but either your mother is going to get hurt or one of the staff will get hurt. Plus, it's not good for your mother's well-being to be so upset. I've seen the CNAs putting diapers on her and she doesn't get upset at all. Sally, I know that it's difficult to see your mother wearing a diaper, but you have to think of what's best for her."

I don't have an ounce of violence in me, but I wanted to hit something or somebody. How dare she tell me to think of what was best for my mother? That's all that I thought about. I felt like I was in the middle of a nightmare and as hard as I tried to wake up, I couldn't. I wanted to blame someone, but there was no one to blame. It wasn't my mother's fault. She couldn't help it. She was afraid she was going to fall again. She already had the fall of a lifetime. I know that she must have been terrified of another one.

I couldn't totally blame the staff either because my mother wasn't cooperating with them. But I'll always think that if they had talked more slowly, more calmly to her for a few minutes before they took her to the bathroom and if they patiently explained what they were doing, that she would have trusted them to help her.

The nurse interrupted my thoughts. "We all have to work together to get your mother walking again. That's the goal we need to be striving for, right? Let's focus on the bigger issues for now, like walking," she said.

I didn't like the way this woman was talking to me, or maybe I just didn't like what she had to say. Did we really have to choose between diapers and walking? I didn't want to have to do that, but I also knew that I had to pick my battles. Since I was the one so upset about the diapers, not my mother, I decided this was a battle that I couldn't win.

"Who's that CNA that's in there with my mother?" I asked. "I've never seen her before."

"She's with an agency," she said, as if I should know what that meant.

"Pardon me?" I asked.

"Sometimes when we're short staffed we use nurses and CNAs from an agency. Some days they'll work here and some days they'll be working at another facility," she answered.

I must have sounded a little snarky when I asked, "Why don't you just increase your staff so that my mother, and all the other residents, know who's taking care of them, and they know the residents? The woman taking care of my mother today doesn't know her in the least. There's more to giving good care than just reading what's in the person's chart. Do you understand what I'm saying?" I asked.

"I understand you and I agree with you but our hands are tied. It all boils down to the budget. Corporate doesn't want to keep people on staff when they're not needed full time," she explained.

"I hope someday Corporate will be lying in a bed and having someone changing his or her diapers—someone they've never seen before," I said.

I had to get out of there. God forgive me but I couldn't bring myself to go into my mother's room again that night.

"Please tell my mother that I called to say I love her but that I was pooped and was going straight home tonight. Tell her not to worry and that everyone is fine. Please remember to tell her or I'm afraid that she'll worry about me," I told her nurse.

She said that she would give my mother the message.

****

Thank God it was finally Friday. We were planning on going out with a couple of other families that night for dinner. It was a tradition that went way back. Our kids had all been friends since they were toddlers. They'd gone to school together, done scouts, had piano lessons, played basketball, ran track, trick or treated at Halloween, slept over at each other's homes, and had been best friends for many years.

As upset as I was when I left the rehab, I was going to do my best to put both my mother and Delia in a corner of my mind that I wouldn't visit again until the morning. That was the only way that I could have a mentally healthy life. I knew that if I didn't give myself some sort of respite, I was going to crack.

Saturday morning came far too quickly. I woke up earlier than I would have liked but it worked out okay since I got the laundry done and the bills paid. I picked up Delia around 10:00. Mom's physical therapy was scheduled for 10:30. When we got to the PT room she was already there in her wheelchair watching the other people going through their therapy. She seemed entertained as she looked on. Today was the first time that Delia had seen her since "the fall."

"What are ye both doing here? Is everything okay?" my mother asked.

"Nan (that's the family's nickname for my mother), we came to watch ye walk. We want to see how far ye will walk today," Delia said with lots of encouragement in her voice. "How're ye keeping, Nan? I heard ye took an awful fall."

"Ah musha, I'll be fine once I'm home again. You've lost a lot of weight, Delia. Ye look like a skeleton. Are ye sick?" Mom said to her older sister.

Ah, sisterly love. Actually, I thought that Delia was looking darn good for someone in her nineties.

The therapist was just finishing up with a patient and walked over to Mom's chair and asked, "Is this your family?"

Mom introduced us as he shook our hands.

"Barbara, now I want you to show your daughter and your sister what a good walker you are. Let's show them what you can do," he said.

"Maybe tomorrow. I'm just enjoying watching the others take their exercise," was her quick reply.

"No, Barbara, I'm off tomorrow so today is the day to show them how well you can walk," he said. "You can do it. I know that you can do it." He was patient and firm with her, and I could see that she liked him and trusted him.

"He's handsome, Sally, isn't he?" my mother asked me as he was wheeling her to the parallel bars.

"Yes he is, Mom," I said loud enough for them both to hear.

He tied some sort of a safety belt around her waist and then helped her to stand up. That's when Delia said loud enough for my mother to hear, "Nan, walk good now."

It was obvious that she was scared that she was going to fall, but to her credit she took about four steps, but then stopped. The therapist said something to her that I couldn't hear. She continued walking. She had a hand on each of the bars and he was holding on to the belt. I wasn't certain how much walking she was doing on her own, and how much he was helping, but nevertheless she was walking. She walked 12 steps, which was beyond incredible, and then she yelled, "I'm going to fall." He helped her back into her wheelchair.

"Barbara, you did a great job. I'm proud of you," the therapist said to her.

"Mom, I've never been more proud of you. I know that it wasn't easy but you did it. You did it! Please keep it up. Please do that every time you come to therapy." I hugged her.

"Ye know what they say, Baby. Where there's a will, there's a way," she said.

"Nan, ye have to do that every day. Do ye hear me, Nan?" Delia asked.

Delia looked at me and asked, "Did she hear me?"

"Every day, Nan. Every day," she said again.

I asked the therapist if she had done that well before. He said that the most steps that she'd taken before that day were four steps. He said that he knew that she was afraid that she was going to fall and that was going to be hard to overcome. He said psychologically and physically, the more steps that she took, the easier it would become for her.

I asked if he was the person who always worked with her and he said, "No." He said that the facility had a really good rehab staff but that she didn't always have the same person. I asked if there was a way that he could always be her therapist. I thought that she did well, not only because Delia and I were there, but because she "clicked" with him. He told me that he couldn't promise that he would be able to work with her all the time, but that he would try as often as possible.

I thanked him and said, "Please try. I think that in the end it will make a huge difference."

Delia and I stayed for lunch with my mother. I was glad that the two sisters were able to spend some time together; it was good for each of them to see the other. As Delia and I left Calafort we were in agreement that our morning in the gym with my mother was a success. I sure hoped that it would be the spark that would help her walk again. I wondered how she would do during the work week when we weren't there.

After our visit I brought Delia straight back to her apartment. I think that the rehab visit had tired her out physically and emotionally, although she never let on that it had. Usually, she went to the grocery store with me, but on that day she asked if I could pick up a few things for her.

I said, "Of course."

Her grocery list was never lengthy. That was because a few times a week she went to the Senior Center and had lunch with her older friends. A couple times each week some of her younger friends would stop by her apartment and would bring take-out lunches for them and for her, and would spend their lunch break visiting with her.

I was always amazed by the number of friends she had. She was like a magnet attracting a wide variety of friends of all ages. She could discuss politics as easily with her adult friends, as she could talk sports with Michael. When she was about 90 years old, she showed Michael and Kathleen that she could do the Macarena. When she was by herself she kept busy reading, knitting and crocheting, and praying. She prayed for the living and for the dead. She seldom complained and never stopped learning. She inspired me. If only she could inspire my mother to take her physical therapy seriously, the road ahead of us would be a much smoother ride.

Chapter 7

"I Love Ye and I Like Ye"

The following week the rehab brought more challenges my way. When I visited on Monday evening I was too late for my mother's supper, so I gave the dinner that I brought for her to the nurse and asked that she give it to her on Tuesday. I knew that my mother would like it—lamb chops, mashed potatoes, and peas. That was the kind of food she ate at home, not that long ago. The nurse du jour told me that my mother was seen by the speech therapist earlier in the day and a decision was made that she could no longer eat the type of home cooked meals that I'd been bringing her.

"Speech therapist? My mother doesn't have any problems with her speech. I don't understand what you're talking about," I said to her.

"We're concerned that your mother is aspirating. You know how sometimes when you're eating and the food goes down the wrong way? Well, it appears that's often what's happening when your mother eats her food," she explained. "That's not healthy for her and could actually slowly kill her. She's been on a mechanical soft diet most of the time that she's been here, except for the food that you've been bringing her. Dietary has changed her food preparation to pureed. And she'll need to drink thickened liquids."

"Why didn't you tell me that there was an issue with her swallowing, rather than telling me after a decision was made to change her diet?" I asked.

"We just did the test today and I'm telling you now," she said, with little patience for my question.

"So you don't want me to bring her any more meals from home?" I asked.

"Let's hold off for now. We'll retest her again and see how she's doing," she answered, a little kinder than her last answer.

"Why is she aspirating? When she was at home she was able to swallow two acetaminophens at one time. She didn't cough or give any indication that she had a problem. I don't get it. What is happening to my mother? Other than the broken hip, she was so much better before she came into Calafort. Now she's in diapers and can't even eat normal food. I don't understand all the changes in her that's happening overnight," I said.

"You have to understand that it's not unusual that when someone is your mother's age, things that were fine just yesterday are no longer fine. Things change quickly at her age. She's been lucky to have done as well as she's done up to now, and I'm sure that you're part of that reason. You've taken good care of her. I often hear what you're saying from families and I know that it's disheartening to see these changes in your mother," she said.

Everything she said to me made perfect sense—perfect sense for someone else's mother, but not mine. She didn't know my mother. How could she make blanket statements about how people should be at a certain age? My mother had always acted years younger than her calendar age. Was I in denial?

"Did she eat the supper that you guys gave her tonight?" I asked.

"She ate about 75%. That's not bad," she said.

"Ok, I'll hold off bringing her food from home for a while. Will you please let me know when you're going to do the test again and then let me know how she does?" I asked.

"I promise I'll let you know," she said.

When I went into her room, she was in her wheelchair facing the wall.

I walked up behind her and whispered into her ear, "Hi Mom, whatcha doing?"

I then turned her chair around so she could see me.

"Hi Baby, I'm just sitting here thinking. I'm not sure where I am though. Is this where I'm staying now?"

"For a while you'll stay here. It's a rehab. That's sort of like a hospital. You need to stay here until you get stronger and you can walk again and then you'll be able to go back home," I said, trying to be convincing about going back home.

"I hope that will be soon. I miss my own little house," she said.

I wondered where she was thinking her own little house was.

"Hey, Mom, it's still light out. I'm going to take you for a walk outside. Let's escape for a few minutes," I said.

"Honey, I'm not able to walk very far. I had a hard day today and I think that it's cold outside," she said, trying to make excuses not to leave her room.

"Don't worry about walking for now; I'll push you in your chair. It's pretty warm out, but I'll put a blanket over your legs, if you'd like," I said.

Ye know me, Baby; I'm always freezing," she said. "But, if ye want to go outside for a little while, we'll go outside."

The weather was nice outdoors and it didn't take long before she seemed more relaxed. I pushed her wheelchair to a little pond on the grounds of the facility that had a few ducks on it. I squatted down next to her and pointed at the baby ducks that were following their mother.

"Isn't nature beautiful?" she said, with a little smile.

"Nature is beautiful," I answered, and then I pointed to a plane high above us. "Mom, look up at the sky. Do you see the airplane way up there? Can you see it?"

"I can see it. Wouldn't it be lovely to be flying some-where now? Would ye and the kids and Dave like to go back to Ireland next summer?" she asked, with hope in her voice.

I knew our days of travelling to Ireland with my mother were over but I said, "Mom, there isn't anything I'd like to do more in the world than to go to Ireland next summer with you."

"Sally, look at the cat running across the street. I hope my little cat is okay. I hope she didn't get hurt when I fell," she said.

"Mom, what did you just say about your cat? About the fall?" I asked, still squatting down next to her.

"Are ye feeding her for me? I think that there's food left for her in the kitchen," she said.

"Mom, did you trip on the cat? Is that what made you fall?" I asked, looking directly into her eyes.

I really wanted to know what had happened. When my mother was in the hospital she said that she was always careful, and I totally believed that she was. Something out of the ordinary caused her to fall.

"She stayed nearby me during the night, all night," she said.

I needed answers. Did the cat cause her to fall or did she mean that after she fell the cat stayed near her when she was on the floor? Our conversation made me think of the night that Dave and I went to her house, and the cat brushed by my legs to get out of the house. Is that what happened with my mother?

"Mom, do you remember what happened when you fell down in your house? Did you trip on the cat?" I tried to calmly pry out some answers.

"I just told ye what happened. That's all that I know, Baby," she said wistfully. Then she added, "What's done is done. I don't want to talk about it anymore."

And she didn't talk about it ever again, no matter how many different ways I tried to bring it up.

I don't know if you'll understand what I'm about to tell you, or if you'll even believe me, but for weeks after I brought Pepper to our house, she looked like she was going to cry. She actually looked sad. I truly believe that she missed my mother. Dave, who definitely is not a cat person, totally agreed with me. Pepper has lived with us now for over 10 years.

I never found out definitively why my mother fell, but I'll always have a strong suspicion of what happened on that fateful July 6th night. Only my mother and Pepper were there and unfortunately neither of them could tell me what went on.

Something else that will always be a mystery to me was why my mother wouldn't take her physical therapy seriously. She had always been a great walker, and since she'd never learned how to drive, walking was often her mode of transportation. When she lived in her home, she never gave a second thought to walking a couple of miles to Delia's apartment or to the grocery store, or to any other destination that was within walking distance.

It made no sense to me why she did so well with her physical therapy the first time that Delia and I watched her, but from then on when I asked her nurse each evening how physical therapy went, I kept getting the same answer—"She refused to walk." It broke my heart that my mother, the great walker, never attempted to walk again, even with encouragement from Delia and from me, even with help from the handsome therapist.

I found the entire rehab situation very sad. Not only was she unable to walk, but she couldn't eat anything other than pureed food, and she was wearing diapers. My mother was wearing diapers. Those are words that I would never have imagined saying. All these changes happened within weeks of moving into Calafort.

Knowing how unpleasant her day to day life was at that time, I tried hard to think of ways to put a smile on her face. What still made her the happiest was getting to spend time with Michael and Kathleen, so I brought them with me on the weekends. They were still her best medicine. We wouldn't stay very long but just seeing them always cheered her up. She would say to them, "I love ye and I like ye."

Michael once asked her why she told them that she liked them. She explained, "God said that we have to love each other and that's why I love all people. God never said that we have to like anyone. But I like everything I see about ye and Kathleen. You're both very nice kids, and I'm proud of ye both. Your mom and dad are doing a good job raising the two of ye."

I sometimes marveled how she could be so articulate, but then an hour later, not have any idea even where she was.

I tried to spend as much time as possible with her outside the building when Michael and Kathleen were with me. I'd wheel her outside and I'd sit on a bench next to her. The fresh air and the sounds of nature were soothing to her. Sometimes the kids would bring their skateboards or scooters. Watching them play was entertainment for her. It was the normalcy of the life she left behind.

Sometimes they would pretend they were dancing old fashioned waltz type dances. In the middle of the dance Kathleen would do a cartwheel or two and then they'd go back to dancing some more. My mother thought it was just wonderful, but in her eyes whatever they did was wonderful. I remember many times watching her, as she watched them. I don't know who was more content—Mom or I.

I hated when it was time to bring her back inside the building, but I intentionally kept my weekend visits short when I had the kids with me. It's tough enough for adults to visit rehab centers so I was appreciative that Michael and Kathleen never complained about going with me.

One of those weekend visits turned into a lesson for me about kids and nursing homes. We had just brought my mother back inside the building and the kids were acting particularly rambunctious. They were teasing each other, and giggling, and were fooling around way too much. One of the residents kept looking at them and I thought that they were probably annoying her. Before she said something to them, I told them that they needed to settle down.

When she heard me scolding them, she wheeled herself closer to me and said, "Please don't make them stop. It's wonderful to hear the laughter of children. There's far too much sadness in here. Too often all I hear are old people hollering for help. Let your children laugh and be happy in here. Let them be children. Most of us don't mind at all."

I was surprised to hear her say those words and I thanked her for putting things into perspective for me. Her sobering comment stuck with me for a long time, and in time I came to realize just how meaningful her words were.

That lady lived in the Meadows Unit. However, she wasn't the typical Meadows' resident. All of the people who lived in that part of Calafort needed long term care, which is another way of saying a nursing home. The majority of those residents appeared to have some degree of dementia or Alzheimer's. She obviously had all her wits about her, and was definitely the exception to the norm.

Mom lived in the Glen Unit of the facility and that was considered the rehab unit. People in the Glen were only there for a few months and then went back home again. A small number of the residents in the Glen had some degree of dementia, but most of them were mentally sharp and were only there long enough to get their rehab. I prayed that as long as my mother would be living in Calafort, that it would always be in the Glen.

Chapter 8

Good Doctors Give Us Hope

My mother made a new friend in the rehab. His name was Dennis. For several days when I arrived at mealtime, the two of them would be sitting at the same table. He was a handsome, well dressed gentleman who looked like he was also in his late 80s. Each day he had on a different brightly colored sweater that accented his thick silver hair. It was cute to watch him flirt with my mother as much as she flirted with him. He seemed to be "with it" mentally, or at least if he wasn't, he hid it well.

One day there was another pretty lady sitting at their table. I never noticed her before that day but as I sat next to my mother, I watched her tuck Dennis' napkin into his sweater and then she poured him a cup of coffee. She obviously knew him.

Uh oh, this woman isn't Dennis' CNA, I thought, half joking to myself.

Next thing I knew Dennis was getting angry at her and said, "You haven't been home in over four days." He told her that he had a new wife now and her name was Barbara. Mom looked pleased as she smiled at the lady who obviously was Dennis' real wife. I wasn't sure if I should laugh at how comical the scene was or if I should cry at how bizarre it was.

The friendship was short lived, however, because of what happened next. The date was August 6th, a month since my mother had fallen. She'd been complaining about pain in her legs for a few days, and had even said, "They've never hurt this much before."

I gave her the "I'm sorry, Mom" response and reminded her that she spent her days sitting in a wheelchair, without doing any walking, and that probably was making her legs hurt more than usual. Since my mother had complained, off and on for years, about pain in her legs, I wasn't too concerned that there was anything out of the ordinary going on. I was wrong.

Minutes after being introduced as Dennis' new wife, she told me that she couldn't stand the pain any longer, and that she needed to go to the doctor right away. When I asked if her arthritis was worse than usual she got angry at me and said that it didn't have anything to do with her arthritis. She said that if I didn't take her to the doctor that she was going to call a taxi. She was making a scene. One of the nurses came over and tried to calm her down.

"Will one of ye take me to the doctor, please," she pleaded, her Irish brogue strong and clear.

There was no calming her down and since she was obviously in a lot of pain, the nurse called the facility doctor who told her to call 911. It didn't take long before an ambulance arrived and rushed her to the hospital. I followed the ambulance in my car. Shortly after she got to the hospital she was brought into the ER and was seen by the doctor. Tests were run, and thankfully it didn't take too long before there was a diagnosis. She had blood clots in her left leg.

She was scheduled for surgery where she underwent a major vein revision. A catheter was placed into her vein and a vein filter was inserted to catch any future clots that may develop. She came through the unexpected surgery fine, and the reason for the severe pain in her leg was gone. I felt terrible that I hadn't been more tuned in to her recent complaints, but I thought that it was just her arthritis. I had heard that same complaint so many times over the years that I didn't think there was anything more serious going on. I vowed to myself that from then on I would always give credence to her complaints.

She stayed in the hospital for a couple of nights and then was brought by ambulance back to Calafort. Things quickly got back to normal for her, her new normal, that is. As crazy as it sounds, I still held out hope that my mother might be able to go back home. The realist in me knew that was something that would probably never happen. She couldn't walk, or use the bathroom, or eat normal food. How in God's name did I think that she could ever go home? I didn't have an answer to that question, but I wasn't ready to give up, even with all those problems stacked against her.

If I could have been at the rehab 24/7, I would have been there 24/7. Since that wasn't possible, I had to depend on the nurses and the CNAs to help her get through each day the best that she was able. I was happy that Calafort had a good reputation, but I came to the realization that what really mattered was which nurses and CNAs were working as to whether my mother had a good day or not.

It was frustrating that I couldn't count on all of them to do the right thing, the kind thing. It made me sad the times that I'd arrive for my daily visit and I'd find her sitting all alone, either in her room or at the end of a hallway, facing a wall. I hated seeing her left like that. My mother had always been a social person and she loved having company. Leaving her by herself, staring at a wall, did nothing but add to her confusion.

I kept asking the CNAs and nurses to make a point to please park her, for lack of a better word, near the nurses' station or near other residents, and to please stop leaving her by herself. That request often fell on deaf ears.

Speaking of deaf ears, I continued asking the staff to please look directly at her when they were speaking to her. They needed to speak slowly and clearly. I told them that she wasn't stupid; she just couldn't hear them or understand their Spanish or Island accents. I asked them to please be patient with her, but I found it disheartening that I even had to make that request.

****

It had been about six weeks since my mother's fall, and I was on autopilot. I was putting in a full day at work, checking in with Delia daily, visiting my mother daily and being her advocate, as well as having a busy home life with Dave and the kids. I definitely wasn't ready for another crisis, but that's not something we get to plan.

My mother recovered totally from the blood clot surgery and was back in Calafort for about two weeks when she faced her next hurdle. She hadn't said anything to me about not feeling well, but she looked like she might be coming down with something. She had a little cough, but that was the only thing that was out of the ordinary.

When I visited her on this particular day and I looked into her eyes I had no doubt that she was sick. When I asked her how she was feeling she said that she hurt everywhere.

"Mom, that doesn't help me to figure out what to do for you, or what the problem is. You need to be more specific," I said.

That's when she started rubbing her upper thighs and said that they hurt. She said that her lower back hurt a lot, too. Suddenly there was a déjà vu of just a few weeks earlier. She was on the verge of tears and said that I needed to take her to the doctor or that she would call a taxi. Her nurse also tried to figure out why she was hurting, but just like with the blood clot issue, there wasn't anything that the nurse could do to help her, or to calm her down. So once again an ambulance was called.

I met the ambulance at the hospital where she was immediately brought into the emergency room. She seemed to be in more pain and was more agitated then she had been prior to the ambulance ride. I regretted that I hadn't asked if I could have ridden with her in the ambulance.

I can honestly say that I had never seen her in that much discomfort in the past. A nurse came to her bedside pretty quickly and checked her vitals. When she asked the nurse to give her something for her pain, she responded to that request by saying that the doctor would be in to see her as soon as he could. I knew there was triage in the ER but it was obvious that my mother wasn't high on the list. This ER visit was a totally different experience from the one just a few weeks earlier.

I felt sorry for her as she waited and waited and waited on a small bed in the ER. She started asking loudly, whenever a nurse walked by her curtained ER bed, for something to help with the pain. I'm not sure why she was so loud—if it was because she couldn't hear well, or if she wanted to make sure that the nurses heard her.

To add to the drama that I was in the midst of, a thin curtain was all that separated us from a man who sounded intoxicated on the bed next to my mother's bed. His language was colorful and he, too, was in pain. He was far more demanding than my mother in wanting to be seen. There was a police officer standing nearby him.

I stood close to my mother's bed and held her hand while we waited for a doctor. Even though I had no idea why she hurt, I knew that she was in a lot of pain, and I wanted someone to make the pain go away. She tugged at my heartstrings when she looked at me and said, "Help me, Baby," but there wasn't anything that I could do to make her feel better.

As the time slowly went by, I continued asking the nurses, "How much longer before a doctor will be able to see my mother?"

"He'll be in there as soon as he can get to her," was the stock answer that I was given each of the times I asked.

What I wanted to say back was, "Of course he'll get to her as soon as he can get to her. I know that. I'm not an idiot. I would just like an idea if we're talking about minutes or hours longer before someone can help her. She's in a lot of pain," but the words that came out of my mouth were, "Thank you. I'm sorry that I keep bothering you. My mother is almost 89 years old and I hate seeing her suffer. I feel really bad for her."

I couldn't just stand there and do nothing, so while we waited for the doctor I kept putting cool washcloths on her forehead and warm blankets on her body because she kept saying that she was "freezing cold." I don't know if either of those gestures helped her in the least, but it made me think that I was doing something for her, even though I couldn't take away the pain.

After what seemed like forever, a doctor finally saw her and admitted her into the hospital. That admission marked the beginning of two weeks of living hell. There were lots of tests—blood work, EKG, chest x-rays, lower spine x-rays, x-rays of her pelvis, a swallowing test, and a Doppler echo of her heart. She was on an IV drip. Oh yea, decisions had to be made—comfort care only? feeding tube? what kind of feeding tube?

I wasn't even aware of all the tests that she had, or the names of all the doctors who saw her, until months later when the bills and her Blue Cross insurance statements came in the mail. That's when I found out that she was also charged for psychiatric care starting on day one of that hospital stay.

The thought of my mother being seen by a psychiatrist was so foreign to me that it was difficult to fathom.

She was diagnosed with a urinary tract infection and pneumonia, neither of which are unusual in elderly people. However, my mother had never been diagnosed with pneumonia before in her almost 89 years, and I knew that particular disease was often the kiss of death in the elderly.

The day after she was admitted into the hospital, I called Dr. Diarmuid. As bad luck would have it, that was when he and his wife were in Germany, and I was told that he wouldn't be returning to work until the following week. Dr. Diarmuid knew my mother better than any of the doctors that were now seeing her in the hospital. I trusted him through and through, and I knew that my mother desperately needed his help.

Unfortunately, she was already on so much medication, including psychotropic drugs, that she didn't have a clue who was taking care of her. That hospital stay had quickly put her in NaNa land. The main doctor who was coordinating her care was a Dr. Limerick. I had never heard the term hospitalist before I met him, but that is what he was. From the moment I met him, I disliked him as much as I liked Dr. Diarmuid. When I saw how some of the drugs were effecting my mother, I told him that I was concerned, and that I didn't want her on them. He ignored my request to take her off those drugs.

After she was in the hospital for just a few days, I was worried how this hospital stay was going to end for my mother. That's when I remembered a conversation that I had had with Dr. Diarmuid several years earlier. He told me that I would never have to worry if there ever was a time that he wasn't available to see my mother. That was because his cousin would cover for him.

As soon as I remembered that conversation, I called their office, and asked to speak with his cousin's nurse.

"Hi Tiffany. I'll be happy when Dr. Diarmuid gets back because he knows my mother so well, but until then, can his cousin please see her? She's really sick and is in the hospital."

In a million years I never anticipated the answer that came from the other end of my phone.

"Sally, I'm so sorry. I wish that he could help but he's absolutely swamped now. He's not only covering the practice here for all his patients and for Dr. D's patients, but he's also covering for two other doctors."

"Pardon me?" I asked, certain that she was wrong. "Dr. Diarmuid told me a long time ago that his cousin would cover for him whenever he wasn't available. My mother needs him now. This morning her blood pressure was 106 over 44. She's really, really sick and I don't have faith in the doctor from the hospital who's in charge of her care. Please, she really needs his cousin now."

"Let me explain what Dr. D meant when he said that his cousin would cover for him. He meant that if your mother needed to be seen in the office here, that his cousin would definitely take care of her. Or if Dr. D had admitted her to the hospital before he went out of town, his cousin would be able to take care of her now. But neither of those things are what's happening. Who's the hospitalist?" she asked.

"Dr. Limerick, but I really don't like him, and I really don't trust him that he's giving my mother good care. Tiffany, my mother has been coming to your office for years. It's not like she's a new patient. Please ask his cousin to see her in the hospital until Dr. D gets back. We're talking about less than a week. Please, Tiffany."

"I'm sorry, Sally, but he won't be able to see her. Dr. Limerick is a good doctor. He's seen some of our other patients before," she said.

"Tiffany, he's not the doctor that I want for my mother," I said.

She didn't respond.

"Hopefully, I'll still have a mother when Dr. D gets back," I added.

I was quiet for a moment, and then ended the conversation by saying, "I don't know what else to say to you. I'll call back next week and talk to Dr. Diarmuid," and then I hung up without saying goodbye.

"God help me," I whispered.

****

Dr. Limerick was a huge man who made me feel like I was bothering him with my questions, suggestions, and concerns. His tall height and his enormous girth, however, never made me feel small, nor did his size intimidate me. I continued to voice my concerns to him about all the medication that my mother was on, and that I wanted her off the psychotropic drugs. Those drugs were turning her brain into mush.

He was coordinating her care while she was in the hospital, so he was aware of all the drugs that the other doctors may have prescribed. She needed to be on antibiotics to cure her infections, but she was also on hydrocodone, lorazepam, morphine, and haloperidol. Hydrocodone and morphine are narcotics that are for pain control, lorazepam is for anxiety, and haloperidol is an antipsychotic drug. I didn't think that she needed all those drugs, and I thought that some of them, along with some of the doctors now treating her were causing far more problems than they were solving. Remember, my mother didn't even like taking acetaminophen when she lived at home.

Dr. Limerick blamed my mother's confusion on Alzheimer's. I told him that she didn't have Alzheimer's; I told him that she had dementia. I told him that she would sometimes repeat things, and was occasionally confused, but that she was a totally different person since she was given all the drugs in the hospital. I told him that before her fall six weeks earlier, she was living by herself in her own home. She knew who everyone in her family was, she was cooking most of her own meals, dressing herself, reading the daily newspaper, writing letters to her family in Ireland, and taking care of her cat. I told him a litany of other things that she was able to do, things that I didn't think someone with Alzheimer's could do.

He told me that dementia and Alzheimer's were basically the same thing. I could not stand that man but I continued to be polite.

"Could she have had a stroke or could this be a reaction to one or some of the drugs that she's on?" I asked. He said that she had not had a stroke but I felt like he gave me a "no-answer" type of answer about the drugs just to shut me up.

The days dragged on as my mother continued to go downhill. I was so relieved when I woke up on the morning that Dr. Diarmuid would be back in his office. I called shortly after his office opened, but I had to leave a message. Throughout the day I continued calling. I knew that he was busy after being out of his office for two weeks, but it was important that I speak with him and for him to see my mother.

I finally reached him around 5:00 o'clock. I was at the hospital, and about to walk into my mother's room, when the receptionist finally put me through to him. I did an about face and found a quiet alcove to have this conversation.

There wasn't any small talk. We went right to the business at hand.

"Hi Sally. I understand that your mother is in the hospital. Tell me what happened," he said.

I tried to be succinct and get him up to speed quickly. "She fell in her home last month, shattered her hip, went into Calafort for rehab, isn't doing well with her physical therapy, had a blood clot in her leg, went to the hospital, had surgery, and went back to Calafort. She's back in the hospital again with pneumonia and a UTI and is doing awful. I really don't like the hospitalist that's in charge of her care. I was afraid that she was going to pass away before you got back. Is there any way that you could see her today? She's a mess, Doctor," I said.

"Who's been taking care of her?" he asked.

"Dr. Limerick. I don't have any faith in him at all. I think that he's hurting her more than he's helping her. You wouldn't believe all the drugs that she's on," I told him.

"I can't see her, Sally," he said.

I didn't like his answer but I understood that since he'd been out of his office for a while that he had a lot of catching up to do.

"What about tomorrow? What time tomorrow can you be there? I want to make sure that I'm there when you're planning on being there," I quickly said.

"I can't take on your mother's care now. The patient that she is now is not the same patient that I've treated in the past. Dr. Limerick is a good doctor and he understands all the various issues that she's having now. I wish that I could help you but I wouldn't be doing Barbara a service if I started treating her at this point."

I couldn't believe the words that I was hearing. I was numb.

"Dr. Diarmuid, please tell me that you're not serious. I've been taking my mother to see you for years in preparation for this day. It's hard for me to believe that you won't take care of her now. Now is when she needs you. Dr. Diarmuid, please help my mother," I begged.

"I'm sorry. I wish that I could help your mom now, but I can't. When she gets out of the hospital and you are able to bring her to my office, I'd love for her to be my patient again, but I can't take care of her now," he said.

I felt like I had been punched, and I wasn't sure how to respond. The words that came out of my mouth were, "And you call yourself a doctor?"

Once again I hung up the phone without saying goodbye.

I stood there for a moment and thought, *What do I do now?*

The answer to my question was that I had no idea what I was going to do. There had been so much anticipation and hope on my part that my mother's care would improve once Dr. Diarmuid returned. In my mind he was the silver bullet that was going to do away with all the unnecessary drugs that had turned her catatonic; in my mind he was going to put her on the correct medication; and in my mind he was going to get her well enough to go back to Calafort.

When I got back to my mother's room, she was dozing off, so I left and went to the chapel. I found solace in that little chapel that I had visited several times that week. Once again I was the only one in there. I prayed, and I prayed, and then I prayed some more. When I finished my prayers, I stayed in the chapel for a while longer and I thought about things.

I thought about doctors in general and how usually they are wonderful people. I thought about how some of them help to bring life into the world. Others are with us until the bitter end helping to make the best of a really crappy situation at the end of our lives. I thought about how good doctors give us hope, even when things seem hopeless. Bad doctors take away all hope, when hope is all we have.

Dr. Diarmuid and his cousin were in the latter category.

****

My mother's personality was changing before my eyes. She was barely talking to me. She just stared a lot, slept a lot, and looked like she was stoned out of her mind. One morning when I visited her, she was in such a deep sleep that I wasn't able to wake her. It took the help of a couple of nurses to finally wake her up.

One of those nurses told me that there was a note in the chart saying "no narcotics recommended." Why then was she on morphine? That was a question that I asked Dr. Limerick. He didn't seem to be as concerned as I was about that note. However, he once again made a point of saying, "This is as good as she'll ever be mentally because of the Alzheimer's." I didn't respond to that comment.

As stressful as that conversation was with Dr. Limerick, something good happened shortly after the conversation ended. I was getting ready to leave the hospital when I saw a lady who worked at the grocery store where I shopped. She said that on some of her days off from the store, she worked as a sitter at the hospital. I told her I didn't know what that meant.

She explained that some patients who had to stay in the hospital were confused and overly anxious, and that there were three ways to deal with those issues. The patient could either be given drugs to keep them calm, or they could be physically restrained, or the hospital could provide a sitter at no cost to the patient. Apparently Dr. Limerick had chosen the first option for my mother, but I didn't like his choice.

This was a no brainer for me. Since I wanted her off the drugs that they'd been giving her to quiet her down, I requested and got a sitter, starting the very next night. Laura stayed in the room with my mother from late evening until the morning. She was a godsend not only for my mother, but also for me. Knowing that she had someone with her, helped me to get a better night's sleep.

Because of the sitter, Mom's meds were slightly decreased, but I still thought that Dr. Limerick had her on too much medication. I wanted to find a different doctor to take over her care, but getting a different doctor was easier said than done. None of the doctors that I spoke with were interested in helping her.

Maybe it was because no other doctor wanted to take on a patient as sick as my mother. They probably thought that it wouldn't be long before they'd be signing a death certificate. Or perhaps there was more loyalty between doctors, than there was between doctors and patients. Whatever the reason, finding a different doctor seemed next to impossible and I didn't know what to do in order to give my mother a fighting chance.

Chapter 9

The Feeding Tube

Since I needed all the help that I could get, I'd gotten into the habit of stopping by the chapel each day and saying a few prayers before I went to my mother's room. One day after I walked out of the chapel, I just stood there for a few minutes deep in thought, leaning up against the wall. I closed my eyes and slid slowly down the wall, until I was sitting on the floor. There I sat thinking about what I needed to do to get a different doctor. I was also thinking about the news that Dr. Limerick had given me the day before. He told me that I needed to start thinking about a feeding tube for my mother.

He said that I needed to decide between a feeding tube and comfort care for her. I told him that I didn't want either of those choices. He said that she was aspirating and not able to get nourishment. He said that that was a decision that I would soon have to make. The thought of a feeding tube in my mother made me sick.

He described two kinds. One kind would be inserted into her nose. The other would be inserted surgically into her belly. He told me that because of her dementia that her hands would need to be restrained so that she wouldn't pull out whichever one I chose. I looked into his eyes and said, "Doctor, what you're describing sounds abusive. I can't imagine putting her through that."

As I daydreamed sitting there on the floor I was getting increasingly frustrated thinking about the many doctors that she had the last week or so, and how their left hands sometimes didn't know what their right hands were doing. There were a few doctors, however, that I trusted. Dr. Rosslare fell into that category. He was a pulmonary doctor, who was kind, made me think that he cared, and what he said made sense to me.

He told me that she was definitely aspirating. I asked him about some of the many drugs that she was on. He told me that morphine causes mental clouding, as well as it suppresses the cough reflex. That was a huge issue because it was crucial that she was able to cough because of the pneumonia. He said that coughing is one way your body works to get rid of an infection, and it also helps to clear the lungs.

After speaking with Dr. Rosslare, I methodically held up notes in front of my mother that said "COUGH" or "YOU HAVE TO COUGH." It was pitiful to watch her trying to follow my directions. She'd make an effort to cough and she'd go through the motions of a cough but as hard as she tried, she wasn't able to actually cough. I could also hear gurgling in her chest.

Dr. Rosslare said not being able to cough or clear her throat was probably contributing to the aspirating. He also said that the meds that she was on could be affecting her ability to swallow. She had a bronchoscopy to clear her lungs. In addition to the lung issues that the morphine contributed to, it also was constipating her. Good God, didn't she have enough problems without being flipping constipated?

I probably sound somewhat calm as I write about this hospital stay. Trust me, I was anything but calm. There were tears, there were sleepless nights, there were incredible headaches, and I was probably short tempered with Dave and the kids.

As I sat on the floor outside the chapel, deep in thought, I heard someone say my name. When I opened my eyes, I saw a man standing over me. I quickly got up off the floor. The man introduced himself as Dr. Cathedra and shook my hand. I didn't have a clue who he was but figured that he was another one of my mother's many specialists.

"May I call you Sally?" he asked.

"Yes, that's fine," I answered.

"I saw you last week in the emergency room with your mother and you were very upset when you were taking care of her," he said.

"I'm sorry. I didn't know that it was so obvious. I was trying to make her feel better while she was waiting for the ER doctor to see her." I paused for a moment, and then said, "Since you know who I am, please tell me who you are. She has so many doctors that I can't keep up with you all."

"No, I'm not any of your mother's doctors but that's why I wanted to talk to you. I understand that you're looking for a doctor to replace Dr. Limerick. If you would like, I'll take over your mother's care," he said.

I was totally surprised by what I was hearing. What was the matter with this guy? Why did he want to help when no other doctor was interested? So, I said, "I don't get it. Why do you want to help me? No other doctor has stepped up to the plate. Don't get me wrong, I can't tell you how much I appreciate your offer, but why?"

"I see the pain that you're in and what you're going through with your mother. I think that I can help both of you," he said, "if you want my help, that is. You can see that I'm younger than a lot of the other doctors at the hospital so I don't have the experience they have."

It was almost like I was still daydreaming and this guy who said he was a doctor wasn't for real. "I'm sorry, please tell me your name again," I said.

"I'm Dr. Cathedra," he answered.

"Dr. Cathedra, I very much would like you to help my mother, but you and I need to talk first. Don't get me wrong. I, I mean we, desperately need help but I don't want to find myself in a worse situation than I'm already in, if a worse situation is even possible. I want to make sure that you and I are in agreement about her care.

"I understand," he said.

"I want her off all the unnecessary drugs that she's on, especially the morphine. She is so doped up that she looks catatonic. I'd like you to find out why she was having so much pain in her legs and in her back. That's what brought her here to begin with. I don't want her going back to the rehab until we know those answers, otherwise she'll be back here again. Also, could the UTI have caused the back pain? And something else I've been wondering about the UTI is whether that could have contributed to some of the confusion that she's having?"

"Yes, to both questions about the UTI. In the elderly, a UTI is often the cause of confusion. Then he added, "I need to know how aggressively you want her treated or are you just looking for comfort care?"

"I don't want just comfort care. Absolutely not. I want the pneumonia and UTI to be treated fully. I hear gurgling in her chest. Could that be congestive heart failure or is that definitely lung related?" I asked.

"If I take over her care, I'll be in a better position to answer your questions. It could be either one. I believe that she has pneumonia so it could be the cause, but gurgling sounds in the chest could also mean congestive heart failure. I would do some additional tests to confirm what's going on," he said.

"I think that they've taken at least two chest x-rays since she's been in the hospital. I need to tell you that I'm paranoid about congestive heart failure. My father-in-law went into the hospital for a broken hip but died from congestive heart failure," I told him.

"Unfortunately, that happens more often than we would like, especially with the elderly," he answered.

"Doctor, I don't want it to happen with my mother. Let me tell you the rest of the story. My father-in-law had been given blood, along with other fluids through an IV. After being on the IV for a few days, his surgeon noticed that the rate of his IV drip was too fast. There was far more fluid going in to him, than what was coming out, but nobody had the common sense to notice it until it was too late. The incredibly sad and frustrating thing is that his intake/output was being religiously recorded, but nobody asked "Why?" about what they had documented.

"I'm sorry," he said.

"My mother is also on an IV. The second day she was on it I had a flashback to what happened with my father-in-law. My mother's drip was set on 175. I had no idea if that was appropriate so I asked the nurse about it, and I told her why I was asking. She told me that if I would be more comfortable that she would turn it down and then she lowered it to a slower drip. That concerned me and I told her that I wasn't asking her to turn it down. I told her that I was just asking because I wanted to hear her confirm that it was where it was supposed to be. I told her that what she did seemed random to me, and to please check and find out what it should be set on. She told me that everything was fine and not to worry. I told her that we thought my father-in-law was fine, too, but that oversight in his care contributed to his death."

I told Dr. Cathedra that I didn't want to put my mother through tests that were invasive. I didn't think that would be right at her age. A very wise doctor once brought to my attention that doctors like to be able to "document a diagnosis" but that doctor's philosophy was that sometimes it was better just to treat the symptoms rather than to put an elderly patient through a lot of very uncomfortable or invasive procedures.

Dr. Cathedra told me that he understood where I was coming from and would honor what I was asking.

"Doctor, the biggest and scariest issue now is that Dr. Limerick is talking about a feeding tube. Since she's not eating, he's concerned that she's not getting the nourishment that she needs. They've also done a swallowing test and confirmed that she's still aspirating. That's what I was thinking and praying about when I was sitting on the floor."

"Sally, before we go too much further, you'll need to make a decision whether you want me to take over for Dr. Limerick. I understand if you want to find a more experienced doctor."

It was a tough decision to make because so much was resting on finding a good doctor, but it was also easy because my mother was going downhill so quickly that if a change didn't happen soon, I thought that she would die.

"Dr. Cathedra, I think that you understand what I'm looking for in a new doctor. You give me the impression that you will care for my mother and that she won't just be a name on another chart. I think that you and I are on the same page about her treatment. Thank you so much for coming up to me and making the offer to help. It means more than words can say. Yes, I would like you to be the doctor who will coordinate my mother's care."

"Ok, I'll talk to Dr. Limerick and let him know that you and I spoke and that I'll be taking over your mother's care. There is one thing that I need you to do for me," he added.

"What's that?" I cautiously asked.

"I'm building my career here at the hospital and I like it here very much. If anyone asks, it's important that you say that you asked me if I would be your mother's doctor.

It wouldn't be good for me if it appeared that I took Dr. Limerick's patient away from him on my own. It must be clear that you asked me," he said.

"Dr. Cathedra, you are the doctor that I want for my mother, and I'm asking you to please take over her care. If anyone ever asks I'll make sure they know that I asked you. I know that my mother has an uphill battle ahead of her, but I think that she's now in a better position to make it through this mess. Thank you so much, Doctor, for your help," I said.

I left the hospital shortly after our conversation, feeling like a weight had been lifted from my shoulders. I went straight home to tell Dave in person the news about the new doctor. He was as happy as I was to finally be rid of Limerick. You would think that this would have been an opportune time for me to clear my mind and to relax for the rest of the evening, but that was difficult for me to do because I still had the feeding tube issue looming over me. It was a huge decision that I would soon need to make. It was difficult for me to imagine my mother living with a feeding tube.

I thought about how there was probably a ton of elderly people who lived for years at home eating the foods that they enjoyed, and didn't have a clue that they were aspirating. It wasn't until they went into a hospital, or a rehab, or a nursing home that someone decided that they needed a swallowing test and before they knew it, they were told that they were aspirating, and that they needed a feeding tube in order to get nourishment.

I also thought about all the social benefits of being able to sit down for a meal with food entering your body through your mouth, not through a tube in your nose or a peg in your gut. Eating had always been one of my mother's biggest pleasures. Before she lived at Calafort, she not only enjoyed going out to eat at a restaurant, but she also got great satisfaction when she cooked a meal for her family and her friends. While she no longer was able to do either of those things, I didn't want to take away the possibility that she'd start eating on her own again. At that point, my mother had little enjoyment left in her life. How could I contemplate taking away food? Then I started thinking about the flip side. If she didn't get a feeding tube, would she die?

Since I knew that ironically my mother wouldn't be a part of this huge decision, I decided that I needed to go to the next best source. The next day after work and after the hospital, I stopped at Delia's. Thank you, God, for my Aunt Delia.

After our hello hug she immediately asked, "How's your mother today?"

I got her up to speed, first about the new doctor, and then about the aspiration issue. Last, but definitely not least, I brought up the decision we needed to make about a feeding tube.

"Delia, I hate to burden you but I don't know what to tell the doctor. You're close to Mom's age. What would you want to do if it were you?" I asked.

She understood that this was an important decision that we had to make for my mother. She thought about it for a few minutes as if the feeding tube decision was for her.

"If it was for a short while, maybe for up to a month, I'd have it. That might give me strength enough to be able to eat again, and to take the tube out. I wouldn't want it for longer than a month," she said.

As simple as her answer was, it helped me. It told me that it wouldn't be something that she would want in her forever. We talked about Mom for a little bit longer and then I asked her if she wanted to go for a little walk. She said that she'd love to go for a short one. She put her portable oxygen tank into the basket on her walker and off we went.

We walked the long hallway of her 5th floor apartment. Delia made a point of walking just as often as she could. She knew that it was good for her to get exercise. The apartment complex that she lived in was in no way assisted living. The residents lived totally on their own, just like in any other apartment complex. The only requirement was that they had to be at least 55 years old to live there.

I didn't stay too long after we got back to her apartment. "Dee Dee, I love you and I hope that you have a good night. Anything I can do for you before I leave?"

"No, go home, eat, and get to bed early. Ye look tired. Let David do the dishes tonight," she said.

"Sounds like a plan to me. Love you," I said as I hugged her goodnight. She was a lot like my mother in that her good-bye wasn't over until her visitor was out of sight. She rolled her walker out to the hallway, waved goodbye, and stayed there until I got on the elevator.

Later that evening, Dave and I talked about the feeding tube and I told him what Delia said. He brought something to my attention that I hadn't thought about. He said that if I decided to have a feeding tube placed in my mother and later decided to have it removed for whatever reason, that it might be difficult to have it removed. The hospital might view it as depriving her of nourishment, and not allow it to be taken out. He reminded me of a similar problem that we had when his father was in the hospital involving a ventilator. What he said added an extra layer of concern in making my decision.

The following day Dr. Cathedra and the gastro doctor each gave me more information to think about that started making the feeding tube decision a little easier. The gastro doctor said that he didn't feel comfortable placing a feeding tube in an almost 89-year-old woman with dementia. Dr. Cathedra said that if she had a feeding tube, that it probably would be permanent.

I was close to making a decision, but I still kept hoping that there would be something else, something more, to let me know that I was making the right decision. It made me sad that I couldn't ask my mother what to do. She may only have gotten an elementary school education in Ireland, but she had an abundance of common sense. I needed her sage advice now, more than I ever needed it before.

The morning after my conversations with Dr. Cathedra and the gastro doctor, I stopped by to visit my mother on my way to work. I sat on her bed and watched her as she sat in a wheelchair waiting to be brought downstairs for yet another test. My heart ached to see how sick she looked and I wasn't sure if she would ever be going back to Calafort; or if when she left the hospital, her destination would be a funeral home.

She knew that I was in the room with her but there were no words spoken between us. Her head hung down and her mouth was open. At one point I squatted down next to her chair and held her hands. I was sad to see her looking the way she looked, but I didn't want her to know that I was sad. I tried so hard not to cry that I started shaking. Somehow she knew. She slowly raised her head and her sad eyes met mine. I felt like she was looking into my soul.

She let go of my hand and reached up to my face to wipe away the tear that was running down my cheek. It was heart wrenching for me as we continued looking at each other. I stood up, bent over, and hugged her. She raised one of her arms and rested it on my shoulder. That was as close to a hug as she was able to give me. As sick as she was, as bad as she felt, she was still being a mother, still trying to take care of me and still trying to make me feel good.

I had to listen carefully as she quietly and slowly said, "Baby, don't cry. I'll be alright. Let nature take its course."

I hugged her again and said, "Mom, I love you most."

I thought about what she had said—"Let nature take its course." Without knowing it, she helped me make the feeding tube decision. As soon as she was taken out of the room, I called Dr. Cathedra and told him that I decided against the feeding tube.

He told me that he believed in the importance of quality of life and emphasized that eating was one of life's pleasures. He made me feel comfortable that I had made the correct decision, but he also wanted to make sure that I understood the reality of the situation.

He said that it was likely that my mother would continue aspirating when she ate, or even on her own saliva, but that he would keep her on antibiotics to keep infection under control. He summed it all up by saying that she could live a short while with this problem, or she could live for years.

I was incredibly relieved that that decision was finally behind me, and that I could focus on my mother instead of feeding tubes. She was still extremely ill, and was on strong antibiotics. Her white blood count was over 20,000. The normal range is 4,500 to 11,000. She still had pneumonia in her right lung, and was silently aspirating. It wasn't clear if her UTI had been resolved. The lung doctor made it clear to me that she shouldn't lie flat in her bed. I'm not so sure that the nursing staff got that message.

When I stopped by to see her the very next morning she was lying in bed, with the head of the bed elevated just a teensy bit, and her nurse was about to put a spoon of medicine into her mouth. When I told her what the doctor had said to me the night before about not lying flat, she said it was elevated enough and that all the medicine would melt in her mouth. I asked her to please humor me and to raise it a little more. She didn't make me feel bad for asking, and she raised the bed to where I would have had it to begin with. It was small guilt-free favors like that one, that sincerely helped me along the way.

I was glad that Dr. Cathedra had taken over my mother's care. He stayed true to his word and took her off the morphine and the haloperidol and even though she was still extremely sick physically, she was more lucid than she'd been since she was re-admitted to the hospital. I later found out that studies showed that elderly patients with dementia who took haloperidol had an increased chance of death during treatment. There were other side effects but I have to say that the increased chance of death was definitely the most egregious. It was beyond me why it was given to her in the first place.

****

There were many days during my mother's two weeks in the hospital that I wasn't sure in what condition she'd be leaving, but on the 15th day, Dr. Cathedra released her to go back to Calafort. He had gotten her infections under control and thought that she would fully recover.

Before she left the hospital, one last swallow test was done and the results were that she didn't aspirate during that test. I was thrilled. However, the lung doctor said that we must proceed cautiously and slowly when she ate. I could proceed cautiously; I could proceed slowly. I just prayed that all her caregivers could follow those simple directions.

We never found out the cause of the pain in her legs, but common sense reminded me what a great walker she'd always been. Overnight she became confined to a wheelchair. I should have realized that her lack of mobility probably aggravated her arthritis and compromised her circulation. And, the UTI probably caused some of the pain in her back. An x-ray of her back also showed that she had osteoarthritis.

I was grateful that Dr. Cathedra sent her back to the rehab with orders for a more comfortable mattress for her bed, as well as a gel cushion for her wheelchair. Mom's total existence took place in and on those two things.

She arrived at the rehab in an ambulance, not nearly as strong as when she left it, two weeks earlier. As I watched the EMTs take her out of the ambulance, I asked myself if it was really necessary for her to have gone through two weeks of hell in the hospital in order to diagnose pneumonia, a UTI, and osteoarthritis. The answer to my question was a big, fat "NO."

I know the reason that she was sent to the hospital was because she said that she had a lot of pain and wanted to see a doctor right away. I have a feeling that if she hadn't made such a scene, she probably wouldn't have been sent to the hospital. Calafort had a doctor on staff. He could have seen her. If the nurse had told my mother that she had called the doctor and that he was coming, she would have been satisfied until he arrived. He could have ordered all the same tests that she had at the hospital, and they all could have been done at Calafort. Even the x-rays could have been taken in her room. She could have been diagnosed and treated without ever having left the facility.

As she was being wheeled back to her room on the stretcher, I walked next to her and held her hand. That's when I decided that I would never subject my mother to another hospital visit. Never, ever again.

Chapter 10

All She Got Was Me

After my mother was settled back in the rehab, she started eating the pureed meals that was served to her. When she was well enough and strong enough to leave the facility for a few hours, I took her for a follow-up appointment with Dr. Robinson, the surgeon who had repaired her hip. It was lucky for us that Calafort had a medical van that took us to the appointment. It was driven by a man named Ben. He was incredibly kind and acted like a tour guide pointing out things along the route that he thought that my mother would find interesting. She conversed easily with Ben, and commented on things that we passed that she was familiar with.

After a thorough exam, the surgeon told us that her hip had healed well and he released her from his care. He also reminded her of the importance of physical therapy, and she responded by saying that she would do better. We ended the visit by him telling me not to hesitate to call him if I ever had any questions concerning her hip.

I knew that she enjoyed her field trip that took her out of the rehab for a few hours. When my mother lived at home, she always loved getting out of the house and going some- where. I didn't know at the time of that doctor's visit, that it would be her last trip outside Calafort.

The day after her appointment I received a call at my office from the nurse du jour saying that my mother had fallen out of her bed. The nurse wasn't sure how it happened but said that my mother appeared to be okay. She sounded almost apologetic when she told me that they were required to call the family whenever there was an incident of that nature. When I asked if I should leave work right away to be with my mother, she assured me that she was fine.

When I visited that evening, Mom was lying on a new bed that was only inches off the ground. There was a large thin pad on the floor next to her bed that would cushion any future falls. There was also a star on her nameplate outside her room. I was told that the star symbolized "falling stars." That made me think that there were enough falls inside Calafort to warrant such a sign.

Later that week was my birthday. It came and it went that year totally unnoticed by my mother. That was the first time that had ever happened. I considered myself extremely lucky, however, for all the many birthdays that she had celebrated with me in the past. I actually considered myself lucky for having a birthday at all.

My mother was 42 when she found out that she was pregnant with me. That was considered a very old woman to be having a baby in those days. She had huge fibroid tumors and her doctor said that there wasn't room for a baby to grow inside her. He also told her that because of her age there was a good chance that her baby would have Down Syndrome. He told her that it could be life threatening for her to try to carry a baby to full term. Her doctor strongly suggested that they "take the baby." That was an old-fashioned euphemism for an abortion.

To say that my mother was strong-willed is like saying that Michelangelo was a good painter. She told her doctor there was no way on earth that she would ever let them take me. She said that we would die together before she would

let that happen to her baby. She saw her baby as a gift from
God. I'm sure that's why she so often said to me, "God knew
what He was doing when He gave ye to me."

I'm not sure what type of surgery my mother had, but
she told me that she had a big operation to tie back the tumors
so that there would be room for me to grow. She had always
wanted to have a lot of children. All she got was me. The day
that I was born she had a caesarian and a hysterectomy.

Now it was my turn to keep her safe and sound.

****

It had now been 100 days since she arrived at Calafort.
That's when I was given two items of bad news. First, I was
told that her insurance had paid the bulk of what they would
be paying for, as far as the cost of staying in the facility. She
would now have to pay over $7,000.00 a month out of her
own pocket. I knew that she would be able to pay for a while,
but I didn't know what would happen to her when she ran
out of money.

She arrived in America the year the stock market crashed.
As she put it "times were tough" and as an Irish immigrant
she took jobs that other people didn't particularly want. She
worked hard and she knew what it meant to do without. She

was thrifty and frugal and over the years she managed to save her money. In my mind's eye I pictured her clipping grocery coupons at her kitchen table.

It was clear to me that she'd probably go through all her hard-earned, hard-saved money in Calafort. In the end my mother wanted her money to go to me and Dave and our children. It would have broken her heart if she knew that she would be spending her life's savings on something she said she never ever wanted.

Part two of the bad news was that I was told that my mother was going to be moved out of the Glen, the rehab side of the facility, and into the Meadows, the long term care side. For some time now, I knew that my mother would be spending the rest of her life in Calafort. But hearing that she was being officially moved into the nursing home side took away any bit of unrealistic hope that I still had that she would somehow, someway be able to go home.

I was concerned that it would be hard for her to adjust to living with a whole new set of total strangers. She may not have remembered all the names of the nurses and CNAs that had been working with her in the Glen, but she recognized them by sight. Now everyone would be new again. I was assured that her new nurse, Sandi, was someone that we'd be happy with. I could only hope.

They didn't waste any time in making the move, and within a few days she was in a new room. Unfortunately, she took some of the same problems with her that she had in the first room. My mother was always cold. I think that's a malady that a lot of elderly people share. To make matters even worse, she had lost a lot of weight since she moved into Calafort so she didn't have much body fat to keep her warm, and obviously she wasn't working up a sweat sitting all day in her wheelchair.

I had brought a lot of her winter clothes to Calafort, in hopes of keeping her warm, but she was at the mercy of the CNAs to dress her, and they weren't always merciful. It wasn't unusual that when I showed up for a visit, she wouldn't be wearing a sweater and her lap blanket was often left on her bed.

After one particularly long day at work I arrived too late to help her eat her supper, and by the time that I arrived everyone had already been taken out of the little dining room. I spotted her near the nurses' station, lined up against the wall with the other residents, all waiting to be taken somewhere.

As soon as she saw me she reached up to hug me and said, "Baby, I'm freezing to death. Can ye find me a sweater to throw over my shoulders?"

I reached behind her and grabbed her sweater that was hanging from the handles of her wheelchair.

"Here you go, Mom," I said as I gently helped her put it on. That was the first time that I really noticed just how frail she'd become. I never thought that "frail" would be a word that I'd use to describe my mother.

I understood that the staff was overworked but it was this type of non-caring attitude that made me count to 10 before saying something that I would regret. The frustrating thing was that it was the simple things, like making sure she was wearing a sweater, that could make her have a much better day. And so, once again I reminded the CNA to please make a point of keeping a sweater on her. Then I thanked her for remembering in the future. This was by far not the last conversation that I would have about sweaters and lap blankets.

The flip side of that coin was that every now and then Calafort did something unexpected that I was grateful for. I was pleasantly surprised to hear that they had arranged to have all the residents' eyes checked. That was great news because I knew that my mother's days of going to her own ophthalmologist were behind her. I was even given a report about her vision test. It said that even though they couldn't determine her visual acuity, her present glasses were satisfactory and that new glasses wouldn't improve her vision. I wasn't sure if that was good news, but thank God it didn't sound like bad news.

****

You would think that as busy as I was with my mother and Delia, that I would limit some of the things that I continued to do for them, but I didn't. I still made a point of going over to my mother's house every Saturday or Sunday. I already had her mail forwarded to my address but I wanted to check on her house each week to make sure that the yardman had mowed the grass and that there were no emergencies in her now vacant home. I also wanted to water the plants on her kitchen window sill. There was something oddly comforting for me to keep the flowers inside her house alive and flourishing.

It was a two-edged sword, however, because I hated hearing the quietness inside her house. As soon as I unlocked the door and walked inside I found the silence deafening. I craved to hear any of the sounds that were familiar to me throughout the years. I wanted to hear my mother happily greet me when I arrived, or her tea kettle whistling, or her pressure cooker cooking, or her toaster popping up the toast. I wanted to hear her quietly singing to herself as she prepared a meal. As silly as it sounds, I would have been happy to hear her gargling in her bathroom.

Now that the house had turned quiet, I realized that those sounds were part of its personality. I also knew that I would never hear any of those sounds again in my mother's hushed house, and that made me sad.

I was also sad that my mother's future didn't look like anything that she would have wanted. Her future would have her surrounded by people that she didn't know. She'd be sleeping on a bed that wasn't her own. And she'd be eating food that didn't look like or taste like anything that she would have made for herself. Unfortunately, there was nothing that I could do to change her future. All that I could do was to make sure that she was getting the best care possible, and to visit as often as I possibly could.

It had been a few weeks since the kids had visited my mother so we stopped by to see her on a Sunday after church. The second she saw them she lit up.

"Mom, Michael was one of the altar servers at Mass today," I told her.

"I'm so proud of ye, Michael. I wish I could have been there," she said. "Maybe you'll be the Pope one day. Would ye like to be the Pope?"

"Grandma, that's something that's never going to happen. Plus, I want to get married and have kids," he answered as he glanced over at me.

"Well ye have a point there, but I think it would be lovely for ye to be the Pope. Remember, there's nothing ye can't do if ye set your mind on it," she said.

The weather was great so we took her outside for a walk. Both kids wanted to push the wheelchair but I told them that it was better for me to push the chair and for them to walk ahead of their grandma, or next to her, so that she could see them and enjoy every moment of them being with her.

"The kids are lovely, Sally," she said. "But the best part of them is that they're just as lovely on the inside as they are on the outside."

"Thanks, Mom. They're good kids. Dave and I are lucky to have them."

"They're lucky to have ye, too, Honey. You've done a good job raising them so far. I'd love to see them in another 10 years but I'll be long gone by then," she said.

"You never know, Ma. You could still be here in another 10 years," I quickly said back to her.

"No, Honey, I won't be around. Remember to say a little prayer for me every now and then," she added.

"I'll always pray for you, Mom," I promised.

When my mother was with me and the kids, her dementia didn't seem bad at all. She always knew who we were and who Dave was. We were able to have conversations. She always asked the kids about school and what they were up to. She asked me about Delia, and about her nieces and nephews. She often asked if I'd heard from any of the family in Ireland. And she'd always ask how my day at work was. That's not to say that she didn't ask the same question, or tell the same story, more than once during a visit, but I didn't mind in the least.

I never told her that she was repeating something she had already said or asked. I reminded myself that when I was a teenager, she often had to repeat the same thing to me more than once before I did what she asked me to do, and she never lost patience with me. How could I not be patient with her at this time in her life?

Chapter 11

Bent Glasses, Lost Glasses, Someone Else's Glasses

It wasn't easy, but I tried my best to look for the good, wherever I could find it at Calafort. My mother's assigned dining room was occasionally one of those places. Even though the Meadows' dining room was small, and loud, and crowded, and even though "the feeders" would sometimes doze off while they were waiting for the food to arrive from the kitchen, it was a destination where I would sometimes find an inkling of satisfaction.

When my mother would feed herself a meal, even if it took a long time, I was happy. It gave me a sense of pride that she was able to do something that most of the others in the room could no longer do. It was in the dining room where I would smile as I watched Michael or Kathleen standing behind her wheelchair, giving her a shoulder massage, like she had done so many times for them. Circle of life?

Other times the bizarreness of that dining room made me shake my head. Sometimes I felt like I was in the Twilight Zone. Let me introduce you to a few of the Meadows' residents and share some mealtime adventures with you.

Mrs. Kennedy would usually push her own wheelchair into the dining room rather than just sitting in it, and letting someone else push the chair. That wasn't a big deal. What was turning into a big deal, in my humble opinion, was that I often saw her crying. When I would ask her if I could get her something or do anything for her to make her feel better she always said, "No." When I asked her why she was crying I always got the same answer, "I don't know why."

On one of her crying days I found myself alone with her and a few other residents, including my mother. The CNAs were all probably in other residents' rooms getting them ready to come to the dining room. While I was having a little chitchat with my mother, I noticed Mrs. Kennedy trying to get up on the table. I didn't know what her goal was; I'm not sure that she knew either. The table wasn't very high, but I didn't want her to fall and hurt herself.

I was torn between running over to her and holding her so that she wouldn't fall, or running outside the room to get help. I sort of did both. I tried my best to hold on to this woman, who was no lightweight, while I hollered loudly for help. My hollers were heard pretty quickly because a nurse, a CNA, and someone visiting his father all ran into the dining room and got her away from the table and back into her chair.

From that day forward, whenever I saw Mrs. Kennedy she was always sitting in her wheelchair with the safety belt fastened. I seldom saw her crying again after that episode but I often saw her dozing off in her chair. I guess they must have gotten her on the "happy medicine." Happy medicine was how I referred to the meds that made some of the residents snooze in their chairs throughout the day.

Another one of my mother's "neighbors" was Elizabeth, who shared a room with her husband, Victor. They lived a few rooms down the hall from my mother, but they didn't look like typical nursing home residents. That's because they were only in their 50s. As sad as it was for them to be in a nursing home at such an early age, they were a lucky couple because Elizabeth's son visited them several times a week.

Apparently, Victor had some serious physical ailments, and Elizabeth had spent years taking care of him. Elizabeth's son told me that he thought that the responsibility of being a fulltime caregiver took a mental and emotional toll on his mother and that she ended up having early onset Alzheimer's. That diagnosis is what caused the two of them to end up in long term care.

Elizabeth appeared to be in good physical shape and was one of the few residents in the Meadows who wasn't confined to a wheelchair. Her mental condition was another story. Even though I had only known her for a short while, it looked to me like she was declining mentally.

One evening while I waited with my mother in the dining room for the food to come, Elizabeth walked in slowly, looking more bewildered then I'd seen her look in the past. Her face was badly bruised and I heard one of the CNAs say that she had fallen the night before. That was the last time I saw her walking by herself. From then on, she either walked with the help of a CNA or she was in a wheelchair with the seatbelt fastened. She also started making yucky sounds. My mother who was extremely hard of hearing, oddly enough, could always hear Elizabeth's sounds.

"Is that woman drunk, Sally?" she'd ask loudly with her lilting Irish brogue.

"No, Mom, she's fine," I'd answer quickly in hopes of nixing that conversation.

"Sally, do ye think she's sober acting like that?" She couldn't let it drop.

"Mom, I think that the woman is sick and she can't help it," I'd say.

"Oh, God help the creature. What's the matter with her?" she'd often reply.

"I don't know what her problem is. I just know that she's sick and I feel sorry for her," I said.

I felt sorry for all of us sitting in that crowded little dining room. I felt bad for the people who called this place home, and I felt sorry for those of us who had to watch what our loved ones had to endure. That same scene with Elizabeth and my mother repeated a handful of times in the months to come.

Then there was Grandma. That's what everyone called the little lady who used to be a teacher. She often would break into song, her favorite being Yankee Doodle. She would try to get everyone nearby her to sing along. It must have been a throwback to her teaching days.

One evening at supper, she was unusually quiet. It took a few minutes before Grandma's silence got anyone's attention. She was slumped down in her wheelchair and one of the CNAs hollered for someone to go get a nurse. Grandma was quiet and her face looked grey. For a moment I thought that she had passed away.

A couple of nurses ran into the room and spoke loudly, "Grandma, can you hear me? Grandma, squeeze my hand."

One of the nurses was listening to her heart with a stethoscope. The scene in the room was surrealistic. While the nurses continued trying to get Grandma to respond, the CNAs went about their business serving the other residents their suppers.

The people sitting at Grandma's table looked in her direction but continued gumming their food. They took little notice of her, as if this was a normal occurrence. After a few minutes, the nurses wheeled her out of the dining room. She didn't look any better at that point than she looked when they first came to help.

I never found out what caused Grandma's problem but a few days later she was back again eating in the dining room. I was happy to see her and occasionally I even heard her singing Yankee Doodle, just without the enthusiasm that she used to have.

Another resident in my mother's new neighborhood who often stood out from the others was Lillian. I never knew what odd thing she would say to me.

One day during lunch I could see her staring at me, and it wasn't a pleasant look. She motioned for me to come over to her table. I was happy to oblige and went over to see what she wanted to tell me.

"I don't like you," she said. "You're a big fake."

"Really, Lillian? Why do you think that I'm a fake?" She had my curiosity.

"Because you're too nice. Nobody's as nice as you pretend to be. You're nothing but a fake! You're a faker!" she said.

"Huh! I'm sorry that you feel that way about me. Is there anything that I can do for you?" I asked, without her noticing the irony of my question.

"No, but tell me about that woman who sits next to you all the time. Can she be trusted?" she asked.

"Oh, she's lovely. I'm sure that you can trust her," I said with a smile, and then headed back over to my mother's table.

Poor Mom. You're living with caregivers who really don't care, and with residents that are whackadoos. What's going to become of you, Mom?

****

To say that my mother didn't adjust well to living in long term care was an understatement. The longer she lived in Calafort the more obvious it was that she didn't want to be there. She had always been an independent woman and had always done what she wanted to do, when she wanted to do it. Overnight she lost the ability to decide how her days were going to be spent. Now she was told when to wake, when to sleep, when to eat, what to eat, where to sit, what to wear, when to bathe, etc. and I knew that it wasn't easy for her to always comply. My mother wasn't a controlling person, but by the same token she didn't want to be controlled.

To make her situation even worse, she didn't know where she was or why she was there. Every now and then when she'd ask me where she was, I'd remind her that she was in a rehab. I told her that she had to stay there until she was strong enough and well enough to go home. That usually seemed to appease her, at least for the moment. In a million years I could never tell her that she was living in a nursing home, and that she would never live any place else.

The powers that be at Calafort were also aware that she hadn't adjusted well to nursing home life. I had no idea, however, that they thought that their on-staff psychiatrist would be the answer to her problems. The way that I found out about this new doctor was when I opened a statement from her Blue Cross insurance and saw charges that he had billed.

I was annoyed that was how I found out about him, but it explained why for the last month or so, I sometimes found her dozing in her wheelchair when I'd come for a visit. It would have been very much appreciated if someone from Calafort had discussed it with me beforehand. They obviously didn't care what I thought, or maybe they assumed that I would tell them that I didn't want a psychiatrist seeing her. The only other time in my mother's life that a psychiatrist had ever treated her was during the two weeks that she was in the hospital, and little good came from those two weeks.

I knew that my mother needed something to calm her nerves, but at the age of 89 I wasn't so sure that a psychiatrist was the answer. I was concerned that a psychiatrist's method of "helping" her would be solely through drugs. I wasn't opposed to her taking a drug, but I was worried that it wouldn't be easy to find the right drug, or the right amount. Delia's primary care physician had prescribed lorazepam for her several years earlier and she and I both were happy with how it made her feel. Plus, she never had negative side effects. I wanted the same for my mother.

Unfortunately, that's not how it worked out for her and the Calafort psychiatrist. He prescribed a variety of drugs for her, but they did more than just relax her; they made her really dopey. I felt like she had become a science project for him as he tried her on lorazepam, and alprazolam, and clonazepam. I think that he was medicating her not only to calm her down, but also to shut her up. When she was doped up enough she wasn't calling my name over and over, which probably made some people happy.

When I read about the possible side effects of those drugs, it described her to a tee. It was apparent that they not only exaggerated problems that she already had, but that they were creating new problems. Some of the side effects were memory loss, confusion, loss of appetite, problems with thinking, sleepiness, and drowsiness. I wanted her to feel less anxious but there had to be a better way than those drugs. I didn't know what the answer was. Well, yea, I did know the answer; but, short of cloning me, I was at a loss.

The stress and the anxiety that my mother was feeling showed in the way she looked. Her appearance changed more in the months that she'd been in the nursing home, than it

had changed in the previous 10 years. One of the most no-
ticeable and saddest differences was her smile. My mother
had always had a beautiful smile, but now when she smiled,
it often looked stilted and unnatural. I'll never know how she
lost her smile; maybe it was because of the drugs or maybe it
was how she felt deep inside, but whenever I'd see that fake
smile I always thought about her saying, "Shoot me first.
Don't ever put me in a home."

I know that my mother would have said that I did all
that I could have done for her, but there's a part of me that
will always feel that I let her down.

She, I, and Calafort were in this ordeal together. One of
the things that I could rely on Calafort to do was to contin-
ually provide some sort of an issue for me to address. The
newest issue was about my mother's glasses. Ever since she
was moved to the Meadows Unit I had heard other family
members complaining about lost glasses, bent glasses, or
ending up with someone else's glasses.

Now it was my turn to complain because her eyeglasses
had vanished, too. I found it maddening that the nursing home took no responsibility for losing her prescription
glasses. I thought that the number of places they could be
was limited, but the bottom line from the staff was that they

had looked everywhere and they couldn't find them. I guess there must have been a black hole for eyeglasses somewhere in Calafort.

I called her ophthalmologist's office and explained what had happened. Since the vision test that was recently done at the nursing home couldn't determine her visual acuity, and bringing her to his office for an exam wasn't an option, her doctor wrote me a copy of her last prescription. His office became the destination of another lunch hour so that I could pick up the prescription. After I got the prescription, I went to a discount eyeglass store, and ordered two new pair of glasses for her. I planned to keep the spare pair safe in my house just in case the other one also went into the black hole.

Her smile and her glasses weren't all that she had lost in long term care. She had already lost so much weight that when I hugged her, there wasn't much of my mother left to hug. Her pudginess was long gone and I felt bones that I'd never felt before. The Dietary Department had started giving her fortified shakes to help her put some weight back on, but I honestly didn't see that they were helping. I really wished that I could bring her some of her favorite foods but I long ago stopped bringing her home cooked meals when they told me that she was aspirating.

All the food that was served to her was pureed. I can't begin to tell you how unappetizing her meals looked, although they were always colorful. There was the brown stuff which was usually some sort of meat and gravy. I think the red globs were Italian dishes with tomato sauce. The whites and the greens were tougher to distinguish. The whites were either rice or bread. Can you imagine pureed bread? If the green was a vegetable, it was usually pretty tasty. If it was a green salad, it was just plain gross.

I always knew when it was a salad because she would scrunch up her face and shake her head the same way Michael and Kathleen used to do when they ate baby food that they didn't like. Even though most of the pureed food tasted okay, it looked like it had already been digested. However, I always told my mother that her meal looked yummy, and thankfully she never disagreed.

****

As you might imagine, it wasn't always easy taking care of both my mother and Delia at the same time, but I was committed to giving each of them all the help that I could give them at that time in their lives. While I was always concerned about them both, thank God usually only one of them had a crisis going on at a time.

It was now Delia's turn. She fell going into her bathroom and tore the thin skin on her leg. She was able to get up off the floor by herself, but didn't call me at work to let me know that she had fallen. When I stopped by to say hello that evening, she showed it to me. It looked nasty enough that I took her to the emergency room. They treated the wound and prescribed an antibiotic to prevent an infection. As bad luck would have it, her leg did become infected. A stronger antibiotic was prescribed and in time, her leg totally healed.

Her carpet didn't do as well, however. I wasn't able to get her blood out of the white carpet where she had fallen, and she never felt up to letting me call a professional carpet cleaner. I think that the stain became an eerie reminder for her to be more careful going into the bathroom.

As tough as some of my caregiving days had been for me, I knew that I wasn't the only one who was on this long term care journey; everyone else in my family felt it, too. I may have been the one going to Calafort every day, but I couldn't have done it without Dave's help. Not having to worry about cooking supper and doing the dishes every night helped me a lot. I didn't realize how much he helped me until he had to go out of town for a week on business.

By the end of the week I was feeling the stress with all that I needed to do for my mother, the kids, Delia, and work. By the time Saturday evening came around I blew my cool. After visiting my mother, visiting Delia, grocery shopping, cooking supper, cleaning up the kitchen, folding the laundry, and cleaning the litter box, I dramatically threw up my hands in the air in front of Michael and said, "I'm doing everything myself for everyone. Nobody is helping me. PLEASE turn off the TV for a few minutes and help me."

He was quiet for a minute but then said, "Mom, I did help you today."

"What do you think you did today, because I see nothing," I snapped back. He was only 13 years old. I shouldn't have been talking to him like that.

"Mom, I went with you to visit Grandma. Didn't that help you?" he asked sincerely.

Wow, his words really put things into perspective. I looked at him from across the room for a moment and then walked over to him. I put my arms around him and gave him a big hug. As I hugged him I thought about him interacting with his grandmother earlier in the day. It's tough enough for an adult to spend time visiting in a nursing home, but Michael was a 13 year old boy who gave up a part of his Saturday morning to go with me.

"Michael... oh Michael... yes, that helped me more than you'll ever know. Grandma loves you and your sister more than words can say. When I see how happy you make her feel, it makes me happy, too. Yes, you helped me a lot. I'm sorry for hollering at you. I shouldn't have done that," I said.

"That's okay, Mom. I know you're busy, and that you have a lot of stuff going on. What can I do to help?" he asked.

"You can give me another hug. That'll help me a lot," I said.

I told myself that I needed to remember that encounter with Michael for a long time. As alone as I felt sometimes with the responsibility of my mother and Delia, I wasn't alone. My entire family was subtly involved right along with me. Thank God I had them.

The holidays were right around the corner, but I was finding it difficult to get into the spirit of Christmas. My mother and I always went Christmas shopping together, and I knew that I was going to miss that tradition. It would also be the first Christmas since Dave and I were married that she wouldn't be celebrating Christmas dinner at our house. I knew that that Christmas season was going to be different in a lot of ways, but I also knew that I needed to make the best of it, and to be festive, for everyone else's sake.

It helped that as soon as the calendar turned to December that Calafort started decorating for the holidays. There were several Christmas trees with twinkling lights throughout the facility. They were each decorated with lots of pretty red bows and garland, a spattering of shiny balls, and of course, an angel or star on the top. There were tin soldiers and nutcrackers carefully placed on tables in the hallways. Bing, Elvis, and Tony Bennett even serenaded the residents through the PA system with traditional Christmas carols.

One evening when I visited my mother, I had some news that I knew that she'd like to hear, and I loved sharing good news with her.

"Guess what, Mom?" I asked, as upbeat as I could sound. No matter how tough my day was, no matter how down I felt when I walked through the front doors of the nursing home, I always tried to look and sound happy when I was around my mother. I saved the frowns and the tears for when I walked back through those doors after my visits with her were over.

"I don't know, Honey. Tell me," she said.

"Michael got chosen for a part in the Christmas pageant at school. He's going to be one of the Three Wise Men, AND he's actually going to be singing one of the verses of "We Three Kings of Orient Are.""

"I am so proud of my big boy. Tell him I'm proud of him. Tell him that I love him. What about Kathleen? What is she going to be?"

"Well, she's only in 3rd grade so they'll just sing as part of a group. I don't know what songs they'll be singing, but I'm sure that it'll be cute," I answered.

This was the first time in a long time that I saw a smile from my mother that looked like her pre-nursing home smile, and I could almost feel her pride. Just hearing about Michael having a part in the pageant perked her up. It made me happy to see her like that, because I didn't see it too often anymore. I thought that it was a shame that she wouldn't be able to see him perform. There were few things that either of the kids had participated in over the years that she ever missed out on seeing.

"Hey, Mom, the Christmas lights on the outside of the building are really pretty. I'm going to put a blanket over you so that you'll be toasty warm and then we'll go outside for a few minutes. It'll do you good to get out of here for a little while."

"Honey, I don't want to wear ye out. You've been working hard all day, while I just sit here on my can. Shouldn't ye go home and eat your supper now?" she asked.

"We won't be outside for long, just long enough for you to see the lights, and then I'll go on home. Dave will have the supper ready by the time that I get home," I said.

"You've got a good husband, Sally. A lot of men would be angry that ye weren't home fixing his supper now," she added.

"I know, Mom, you're right. I am lucky," I said.

I bundled her up from head to toe and we went outside. That's when I had a flashback to the prior Christmas. I remembered us walking side by side up my street, and her wanting to walk further than she had walked in a long time. I thought about her telling me that she didn't want to turn back to my house because "we don't know where we'll be next year at this time." In retrospect, that was her subtle prediction of what was to come.

As I pushed her wheelchair around the building, she asked, "How are the kids? I miss seeing them."

I told her again about Michael's part in the Christmas pageant. She sounded as happy and proud then as she sounded when I told her just a few minutes earlier. I wondered if she was just making conversation with me, and didn't want to say, "Ye just told me that story" or if her dementia caused her to totally forget our earlier conversation. Either way, I could see that thinking and talking about the kids made her happy no matter how many times we had basically the same conversation.

Chapter 12

Getting "Medicaid Ready"

It was tough enough keeping up with my mother's medical issues, but once she hit her 100th day and became "private pay" I made a point of taking the time to scrutinize the monthly bills that were coming from Calafort. It wasn't unusual for there to be an error on the bill, and it sometimes took months for it to be corrected.

The first billing mistake I found had to do with her medications. Instead of Calafort billing my mother's Blue Cross insurance for her medicine, they were billing her directly for the Cifdano's Pharmacy bills. I refused to pay those bills. It took two billing cycles before I could get them to start sending her pharmacy bills to Blue Cross. However, it took even longer before I could get them to submit the initial two months' bills to her insurance. In the meantime, Cifdano's Pharmacy was threatening to not send my mother's medication to the nursing home. That threat was all that it took to get me to pay the bill.

In my mind there were three issues going on. The most important was that she received her medication timely. The second issue was that the medication be properly billed. The third issue, on my mind and in my heart, had to do with my mother's financial reputation. She had always worked hard and paid her bills on time. At that point in her life, I didn't want anything to blemish her impeccable financial history. I knew that she didn't have a clue what was going on in the business office but it was important to me because if she understood what was going on, it would have been important to her.

Keeping up with the bills had become one more facet of her long term care that I needed to make sure was right.

Then one day it hit me that I should probably have already spoken with an elder care attorney concerning my mother's finances. She didn't have a lot of money, but she had worked hard throughout her life to save what money she could save. I didn't want to blindly spend it all on the nursing home if that could be avoided. I made an appointment with Kennedy Naughton, an attorney whose expertise was in elder care, and getting people Medicaid ready for institutional care.

The time and money I spent for the consultation was time and money well spent. My friends and relatives had been telling me that I should have my mother's house put in my name so that she wouldn't lose it. They told me that when she ran out of money, that if the house was in her name, that it would have to be sold to pay for the nursing home bills. I was naïve and what they told me made sense.

Kennedy allayed my worries about the house. She explained that my state is a Homestead state and as long as my mother wanted to go back to her home, even in the condition that she was presently in, the home would be safe in her name. She explained at a level that I could understand why it would have been counterproductive for the house to have been put in my name.

She also explained to me how to get my mother "Medicaid ready" which would allow some of her money to be preserved so that it would be mine after she passed away. Her legal knowledge as an elder care lawyer was invaluable. I can't suggest strongly enough what a crucial resource that type of lawyer is for anyone who has an elderly spouse or family member.

She made it clear that people who are very poor are already on Medicaid. She said that people who are wealthy can afford to pay for long term care indefinitely. It's the middle class that first must go through their entire life's savings before they will qualify for Medicaid. With her legal advice I was able to get my mother on Medicaid before her savings were depleted.

However, there was a lot of homework that Kennedy assigned to me that needed to be completed before my mother would be eligible for Medicaid. A few of those assignments included using my mother's money to complete any repairs or work that needed to be done to her house while she still had money left to do the work. I also needed to provide recent copies of all her bank statements and CDs, as well as proof of her income from my dad's annuity and her monthly social security. Kennedy also needed a copy of my mother's birth certificate from Ireland, a copy of the deed to her home, and a durable power of attorney.

None of the above was hard to accomplish. However, there was one thing that she wanted me to do that wasn't easy for me, and that was to make irrevocable funeral plans for my mother. I can't begin to tell you how upsetting that was for me to do. Several times over the next few weeks I turned down lunch plans with friends at work so that I could visit different funeral homes in order to buy my mother's casket and to make her final arrangements.

I found it bizarrely uncomfortable to be left alone in a showroom of caskets. I felt like I was taking part in an episode of the Adams Family, but there was nothing funny about it. I learned far more than I ever wanted to know about caskets, including the ones with false bottoms that could be rented. I also had to decide on a vault. Until then I thought that a vault was something that you put your valuables in in the bank. Eventually I bought a casket and put that unpleasant task behind me. When Mom asked me that evening if I had a nice day at work, I hugged her and told her it was sort of a tough one.

It took a few months before I got all the documents that I needed to get and completed all the tasks that Kennedy wanted me to do. I continued paying the full nursing home bill each month, but additionally I was supposed to transfer a specified amount of money (thousands of dollars) from my mother's account into a new account that was in my name.

I was to do that monthly transfer until she had less than $2000.00 left in her name.

That's when she would qualify for Medicaid, but she was still several months away from that happening. I regretted not having started the process much sooner because she would have been able to save a lot more of her money, but I didn't know any better at the time. It sure would have been a great bit of advice for Calafort to have shared with me, as well as with all the other families whose loved ones called Calafort their home. In retrospect, I don't know why they didn't.

The thousands of dollars that my mother paid to Calafort each month went to a variety of things. The bulk of it went to her room and board and a cadre of doctors. She had the psychiatrist, a podiatrist, Dr. Shrinirk, and Dr. Cathedra, which were more doctors than she ever had at one time when she lived in her own home.

You already know what I thought about the psychiatrist; I was thankful that there was a podiatrist but I didn't give him too much thought; Dr. Shrinirk was the on-staff doctor that was used by the facility for the residents who could no longer leave the nursing home in order to see their own doctors; and then there was Dr. Cathedra. The only reason I knew that he was still in the picture was because I saw that he was billing my mother's insurance for occasional visits. It's not an overstatement to say that I thought that he had saved her life when she was in the hospital, and for that I will be forever grateful, but I hadn't seen him or spoken with him since he discharged her from the hospital.

He never communicated with me when he saw her in the nursing home which made me think that he no longer had the same interest that he had when she was his patient in the hospital. He was fully aware that I didn't want her to be overly medicated, yet he never questioned the drugs that the Calafort psychiatrist had prescribed for her, at least not to me.

I thought that because of all that we had gone through with him when my mother was in the hospital, that this doctor/patient relationship was different from the run of the mill. I guess that I was wrong because he never even told me when he severed their relationship. I just stopped seeing his name and services on her insurance statements.

****

During that season of my life, I was kept pretty busy taking care of my mother and Delia, and working full time; I also had a busy home life. We lived on a lake and had recently purchased a motor boat. Even though it was still winter and the weather was nippy, the kids didn't seem to feel, or at least mind, the cold weather. Dave and I spent many weekend afternoons towing Michael and Kathleen and their friends around the lake as they went tubing.

Their screams of sheer delight as they were pulled behind the boat were juxtaposed by the hollers I heard later in the evening at the nursing home. There was always one or two residents hollering for a nurse or a CNA to help them. It's funny how two different yells could evoke such different emotions in me.

It didn't seem like it was that long ago that my mother's body was strong just like the kids that we were towing around the lake. Now she had legs that no longer walked, and her arms and hands were stiff and didn't work like they were supposed to work. I asked the physical therapy department to please screen her for some sort of physical therapy on her arms and hands before they became any worse. I was pleasantly surprised that they not only approved her to get physical therapy, but occupational therapy as well.

I was thankful that they saw the need because her arms had become so stiff that it was difficult for her to lift them over her head. It was quite the challenge for the CNAs to dress her with clothes that needed to go over her head; even cardigan sweaters were getting harder to put on her. I didn't understand why one of the nurses hadn't already made the request for physical therapy, rather than me being the one. How stiff did she have to become before someone from Calafort would have asked that she be screened?

My mantra with the doctors, nurses, and CNAs had always been, "Please, let's be proactive so that we don't have to be reactive down the road." Unfortunately, my concerns weren't always their concerns. I truly believed that the stiffness in her arms and hands could have been avoided. Now my mother was in a position where she was trying to work her way back to where she was physically, just months earlier.

Would it have killed them to have taken a few extra minutes each day over the past several months to do some stretching exercises when they dressed and undressed her? This could have been accomplished by a CNA. Now a more skilled, more expensive staff member had to be involved. Over the following months her insurance was billed thousands of dollars for the physical and occupational therapy on her arms and hands.

****

I tried to visit my mother nearly every day and it often worked out best for me to see her during my lunch break. That way, I'd have time to stop at Delia's apartment on my way home from work. Sometimes, however, I used my lunch break to take Delia to her doctors' appointments. One of her regularly scheduled appointments was with Dr. Roundstone, her dermatologist. Her fair, Irish skin had seen over nine decades of sun and she had had her share of skin cancer.

Dr. Roundstone was a sweetheart of a doctor, and he and his staff were always kind to her. During one of her regular visits he saw something suspicious on her right shin and did a biopsy. When the results came back, he confirmed that it was a squamous cell carcinoma.

Since her skin was so thin, he didn't want to surgically remove it. His recommendation was for radiation treatment, and he was adamant about that recommendation. I trusted him immensely so I made an appointment with Dr. Paul. He was the doctor who did her radiation therapy five years earlier when she had breast cancer. I've already told you how I describe good doctors vs. not so good doctors. Dr. Paul topped the good doctor list.

When I took Delia for her consultation at the Tasuil Cancer Center, I was reminded of just how great Dr. Paul was with her. We had to wait in a crowded waiting room for a long time, but their reunion was worth the wait. Even though they hadn't seen each other in several years, he hugged her when he entered the exam room and he talked to her like a long-lost friend. Well, actually he talked with her like a grandson would talk to his grandmother. After the medical part of the visit was over, she remained in her wheelchair and he sat up on the exam table. It was as if I was invisible as they talked for several minutes.

Finally, she said to him, "Doctor, don't ye have other people waiting to see ye?"

He appeared to be so interested in talking to her that he actually forgot for a short while that he had a waiting room packed full of other patients. In response to her question, he hopped off the exam table and explained to me the radiation schedule for the next several weeks. He said that in spite of her age that the prognosis was good. I knew that he cared about her and I told him that I was glad that he was her doctor. Once upon a time I had said those same words to Dr. Diarmuid.

She was a trooper for the next six and a half weeks, as I took her for her radiation treatments every Monday through Friday. I never told my mother what Delia was going through;

no good would have come from her knowing that information. It would have upset her to hear the news, and she would probably have soon forgotten that I told her.

The two sisters hadn't seen each other in months, but every day they each asked me how the other was doing. I knew that Delia felt bad that my mother was living in long term care, but she knew that there wasn't any other choice. Shortly after her radiation treatment was behind her, she told me that she wanted to go see my mother.

Several times we made plans to visit Mom, but each time Delia would back out at the last minute for one reason or another, and then would ask if we could go the following Saturday or Sunday. I think that she worked herself up so much anticipating a visit with my mother that her anxiousness would actually make her sick. I hate to admit it, but I was always a little relieved when she didn't go because I knew that it would break her heart to see the way my mother looked at that point.

It was around this time that my mother got a new roommate. Unfortunately, roommates come and go on a regular basis in a nursing home. I thought that this lady would be a good one for her because every time I visited, she was asleep in her bed. She was such a deep sleeper that I didn't think that my mother hollering my name would disturb her in the least.

One evening when I walked into their room I gave my mother my usual, "Hi Mom, I'm here!"

She was sitting in her wheelchair next to her bed and when she saw me, she quickly put her index finger over her lips and shushed me. She quietly said, "Don't talk too loud, Honey. Delia's taking a little nap and I don't want to wake her."

Well now, that wasn't something that I anticipated hearing.

"Really? Has she been sleeping for long?" I played along because, well just because I didn't know what to say.

"She had a very bad night last night. I don't know what's the matter with her, but the sleep will do her good. Let her sleep for a while longer," she whispered.

"Good idea," I confirmed.

"Are ye hungry?" she asked softly.

"Yea, a little bit, but that's okay. Dave'll have supper ready by the time I get home," I said.

"It'll be something good, I'm sure. Be happy that ye don't have to cook after a long day at the job. He's a good man to do the cooking for ye. How're the kids?" she asked.

"Everyone is good." I bent over her chair and gave her a hug and kissed her. "I've been wanting to give you that hug all day. That's really the only reason I stopped by tonight. I just wanted to stay long enough to say, 'Hi' and to tell you that I loved you, and to make sure that you have everything that you need. Is there anything that I can do for you or get you before I leave?" I asked.

The way she looked at me at that moment and the way she responded to my question reminded me of "my old mom."

"Ye know that I love seeing ye but you're a silly ass to come all that way for just a few minutes. Ye know that they'll call ye if anything's the matter. Don't worry so much about me. I have everything I need. Be careful on your way home," she said.

One more hug and I said, "I love you most, Mom."

"Baby, I'll love ye till the day I die. Tell Dave and the kids that I love them, too," she said.

"I will," I said as I squeezed her hand. I smiled at her and then I turned around and left.

"Safe home," I heard her say as I was walking away.

On my drive home I smiled to myself as I thought about her thinking that Delia was sleeping in the room with her. I hoped that that lady didn't pass away any time soon. She could actually be therapeutic for my mother, at least until she wakes up and gets out of bed.

My entire visit probably lasted all of 10 minutes, but those 10 minutes of her getting to see me, satisfied her for that day. It didn't take long for me to figure out during each of my visits, if the visit could be for just a few minutes or if I needed to stay for a couple of hours. I was happy to give her whatever time she needed.

We never had much money when I was growing up so I didn't have a lot of "things." What I did have, however, was invaluable and that was all the time my mother gave me. Now I was giving some of that time back to her.

****

It had been over nine months since the first time I met with attorney Kennedy Naughton. I had already completed everything that I needed to do in order for my mother to become Medicaid ready for institutional care, and her savings account now had less than $2000.00 left in it. It was time for Kennedy to submit the written application.

It wasn't long after the application was submitted before an interview was scheduled for me with the Department of Children and Families. During the interview I was told that

Calafort needed to provide statements showing all the bills from the time she entered the nursing home. They gave me a short amount of time to get the information to them. Sounds like an easy request, right? It was like pulling teeth to get the needed information.

Once the paperwork was provided to DCF, in less than a month, my mother was approved for institutional care and Medicaid. Upon approval, she could no longer have more than $2,000.00 total in her accounts or the Medicaid would be in jeopardy. Her monthly room charge to Calafort was reduced to a small fraction of the $7,000.00 that she'd been paying since she hit her 100th day; the new amount was based on her Social Security check and her monthly annuity check from my dad. The only money that she would be allowed to keep out of those two checks was $35.00 a month for "personal needs." (I believe that amount has been increased, but not significantly).

I'm not sure what the government thought $35.00 would buy; a trip to the nursing home beautician was $25.00 for just a haircut. That being said, I was happy and relieved that she was approved and that I was able to preserve some of her savings. She would have been happy, too.

A month after she was approved, I received a bill from Calafort saying that my mother's account was $8000.00 past due. Their records indicated that she was Medicaid pending, but not actually on Medicaid. This was frustrating because the day that I received the approval letter from Medicaid, I brought a copy of it to the business office at Calafort. Four phone calls later, they corrected their mistake and my mother's account was no longer past due. At that point, I was hopeful that things were permanently resolved with Calafort's business office and my mother's account.

I also made a point of notifying my mother's Blue Cross insurance that she was now on Medicaid. I guess that the wheels of bureaucracy sometimes turn slowly because they continued deducting her coverage from her monthly annuity. That also took a few phone calls to get them to stop deducting a monthly premium for insurance that she no longer had. Eventually I received a letter saying that she was no longer covered by Blue Cross and that she would see a refund for the premiums that she was wrongly charged.

Chapter 13

Last Rites

Have you seen the movie *Groundhog Day*? If so, you'll understand why the nursing home made me feel like I was a character in that movie. That's because I kept reliving the same scenes and having the exact conversations over and over again with the people who took care of my mother.

I don't know how many times I said, "Please make sure that you put a sweater on her. She's always cold. She depends on you to do that for her because she can no longer do it for herself."

I also continued asking that they please keep her fingernails short. Her skin had become thin like Delia's and her fast growing nails would break the skin if she scratched too hard.

I never understood why I even had to make that type of request.

I still had to remind them to please not leave her sitting in her wheelchair, facing a wall. I don't understand why my mother wasn't able to maneuver the chair so that she wasn't in that position, but no matter the reason, she wasn't able to do it.

Some days I wanted to gather the staff that was working when I was there and say, "Don't you people get it? What are you doing here? Don't you understand that my mother and all the rest of the residents are here because there is no other choice for them? They depend on YOU for EVERYTHING. Wake up and treat them the way you would want your mother and your father to be treated, the way that someday you'll want to be treated!"

Of course, those words never went beyond the confines of my mind. If I thought that saying those things would have made any difference, I would have said them, and more. But I knew that I had to be forever diplomatic, because I would never want to risk any repercussions towards me, landing on my mother.

Another issue that concerned me was that I didn't always see the staff wash their hands or put on gloves before or after they were with a resident. I knew that nursing homes are notorious for spreading germs, which is what was happening at that time. For weeks I had been hearing a lot of the residents, as well as the staff, coughing. Many ended up with bad colds, bronchitis, or worse. I prayed that Mom wouldn't catch whatever was going around. For some reason she was able to stave it off longer than many of the people who lived and worked at Calafort, but eventually her luck ran out and she caught "it", whatever "it" was.

She had been a three pack a day cigarette smoker for over 40 years before she quit cold turkey. Her cigarette of choice was potent and unfiltered. After all those years of smoking, I didn't think that her lungs could have been in the best shape possible.

As soon as we noticed that she was getting sick, a chest x-ray was ordered and it showed that she had bronchitis. She was immediately put on an antibiotic. Several days later a second x-ray was ordered because she didn't seem to be getting better. At that point it was apparent that she needed something different, something stronger, so they changed the antibiotic.

Over time she recovered from the bronchitis, but it had become obvious to me that whenever she got sick now, the recovery took a little longer and she seldom improved to the point that she was at before the newest diagnosis. Even though I always breathed a sigh of relief when she felt better, it saddened me that she often looked a little frailer, and a little weaker, than she had been just a month earlier.

I was thankful that my mother was feeling better before the start of the holidays. One of my best friends from the time that we were 10 years old and her family spent Thanksgiving with us that year, Mom's second Thanksgiving in Calafort. While the turkey was still in the oven, Ninetta went with me to visit my mother. When we were kids we spent lots of time at each other's houses and we were more like sisters rather than friends. It had been a few years since she had seen my mother and I told her that my mother had changed dramatically. I wanted to prepare her for what she was going to see.

As we walked down the hallway towards my mother's room, we could hear her calling, "Sally, Sally, Sally." We each stopped in our tracks when we first heard her calls and just looked at the other. I was used to hearing it, but it was the first time for Ninetta. She knew that my mother hadn't seen me yet.

"Sally, how long do you think she's been calling for you?" she asked.

"I don't know. Once she sees me, she usually calms down pretty quickly, but this is how she often is when I first get here. I've heard it a hundred times, but it still makes me sad. It's killing me to see her like this. Other times it's just the opposite, and I don't hear a peep from her as I'm walking down this hall. Those days I sometimes find her sitting in her wheelchair with her head hanging down. Those are the days that I think she's overly medicated. But then... once in a blue moon, I'm thankful to find her pretty much like she used to be. I relish those visits."

I paused for a moment and then said, "Let's keep going."

As soon as she saw me, she stopped calling my name. She hadn't noticed Ninetta yet.

Her eyes teared up as she said, "I didn't know where ye were and nobody would tell me. Are ye okay?"

"I'm fine, Mom. You never ever have to worry about me; I'm always fine even when I'm not here with you," I said. I gave her a strong hug, and then rubbed my hands up and down on her back. A hug from me always soothed her.

"Mom, look who's here with me. It's Ninetta, and she wanted to come see you. Do you remember Ninetta?" I asked.

She had already calmed down, and when she saw Ninetta, she smiled a real smile, and said, "Don't be silly, of course I remember Ninetta. Didn't she do a lot of growing up at our house? How are ye, Baby?"

"Hi, Barbara. I'm good. How're you?" she asked as she bent over and gave her a hug.

"I'm good, too. It's so nice to see you," Mom answered.

Since it was time for lunch, we wheeled her down to the pretty dining room in the Glen Unit. I wanted her to have a nice Thanksgiving dinner, although I was pretty sure that she had no idea that it was any holiday.

I was surprised at how much Mom remembered about Ninetta. When she asked her how her parents were doing, she seemed sincerely sorry when she learned that they had passed away. Ninetta reminded my mother how much she used to love the great pot roast dinners my mother used to make.

As the three of us sat at a table next to a window in the Calafort dining room, it reminded me of all those meals with Ninetta in my mother's kitchen, sitting next to the kitchen window, laughing and joking and enjoying her great cooking. I could see the sadness in Ninetta's eyes as she looked at my mother. She probably thought this would be the last time she'd see her.

We had a really, really nice visit and I was so thankful that I could spend a part of Thanksgiving with Ninetta and my mother.

After we had said our goodbyes to my mother and were walking out to my car Ninetta said, "Sally, I don't know how you can stand it. It's so sad to see her like that. She's lost so much weight. Do you know what she weighs?"

I took a deep breath and said, "She's down to 92 pounds; she weighed about 140 pounds when she came in here. They're giving her an appetite enhancer but I'm not sure how much good it's doing. Ninetta, I can't stand seeing her like this. I hate it. The day that she passes away will be the saddest day of my life but I would never ever try to keep her living just to know that she's alive. That's why I signed the DNR, but as long as she's still with us, I will work non-stop to make things as good as they can be for her."

She gave me a hug. We both loved my mother, each in our own way. It was a pretty quiet ride back to my house.

A few weeks after Thanksgiving, I got a call from Mom's nurse, Sandi. I never liked when my phone would ring and the caller ID said "Calafort." It was seldom a call that I wanted to hear. This time Sandi was calling to suggest that I get my mother on hospice care. My heart dropped as I wondered if that call signified that this was the beginning of her end.

I was upset initially because I thought that meant that they had given up on her. Sandi explained that they'd never give up helping my mother and that they had some residents who had hospice care for years. She said, however, that a doctor would have to say that she was terminally ill, in order for her to be eligible for hospice.

Sandi said that if my mother had hospice care that things might be easier for me because I may not feel so compelled to visit her every day. If she was on hospice there would be someone else who'd be spending time with her. There would be someone else to take her for walks outside. It would be company for her. She made it sound like it might be something that would help both of us.

I talked to Dave and Delia and some of my closest friends. This was another tough decision for me to make. It would have been much easier to make a decision if she had some sort of terminal disease and needed lots of help with pain control. Thank God that wasn't the situation with her, at least not at that point. She wasn't terminally ill; she was simply elderly and desperate for company. She also longed for her life as she once knew it. Institutional care was what had taken the biggest toll on her.

I made the time to speak with a hospice representative and she explained that hospice care could not provide any extraordinary means to keep my mother alive. I was totally in agreement with that philosophy. When she was in the hospital I made the decision against a feeding tube. Nor would I ever have wanted her on a ventilator. And I would have been upset if they ever "sent her out" to the hospital.

All that being said, I was still having problems making a decision. It helped that Sandi didn't pressure me, and told me to just think about it for a while. She said it wasn't anything that I had to decide right away. For the next few weeks I thought about it every now and then, but then I put it out of my mind. I guess I didn't think the time was right for my mother to have hospice care. In my heart I thought that I would know if the time would ever be right.

****

At that point, it had been more than a year and a half since my mother lived in her home, but I still stopped by her house every weekend to water the plants and to make sure there weren't any problems. Sometimes I asked myself what was the real reason that I went to her house. It was difficult to come up with a good answer. I think that in some odd way, however, it kept the connection to my pre-nursing home mother alive in my mind. If nothing else, it was somewhat therapeutic for me.

I was still bothered about how quiet the house was but I'd accepted that's how it would always be. As empty as the house was of sounds, however, it was chocked full of memories. Each week as I walked from room to room to make sure that everything was okay, in my mind's eye I saw all sorts of memories from my childhood, adolescence, and even in my role as a mother. It was as if I was now a spectator watching scenes from my life.

One of my memories that rose to the surface was of a Saturday afternoon that I had both kids with me. Kathleen and I were doing something at the dining room table. Mom and Michael were in the kitchen. Kathleen was only about four years old and had gotten on my last nerve. I seldom spanked my kids but on that day I took her off her chair and paddled her a few times. My mother and Michael could hear the spanks and could hear her crying. I think her pride was hurt probably more than her fanny, and she dramatically ran into one of the bedrooms.

Michael was in the dining room almost immediately wanting to know why she got into trouble. He wasn't cocky or disrespectful when he looked me in the eye and said, "Grandma never spanked you. That's what you've always told us. Why did you spank Kathleen?" I think he was sincerely curious for an answer.

I couldn't be upset with him for asking his question. He was correct. Only once in my entire life was I ever spanked and I think that my mother regretted it, as soon as she did it.

She used to tell me stories about all the slaps that she got as a child in Ireland from her mother and from the schoolmaster. She said she often didn't even understand why she was being hit. She told me that she vowed that if she ever had children that she'd never hit them, and that she'd "scratch the eyes out of anyone who laid a hand on any of my kids."

"Michael, this is between Kathleen and me," was the answer I gave him. That wasn't a good answer, but I didn't want to tell him the real reason which was simply because I lost my patience with her.

A while later my mother walked through the dining room. I could tell that she wasn't happy, but she never once criticized me for spanking her granddaughter. She knew that I knew how she felt without having to tell me. I think that

was one of the few times I ever raised a hand to either of my
kids.

Memories of those days gone by with my mother and
my kids helped me to get through the Calafort days. As I left
her empty house that day and backed out of the driveway, I
glanced over at the front porch. I imagined her waving goodbye to me, and telling me, "Safe home."

****

Over the next few months I watched as she continued to
slowly go downhill. There were more chest x-rays and more
diagnosis of bronchitis and pneumonia. There were also more
urinary tract infections. In my mind, I blamed the UTIs on
the diapers. The intervals of time between her getting better
and the next diagnosis got shorter and shorter. I'd ask the
nurses if she was really better when her antibiotic was gone.
They'd say, "Yes" based on an x-ray or urine test. I, however,
remained skeptical because her cough sometimes lingered
and never seemed to go away entirely. The nurses told me
that she was probably aspirating.

One night when I stopped by after work, her blood pressure was only 60/40. Even though the nursing home hadn't
called me to say that there was a problem, I had such an

uneasy feeling about it that when I left Calafort that evening, I called my good friend, Bob, who had sung at my wedding. I was calling him now to ask if he'd sing at my mother's funeral when that day came. Of course, he said, "Yes." I hoped that that day would be a long way off, but only God knew the answer to that question.

Not many days after I had spoken to Bob, I noticed that my mother's cough was changing. It sounded like the kind of cough that she would get that often turned into bronchitis. I asked her nurse to please let the doctor know right away so that he could prescribe an antibiotic, if he thought she needed one. This was the time to be proactive.

I felt like I was coming down with something, too. I really didn't have time to go to my regular doctor so I fought it off for several days. When it started to get worse, instead of better, I decided to go to a walk-in clinic. I knew that I needed to be healthy because I felt like I was always on-call for my mother and for Delia.

After a long wait in the waiting room, I was brought to an examination room, but then it took a while for the doctor to come in. Shortly after he walked into the room, I got a call on my cell phone from the nursing home. It was Sandi and she said that my mother was declining rapidly and to please come as quickly as possible. As many times as I'd received calls from Calafort, I'd never heard the words "declining rapidly" and I thought that it meant that she was about to die. I apologized to the doctor as I got off the table and told him that I had to leave right away.

I drove much faster than I should have driven and cried all the way to the nursing home. I prayed that I would get there before she passed away. It was important to me that she didn't die by herself. We were together when I came into this world and I wanted to be with her when she left it.

When I arrived at Calafort, I ran to her room. Sandi had just finished taking her vitals, and was leaving her room as I walked in. She told me to let her know if I needed anything. My mother appeared to be in a deep sleep. I knelt down on the padded cushion next to her bed as she lay in her bed that wasn't high off the ground. I could see that she was breathing but I couldn't wake her. I held her hand and asked her to squeeze my hand. There was no response.

She had a blanket on her to keep her warm. I peeked under it because I wanted to see her chest moving up and down. I wanted to see every sign of life while there was still life in her. That was the first time I'd seen her so scantily clad since she'd been in long term care. I was shocked to see what had become of her body. She looked like the pictures I'd seen of people who had lived in a concentration camp. I knew that for months she had been given an appetite enhancer, and I was told that she'd been eating better. How could she be eating better when she looked like a skeleton with skin covering her bones?

When I couldn't kneel any longer, I sat on her bed close to her. I did this for hours and talked to her as if she could hear me. I told her what a great mother and grandmother she was. I told her that I hoped that I could be as good a mother to Michael and Kathleen, as she had always been to me. I told her that if she had pain, I wished that I could take it away. I told her over and over how much I loved her. I told her that she needed to rally and get better because Michael and Kathleen and I still had plenty to learn from her. In the overall scheme of things, it wasn't important in the least, but I told her that I wanted to know how to make her pot roast.

When I was younger she told me that death was just one part of life. As I sat with her that day, I wanted to know why dying had to be so hard. No nurses entered the room during the day. They could probably hear my soliloquys and wanted to leave us alone.

Throughout the day I stroked her hands and craved to feel a squeeze from them, no matter how slight. I looked carefully at her hands and thought they told a part of her life's story. Those two old hands had milked cows, caught and filleted fish, painted houses, mastered chopsticks, and nursed my pet rooster back to health. They sewed, knitted, cooked, and cleaned. They caressed and they prayed, but they didn't spank. Those wonderful hands dried many tears, held a lot of hands, and gave lots of tickles and backrubs. The more things I thought about her hands doing, the more I wanted to feel her squeezing my hand just one more time. I waited all day for her to open her eyes and smile at me or to take her last breath and go to Heaven.

At some point during that long day, I left her room long enough to ask her nurse to call a priest. I knew that my mother would have wanted to have Last Rites. It would have been important to her. As sad as I felt, I was preparing both of us for her to die.

It didn't take long for the priest to arrive. He and I made small talk for a few minutes and then the focus turned to my mother.

I remember that he had a crucifix, holy water, and holy oil. I think that there may have been candles but this was such a somber few minutes that some of the details are now foggy in my recollection. For some reason, I do remember some of his words as he anointed her with the oil...

"Through this holy anointing may the Lord in his love and mercy help you with the grace of the Holy Spirit. May the Lord who frees you from sin, save you and raise you up."

My mother had been lying perfectly still and quiet for hours. What happened next was eerily well timed.

The priest continued, "Barbara, if this is the time that the Lord is calling you home..."

At that point she started coughing. The priest stopped talking and looked over at me. Neither of us said anything to the other.

He waited for her to stop the coughing and then he started again, "Barbara, if this is the time that your Lord and Savior is calling you home..."

She started coughing again. He looked at me once again and said, "Maybe she doesn't want this to be the time." He and I smiled at each other and then he finished the blessing. After the sacrament was over, we talked for a few minutes longer. He tried to give me some words of encouragement. I wondered how many times he had that same conversation with families as they awaited their loved ones' departure from this earth.

Shortly after the priest left me, the nurse came into the room and asked if I needed anything. I told her the only thing I needed were prayers for my mother. She told me that she had been praying for her. I sincerely believed that Sandi cared about my mother.

I heard no more coughs from my mother. I stayed with her until my back ached and I was physically and emotionally drained. I was talked out and cried out. I gave her one last kiss on her forehead and told her that I would see her tomorrow. I wondered if she heard me. I wondered if she would be alive tomorrow.

Even though I was exhausted when I got home, I wasn't able to relax or to get much sleep that night. I couldn't stop thinking about her so I called the nursing home a few times throughout the evening and the night just to make sure that she wasn't "declining rapidly" again.

When I called the first thing in the morning the nurse told me that she was much better than when I left her the evening before. She said that her blood pressure was stronger and that she was even talking a little. I contemplated staying home from work and spending the day at the nursing home, but after Dave left with the kids, I decided to go to work. However, I couldn't go to the office until I first stopped by Calafort to see for myself that she was doing better.

When I got to her room, she was sitting up in her bed and the CNA was trying to get her to eat a little pureed breakfast, but it was apparent that she ate all that she was planning on eating at that time. The CNA said that she had eaten about 10% of her breakfast. I knew that wasn't much but I was amazed to see her eating anything at all.

I felt relief the moment I saw her and I thanked God for letting her live through the night. I knew that she was weak from yesterday's ordeal and I didn't want to wear her out by staying more than just a few minutes. I told her that I loved her, and she mouthed those words back to me.

Before I left her room I gave her some news that I thought she'd like to hear. I told her that another one of my best friends would be coming from Texas the following month and that she wanted to visit her. Amy was another childhood friend that was like a sister. The only response from Mom was a slow nod. I hoped that she'd still be with us when Amy arrived.

When I left my mother's room I looked for Sandi. When I found her I told her that I thought that it was time for hospice. When hospice care was first broached with me months earlier, the timing didn't feel right, but I believed that I would know when it was right. That time was now. She needed more help than I could give her and I needed help. I didn't think that I could continue doing all that I did for my mother all by myself any longer.

I was on the verge of a breakdown. I felt helpless in trying to improve the quality of her life, and that made me sad. It wasn't unusual that at the end of a long day at the office, and a long visit with my mother that I would have a meltdown after I left the facility. I would cry on my drive home, but I always made sure that by the time I pulled into my driveway, my meltdown was over and that my tears were gone. I didn't want my family to know.

The day after I told Sandi that I wanted my mother to have hospice care, I signed the papers and she was officially on the program. As the days went by, she continued to get stronger and was able to get out of bed, eat in the dining room, and even go outside for wheelchair walks. I hoped that with my mother on hospice I would have more time to help Delia, and maybe even a little more time for myself.

Sandi told me that she knew when my mother had "turned the corner" and started getting better. That was when she once again started calling my name repeatedly. As annoying as it had been in the past, Sandi said that she and the rest of the staff were happy when she started doing it again because that was a sign that she was improving.

Even though she continued going in the right direction, I knew that my mother would never be as well as her older sister. It was hard for me to believe that Delia was 94 years old. I seldom thought of her as elderly, maybe because she continued to be such a great source of strength for me. On days that she sensed that I was down, she knew the words to say that would cheer me up. Every now and then she'd lecture me about taking care of myself and about making time for myself. I knew that she was absolutely right, but it was far easier said than done.

After my mother had been on hospice for a while, I decided that it would be okay for me to occasionally skip a day's visit with her, and to spend that time with Delia. The nursing home staff, however, never knew when I wasn't going to be there. I felt confident that my mother would get better care if neither Calafort nor hospice knew when to expect me. They both were charging her insurance for quality health care, so I hoped and I prayed that's what she got whether

I was there or not. Unfortunately, that's not how it always was.

I found that out one evening when I arrived for a visit, and Sandi said that she wanted to tell me something before I went into my mother's room. She said that my mother was extremely upset earlier in the day and that she wanted me to know what had happened before I saw her. She said that the CNAs had already been spoken to and they were aware what they did was wrong and that it would never happen again. I could feel my heart beating fast as I waited for her to tell me what had happened.

It turned out that there was a woman named Sally working in the laundry room. After listening to my mother repeatedly calling my name, a couple of the Calafort CNAs thought that it would be funny for them to bring "laundry room Sally" to her. When she walked into the room, one of the CNAs announced, "Here's Sally." My mother didn't find the humor in their joke at all, and put them in their place.

Sandi said that she just happened to walk into the room in the middle of this scene and heard my mother say, "What sort of a fool do ye think that I am? Do ye think that I don't know my own daughter? Get out of my room and don't ever do something like that to me again. Now get out of here!"

As Sandi was telling me what happened, I vividly pictured my mother's Irish temper flaring up.

What was the purpose of their joke? What did they think my mother would say to them? Did they think that she would think that it was funny? Maybe a decade earlier she may have thought that it was funny, but it definitely wasn't funny at that time, considering her state of mind and her mood.

I was upset by what the CNAs had done, but I was proud that she still had the strength and wherewithal to respond the way that she responded. Sandi assured me that they would never do anything insensitive like that again.

Of course, when I went into my mother's room she was quick to tell me her version of the same story. It was pretty much the same as what Sandi had told me. I was pleasantly surprised that her memory was so vivid of the event and I wondered why her short-term memory was good sometimes, and other times it was like a sieve.

I didn't want her to dwell on that unpleasant incident so I took her outside in hopes of getting her mind off "laundry room Sally" and on more pleasant thoughts. It was refreshingly quiet outside the building, and I sat on a bench with her facing me.

"Gosh, Mom, it's so nice sitting out here for a little while, isn't it?" I asked as I gave her knee a little pat.

"You're too good to me, Baby," she said, but I could tell that she was still thinking about what had happened earlier in the day.

She continued to vent, "I don't know what in the name of God was the matter with those women. Are they crazy, or did they think I'm the crazy one?"

"Some people just don't have any common sense. You know that. I'm sorry that it happened, but I don't think that'll ever happen again. I want you to always tell me if anything happens to upset you when I'm not here with you. Do you promise that you'll tell me?" I asked.

"Ye know that I will," she said.

"Mom, are they nice to you here? Are they kind to you?" I asked.

She was quiet for a moment and then said, "I think so."

I would have been happy to hear a more definitive answer but for the moment I was satisfied with the answer that I got.

I missed the great talks that she and I used to have, but that didn't keep me from trying to still have them. I tried to keep her as involved as possible in Michael's and Kathleen's lives, although she could no longer have the type of involvement that she once had.

I wanted to stop talking about the nursing home so I switched gears and said, "Let me get your opinion on something."

She looked at me blankly, which made me wonder if she was still thinking about what happened earlier with the CNAs or if she was paying attention to what I was saying.

"Mom, the youth group that Michael belongs to at church is planning a trip for a week over the summer to Georgia. They are going to be doing all sorts of volunteer work there. He's never been away from home for a week before without us. What do you think? Should we let him go?" I asked.

I wasn't sure if she was at all focused on what I was saying.

"Mom, are you hearing what I'm asking you?" I asked.

It took a moment, but then she answered, "Honey, I was thinking about the right answer to tell ye." Another pause and then, "Ye and Dave have taught Michael right from wrong. He knows what the right thing to do is. He's a big boy now and before ye know it, he'll be a man. If there will be grownups on the trip with him, I say that ye should give him the chance to be away from ye. I've always told ye that travel is a great education. He'll see things in Georgia that he would never see here." And then she posed the same question to me, "What do ye think?"

"I think that's really good advice. He's in high school now so he's definitely old enough to do this sort of thing. I just wondered what you thought. Dave and I will talk some more but we'll probably let him go," I said.

It was nice for me that I could still occasionally have that type of conversation with her. Her answer really didn't surprise me. She always gave me my wings, my independence. She was the one who encouraged me to finish college, to travel, to get my own apartment. She said it was important to do those things before getting married. I'm certain that she missed me tremendously when I moved out of her house, but she never made me feel guilty. Now she was encouraging me to give my kids a taste of independence.

Chapter 14

Second Class Residents

On my drive home the night of "laundry room Sally" I came to the conclusion that as long as my mother lived in Calafort, there would always be issues. Thank God that most of those issues weren't life threatening, but I thought that if they were addressed, that the lives of the residents who lived in the Meadows Unit could be more pleasant. I guess you could call those issues "creature comforts."

One of the things that I looked into wasn't a huge issue, but it bothered me nonetheless. It had to do with utensils. The residents in the Meadows Unit would sometimes go without correct utensils for a week or more at a time. They'd be given large soup spoons instead of a regular size teaspoon.

Just imagine eating your cereal, ice cream, pudding, cottage cheese, whatever, with an oversized spoon. Sure, you could do it, but would you want to do it?

When I found out that the dining room for the Glen Unit, the rehab portion of the facility, had teaspoons, I complained. My complaint was addressed, but Calafort's solution wasn't my solution. Their solution was to replace the utensils in the Meadows Unit with plastic utensils. That's when I became more vocal that my mother and the others in the nursing home part of Calafort were being treated like second class residents, and that the rehab residents were treated like they were in first class.

When I thought about all of my mother's monthly income, except for a whopping $35.00, going to Calafort, I thought that it was only right that she should have real utensils to eat her colorful blobs of food. The unit supervisor told me that the flatware and cups kept disappearing. She said that they didn't know if they were lost in the garbage or if they were being taken.

I told her that I really didn't care the reason that they didn't have enough flatware or cups for the entire facility but if this was an ongoing problem that they should think about being proactive and order more before they ran out. I guess that I must have complained to the right person, because that problem got resolved and didn't surface again while my mother lived at Calafort.

Another topic of discussion having to do with the dining room wasn't a complaint at all. I was just curious why there was a large television set in there, but I never once saw it turned on. There was also a storage container that never budged from one of the corners of the room that was filled with DVDs. Obviously at one time they were showing those DVDs to the residents, and I wondered why they no longer did.

Since there was always other fish to fry, I never went out of my way to look into it. One day, however, when I ran into the Activities' Director I asked her about it. She said that a while back they used to play old movies, but few of the Meadows' residents showed much interest in watching them.

I thought about her answer for a moment or two and then I gave her my opinion. I told her that I could understand why they didn't like watching the old movies. As much as I didn't like to admit it, I said that a lot of the residents in the Meadows Unit weren't as mentally sharp as the people who lived in the Glen Unit. I said that a lot of them had pretty short attention spans and that it was probably difficult for them to follow the plots of movies. Plus, many of them were hard of hearing, although few of them wore hearing aids.

I suggested that they try to get DVDs for old Lawrence Welk shows or National Geographic shows, or even DVDs about animals. I thought that any of those suggestions might hold their attention longer than the old movies did because it wasn't necessary for them to be able to follow closely in order to enjoy it.

We talked for a little bit longer, but when we said goodbye I thought that that was the end of the TV discussion. I was surprised when I found out that she had taken my suggestion seriously and purchased additional DVDs. For a month or so my mother would sometimes happily tell me that she went to the movies during the day.

I don't think that there were a lot of residents who watched the DVDs, but it was a pleasant diversion for those who did. Unfortunately, over time I had the feeling that the movie days were happening less frequently, and then they totally stopped.

I was disappointed when I heard that they weren't doing it any longer, so I asked the Activities' Director why they'd stopped. I told her that I knew that at least some of the residents enjoyed the entertainment. She said that there needed to be someone to stay in the dining room with the residents while they were watching the TV and that created a problem because often the CNAs were needed in other areas.

She said that they had to temporarily stop playing the DVDs, but she was hopeful that they'd be able to start it up again down the road. I think that it was a very long road because the DVDs found a permanent home back in their container. I decided that this wasn't a battle worth fighting, so I didn't bring it up again. There were far more serious issues on the horizon.

I was glad that things were somewhat stable with my mother at that moment in time because that gave me a little more time to spend with Delia. We enjoyed each other's company, and looked forward to our chitchats over a cup of tea. I was greatly appreciative that she had made things so much easier for me than they could have been. A few years earlier she wisely realized that there were some things that she could no longer safely do without assistance, so she searched out ways to get that extra help.

Without me even being aware that she was looking into it, Delia found out about a great organization called Community Care for the Elderly. Through them she was able to get an aide who came to her apartment a few times a week and helped her take a shower; another lady came and did light housekeeping. Usually she'd ask them to go for a walk with her so that she could get some exercise.

She also discovered an organization that provided frozen food to senior citizens. At the beginning of each month she received a variety of meals delivered to her apartment. She was the one who chose the meals from a fairly large menu. An added bonus was that the kind delivery man didn't just stack the meals on her kitchen counter; he put them away for her, just the way she wanted them put away. Those frozen meals supplemented the home cooked meals that I brought her.

In spite of all the help that she was getting, however, she and I both were concerned that she didn't seem as strong as she had been, nor was she as steady on her feet when she walked. I never wanted her to go through a fall like her sister had, and then end up living out her days in long term care.

The next time she had an appointment with her doctor we discussed these concerns with him. He suggested at-home physical therapy to help her get stronger, and to walk more safely. Delia and I both told him that we thought that would be a great idea. He ordered a physical therapy evaluation which was a prerequisite for getting PT.

I didn't know what criteria was used in determining who qualified for PT but thankfully she did qualify. As a result of that evaluation, occupational therapy was also ordered for her. Three times a week an occupational therapist and a physical therapist came separately to her apartment and worked with her.

She even received a nice new walker that had a seat that she could sit on, in case she needed to rest while she was on a walk, or out with her friends. If she lifted the top of the seat there was a small compartment that she could store things in while she was walking, like her portable oxygen tank, or a bottle of water or a box of tissues. She called it the Cadillac of walkers. It became her constant companion around her apartment, as well as any time she went out with me or with her friends. At 94 years old, she acted decades younger.

I compared the physical therapy that Delia received in the comfort of her own home to the physical therapy that my mother received in the nursing home. Delia was getting it proactively to prevent any future problems, and she was thriving. Mom was getting it reactively to help with the stiffness that had developed in her arms and her hands since she lived in Calafort. I wondered whose physical therapy did the most good.

****

I think that I may have jinxed things when I told a few of my friends that my life had gotten a little less stressful since my mother had started receiving hospice care. That must have been the calm before the next storm because my reprieve ended when she came down with her next UTI and bronchitis. Those two infections made her deathly sick.

When I signed her up for hospice I thought that it would be her ally, and that it would help her overcome medical bumps in her road. That, unfortunately, wasn't what happened. For several days after she was diagnosed with the newest infections, I kept asking them to give her the antibiotic that I knew had worked well for her in the past. They refused to go along with my request.

I'm sure that when I signed her up for hospice we all knew that she'd have future infections and other ailments before she passed away, but it was my intent that she would always be treated fully; I never wanted just comfort care. I was totally in agreement with hospice from the very beginning that I didn't want her to have extraordinary means to keep her alive. I was about to find out, however, that their idea of extraordinary means wasn't the same as what I thought that it was.

Their refusal to give her the antibiotic that I wanted them to give her stemmed from her aspiration issue. Ever since it was noted that my mother was aspirating, all her pills had to be ground and then mixed with applesauce. That presented a problem with hospice because the antibiotic that had worked best in the past to clear up her UTIs and bronchitis could not be ground. It had to be given through an IV.

Her hospice nurse said that an IV would be considered an extraordinary means to keep her alive and for that reason she couldn't be given that drug. As the days went by she was getting sicker and sicker even though hospice had ordered an antibiotic that she was able to take orally.

I pleaded with the nurse until I was blue in the face, begging her to please give my mother the antibiotic that I had requested. I tried to get her to understand that if she wasn't aspirating, that she could have taken that antibiotic orally. I was just asking that she receive that same medication through an IV. The medication that could save her life wasn't an extraordinary means. She continued to deny my request.

Things came to a head when I arrived one evening after work. I was walking quickly to my mother's room when I saw the hospice nurse heading down the hallway in my direction.

We already had had enough interaction with each other that we both knew that we didn't care for the other. It would have been easy for me to walk past her without saying a word.

"Sally, I'm glad that I ran into you. Do you have a minute that we can talk in private?" she asked.

"Has something changed with my mother?" I asked anxiously.

"Let's go into this little conference room," she said as she led me into a small room with a table and a few chairs. "There's no change with Mom, but I think that we need to talk about something that's very difficult for you to accept. It's clear that you love your mother very, very much," she said in a professional but not comforting voice.

I wondered where in the name of God she was going with this talk. She didn't need to tell me how much I loved my mother, and frankly I didn't care whether this woman noticed or not. I also didn't like it that she referred to my mother as "Mom."

She continued, "There comes a time when we have to let go of the people we love. We have to let go because we love them. It's not unusual that a person will actually will themselves to stay alive for the sake of someone that they love. You don't want your mother to suffer any longer. Let her know that it's okay to let go. She's in a lot of pain and even the morphine isn't helping. Even with the morphine she still says that she's never been in this much pain in her entire life. The other day she lifted her arms and said, 'Take me. Please take me.' Sally, she's asking that God takes her.'"

I covered my face with my hands and broke down and cried. She came closer to me and I thought that she was going to hug me.

"Don't touch me," I said as I emphasized each word. I composed myself the best that I could and then I said to her, "I thought that hospice care was going to help my mother and me, but that's not what's happening. You're letting her die. I keep expecting to get a call saying that she's passed away. You don't know my mother one little bit. Let me tell you a couple of things that you took the wrong way. My mother telling you that this is the worst pain she's ever had in her life doesn't surprise me in the least. For the last decade, that's how she described her arthritis pain—it was the worst pain she'd ever had in her life, yet the strongest pain medication she took for it was acetaminophen.

"And as far as her lifting her arms and saying 'take me' you have that totally wrong, too. I don't know if it's an old Irish saying or if it's just something that my mother has always said, but from the time my kids were babies she would say to me when they were in their cribs or just underfoot, 'Take them, Honey.' It was her way of saying to lift them, to hug them. That's what she wanted from you—a hug. She wasn't asking to die."

My heart was pounding as tears ran down my cheeks. I don't think she knew what to say, and I really didn't give her an opportunity to talk at that point.

"When I signed her up for hospice, it never occurred to me to tell you not to give her morphine. I thought that everyone involved with her care knew that I didn't want her on it because of the awful time she had with it in the hospital. I thought that sort of information would have been in her chart. I was wrong—you didn't know. I should have also remembered that's a big part of what hospice is known for—to help control pain at the end of a person's life.

"I'm telling you now what I should have already told you. I don't want my mother on morphine, not unless you discuss it with me first. My mother has bronchitis and the morphine is suppressing her ability to cough. You know that, right? I went through this two years ago when she was in the hospital. I want her off it today," I said.

She just glared at me.

"And one more thing. I want her off the antibiotic TODAY that you have her on, and I want her back on the one that worked in the past, the one that I've been asking you to put her on."

I knew that she was as annoyed with me as I was with her. I also knew that hospice is almost always a godsend to their patients, and to those patients' families. This woman standing in front of me, had to have been the exception.

"I've already told you that we can't use an IV to give medicine. I told you that it's extraordinary means and we can't do that," she said.

"I don't understand the difference between an antibiotic that's ground in applesauce and that same antibiotic given through an IV. Either way it's the same antibiotic. It's not like a feeding tube or a ventilator. It's an antibiotic!" I said.

"You'll have to take your mother off hospice because we can't do what you're asking," she said stubbornly.

"Bring me the papers right now and I'll sign whatever I need to sign. I should have done that as soon as I realized that your plan wasn't working," I said.

"Sally, I understand that this is an emotional time for you but please think about what I've said. If you're sure that you don't want your mother on hospice, I'll do what's necessary to have her taken off. I'm sorry that things worked out like this. I enjoyed working with your mother," she said as she tried to shake my hand that I didn't extend back to her. That was the last time I saw that woman.

I hoped that I had made the right decision. Sometimes I wished that my mother was able to have had more children so that I had help on days like that one. Rationally, however, I knew that even if I had siblings, I may still be the one making the decisions. Over the course of the last couple of years I saw brothers and sisters, each with their own steadfast opinion, arguing with each other about what needed to be done for their mom or dad. I also saw families that had several sons and daughters, but only one was involved in the care of their mom or dad.

I was so upset after my conversation with the hospice nurse that I wanted to leave without visiting my mother. I knew, however, that if something happened to her before I saw her the next night that I'd always regret it, so I headed towards her room.

I found her sitting quietly near the nurses' station. I swear she looked even tinier than the day before.

"Hiya, Mom. How're you feeling? Any better?" I asked as cheerfully as I could be.

"Hi, Baby. I don't feel too good. How'd ye know I was here?" she slowly asked. She was pale and her eyes looked sad and droopy.

"I'm sorry, Mom, that you don't feel well. I'm going to bundle you up and take you outside for a few minutes. Maybe that'll make you feel a little better."

"No, Honey, it's too cold outside. I'm already freezing," she said.

"Believe it or not, I think that it's actually colder in here than it is outside. I promise that I'll bring you back inside if you tell me that you're cold outside. Deal?" I tried to be persuasive. I thought that a few minutes outside might make her feel a little better. I didn't think that it would hurt.

"Do what ye think is best," she whispered.

The days were getting longer so it was still light outside. I was able to point out the pretty red purple sky, a few squirrels, the pond, the stream in the sky that was left by a passing jet, and the Spring flowers that had started blooming. I knew that she felt miserable physically, but the few minutes we were outside helped her mentally and emotionally. Surprisingly I spent more than an hour with my mother that night, a night that I almost didn't go into her room.

When I brought her back inside I left her where I found her near the nurses' station. I expected that I would be given the hospice papers to sign to take her off the program, but nobody said anything to me about it.

I gave her a kiss and a hug and told her that I'd see her the next day. As I was about to leave she took both my hands and whispered, "God knew. Safe home, my baby."

"I love you, too, Mom. You're the best," I said as I left her for the night.

Dave and I had no plans that evening which I was thankful for. It was nice to be able to go home, eat supper, and not have to go anywhere else for the rest of the night. I told him about the argument "du jour" with the hospice nurse, but then I kept thinking about it until it was almost time for bed. Did that woman actually think that I was going to go along with depriving my mother of an antibiotic that I knew had worked for her before? If so, she and Jack Kevorkian must have been related.

The following night when I walked into my mother's room I was relieved to see that she was hooked up to an IV, although I didn't make an issue out of it in front of her. I wondered how that came about.

"Hi, Mom," I said as I walked over to her and gave her a hug. "Have you already eaten your supper? It's sort of early for you to be back in your room."

"I'm not hungry. Go get something for yourself. I think there's something in the icebox for ye. I don't want ye to be hungry," she said slowly.

I just went along with her conversation.

"Thanks, Mom. I'll eat when I get home. I'm going to go down the hall for just a few minutes but don't worry, I'll be right back," I said.

I needed to talk with Sandi about getting her off hospice since nobody had said anything to me about it. I was expecting to have gotten a call at work during the day, but for some reason that call didn't happen.

I was amazed by the news that Sandi told me. She said that the Assistant Director of Nursing was standing outside the conference room when the hospice nurse and I were talking. She said that she was disturbed by the way the nurse had spoken to me. After hearing our conversation, she talked to Tom, Calafort's administrator. He called hospice and told their administrator that he no longer wanted that particular nurse working at Calafort. Sandi told me that a new nurse had already been assigned.

"Really? Sandi, I am shocked that you all did that for my mother. Thank you so very much. I really, really mean it. Thank you. But that doesn't explain why she's on an IV now. The nurse yesterday told me that she couldn't be on an IV if we wanted her to stay on hospice. Don't I need to sign some papers to get her off it? That conversation with that nurse was so unpleasant for me, that I don't want to have to have it a second time. Please bring me whatever I need to sign," I said.

"We checked with hospice and they said that she could get this medicine through the IV. It just isn't something that they will keep doing over and over again. They've also taken her off the morphine," she said.

"You have made my day. Thank you," I said once again.

Then she dropped the next mini-bomb. "Did you know that she's been off the appetite enhancer since she's been on hospice?"

"What do you mean she's off the appetite enhancer? What are you talking about?" I asked, and then I breathed a loud sigh.

"Sally, I thought that you knew that once a patient goes on hospice care, their care is primarily coordinated through the hospice doctor from then on. I thought that you knew that they took her off the enhancer," she said.

"Sandi, I had no idea that she was taken off it. Nobody said anything to me about it. Do I need to ask to see her chart every day to see what's going on with her? You guys all know how much weight she's lost since she's been in here. She's eating like a bird. I want her back on the appetite enhancer. I don't understand why she was taken off it, but I want her back on it today. Who do I need to talk to, or can you do that for me?" I asked, totally exasperated.

"Don't worry, I'll do that for you," she said.

"I need to give some serious thought about hospice. I need to decide whether my mother is better off now or if she was better off before going on it. I'll let you know what I decide," I said, slowly shaking my head.

I paused for a moment and then asked, "Why is she in her room now? Everyone else is in the dining room. Did she have to get the IV medicine now?"

"Actually she was in the dining room earlier but she said that she didn't want to eat. You know your mother. When she doesn't want to eat, there really isn't anything that we can do, so I decided to give her the medicine now and I'll try again later to feed her in her room."

"Sandi, please try hard to get her to eat later," I said.

"Keep in mind that she doesn't feel well so I understand that she doesn't want to eat. But the good news is that she ate about 25% of her breakfast and about 25% of her lunch, so she has eaten something. I promise you that I'll try again later," she said.

"Thank you. I'm going to go in and say goodnight to her. I know that I just got here a little while ago, but I'm really worn out. Please don't forget to get her back on the appetite enhancer," I said.

"Don't worry, I'll check on it for you," she said. "Sally, why don't you bring her out here so that I can keep an eye on her? I'd feel more comfortable if she and I could see each other."

I went back into her room for a few minutes and squatted down next to her wheelchair. She spent her day having to look up at people, so for now I wanted to be eye to eye with her. I told her how much I loved her.

"I love ye too, Baby. I'm so sorry I'm putting ye through this," she said slowly.

"Mom, you're not putting me through anything. It's you that I feel bad for. This new medicine that you're on now will make you feel better. I promise. I'm going to bring you out by the nurses' station. Sandi can use some company," I said.

Then there was one last hug for the night and one last "I love you."

"Safe home, Baby," she said, almost in a whisper to herself.

When I got to my car I couldn't help but cry. I was both frustrated and discouraged. I knew that her days were numbered, and I wanted those days to be good ones. I prayed that God would help me to help her, and to protect her.

Chapter 15

"Where Should I Stay Tonight?"

By the time my mother had completed the IV antibiotic regimen, she was visibly better from her infections. I thanked God that she had rallied once again. She continued to lose weight, however, which was disheartening because she didn't have a lot of pounds left to lose. I tried everything that I could think of to encourage her to eat more food. I often stopped by Steak and Shake on the way to Calafort and bought her a vanilla milkshake. She used to love milkshakes. Now if she drank half of one, I called it a success.

Every now and then I still brought her food from home that I had cooked just for her. They weren't full meals like I used to bring; they were just side dishes like mashed potatoes and mashed carrots. In the past she used to love anything that I cooked for her, but now, as hard as I tried, seldom was I able to get her to eat more than just a few bites. I even tried baby food, different brands and different varieties, but she would usually say that she wasn't hungry, and then tell me that I needed to eat something.

I thought about her day and night, and I was getting more worried with each passing day. Things would have been far less worrisome for me, however, if I felt like the staff and I were always on the same team, but aside from Sandi and a couple of the CNAs, that's not how it was. There were times that I actually felt as if I had an adversarial relationship with the staff. I knew that wasn't how a family member should feel about the people taking care of their loved one, but unfortunately that's how it sometimes was for me. Other sons and daughters voiced that same complaint.

No matter the relationship between the staff and me, I was my mother's advocate and there were occasions that if I hadn't spoken up on her behalf, things would have been even tougher for her than they already were. I didn't nitpick. By this time, I'd been on the nursing home journey long enough to know when it was best for me to overlook something, and when it was important for me to make an issue out of it.

While my mother was always my number one concern, she wasn't the only person that I looked out for. If one of the other residents needed help, I never looked the other way. The more that I got to know some of the people who now called Calafort their home, the more I imagined what they were like in their younger years. I figured that most of them probably had vibrant and productive lives. Once upon a time they probably had pep in their step. They weren't all wrinkled, and they probably didn't have a lost look in their eyes. I doubted that they spent their days crying, or drooling, or needing to have a diaper changed.

I often wondered if the staff ever considered that there was a time when the residents in Calafort were just like them. That one day, they themselves might be just like those residents. There were many times that I wanted to get on the public address system and say, "Dear doctors, nurses, therapists, and CNAs, someday your healthy body will no longer be strong. If you live long enough, you too, may be in the exact situation that the residents you are taking care of today are in. Treat them the same way that you'll want to be treated, because one day, you or someone you love dearly could be sitting in their wheelchair."

****

I needed a vacation. I needed a vacation with my family, and away from Calafort. For months Dave and I had been planning a summer family vacation to the Grand Canyon. We thought that it would be a great experience that we'd thoroughly enjoy and that the kids would always remember. Normally when we planned our vacations we'd book the flights and make hotel reservations way in advance. This vacation was different. Even though we'd sit around and talk about all that we wanted to do at the Grand Canyon, we never followed through and made travel arrangements to get there.

When it came down to it, Dave and I both knew that we couldn't be that far away from my mother and Delia. We knew that emergencies were always popping up with them, and in reality it didn't matter how breathtaking the scenery was, I'd be worried about what was happening back at home with my mother and aunt. I was disappointed when we officially decided "not this year" and then had to tell the kids that we were totally changing our plans, but I knew that it was the right decision.

We gave it a lot of thought and in lieu of the Grand Canyon we decided to take a trip to Washington, D.C. for 8 days, which included the time that it would take to drive there. I knew that I would still worry about my mother and Delia while we were away, but if necessary, I could fly home in less than a couple of hours. I also knew that my family deserved a family vacation. Last, but not least, I knew that I needed one, too,

A few weeks before we planned to leave on our vacation, I took Delia to see her doctor for a routine exam. She made the doctor and me smile when she asked him if she should take something to help her with her memory. He and I both knew that there wasn't a thing the matter with her memory, but the conversation continued.

"Dee Dee, I know exactly the pill that you're talking about. It's over-the-counter and from what I've heard, it works really well. Darn, I can't think of what it's called, though," I said as I glanced over at the doctor.

"There must be something in the air, because I can't think of the name of it either," the doctor said as he folded his hands on the top of his head and thought about what he couldn't remember.

"Good grief, it's on the tip of my tongue. I think that it's two words," I added.

"What's the matter with the two of ye? I think that ye both need to take it. It's ginkgo biloba," she said with a little twinkle in her eyes.

The doctor and I both laughed.

"Delia, I'd say you really don't need it. Sally and I are the ones who should be taking it. Oh, by the way, how's Arthur been treating you?" he asked.

"Who's Arthur?" she asked.

"I think that Arthur has been spending more time with you than you'd like," he answered.

"Who's Arthur?" she asked again.

"You probably know him as Arthur Ritus. I mean arthritis," he joked.

"Very funny," she said as she smiled back at him. I could see that she was thinking about what he had just said. "Doctor, I think that everyone has arthritis when they get to a certain age. It's worse for me the first thing in the morning. Sometimes it's so bad that I could cry."

The doctor was listening to her and nodding his head.

She continued, "I suppose that I could sit around all day and complain about it and nurse it, but I know that would only make it worse. Once I get up and get the bones moving, I feel better. And, if it doesn't get better then I take something for the pain. There's no use complaining about it. Besides, a little pain lets ye know that you're still alive."

"You're right about that, Delia. You're very wise," the doctor said.

"Are ye making fun of me?" she asked, although the doctor and I knew that she was right.

"I'd never make fun of you," he said. "You are right on the money about not sitting around all day when you have arthritis. It's an easy thing to do, but it just makes the problem all the worse."

"Okay, Doctor. While we're here, I want to tell ye about my breathing. It's always worse in the morning, too. And the phlegm. Sometimes I think that the phlegm is going to choke me. Do ye have anything for that?" she asked.

"The morning is usually the most difficult time of the day for people with breathing problems like COPD. I remember you told me that you smoked for most of your adult life. There's nothing you can do to undo all those years of smoking but there are a few things that will help with the symptoms. Make sure that you don't skip using your inhaler when you're supposed to use it. And make sure that you use more than one pillow so that you're not lying flat on your back when you're in bed," he said.

I interrupted. "Doctor, Delia actually has a large foam wedge that she uses every night under her upper body. She also puts at least one pillow on top of the wedge. She's definitely not lying flat. But I know that sometimes in the morning it's still hard for her to breathe."

"Delia, I'm going to give you something to take that will help with the phlegm, and I want you to make sure that you drink enough water during the day. That'll help loosen the phlegm. If that doesn't help you, the next time that you come in to see me, we'll talk about getting you on oxygen during the night," he said.

He also asked her if she thought the physical therapy helped her. We both commented that she seemed to be stronger than she was before the therapy, and more steady on her feet.

He looked sincerely happy that things had improved in that regard.

"Doctor, I know that you're busy but I have one more question for ye," Delia said, knowing that he still had other patients left to see. "Do ye think that I should get off my nerve pill?"

He looked a little surprised and said, "Before I answer your question, let me take a look at your chart."

He looked thoughtfully at the chart for a minute or two and then said, "You've been on lorazepam for a long time. Why do you want to stop taking it?"

"I know that it's no earthly good for me. Maybe I've taken it for too long. Maybe I'll be okay without it. What do ye think, Doctor? Am I foolish to get off it?" she asked.

She was right in that she'd taken lorazepam for many years. Before taking it, however, she suffered from anxiety and panic attacks. She seldom had either anymore and I never noticed any negative side effects from her being on that drug. It never caused her to be lethargic or dopey or confused. Getting off it wasn't something I ever thought about suggesting to her, but it appeared that this conversation was between her and her doctor so I stayed quiet and just listened.

"I think that it might be a good idea to get off the lorazepam but I think that you do need to take something. How about if we try you on alprazolam and see how you do on that?" he suggested.

"You're the doctor. If ye think that it's good, I'll trust ye and try it," she said.

"Okay, I'll have the nurse call the prescription into your pharmacy. If you have any problems or questions, I want to hear from you, okay? Otherwise, I want to see you again in three months," he said.

Before we left she showed him a small wound on her left shin. She said that it didn't hurt but she noticed it a few weeks earlier and that it wasn't going away. She told him that she didn't remember bumping her leg, but thought that it was odd for it to be there for no reason. The doctor didn't seem concerned but said to keep an eye on it.

On the drive back to Delia's apartment she asked if I thought she made a mistake about getting off the anti-anxiety pill that she was on.

"I don't think that you made a mistake. I was just a little surprised that you suggested it since you weren't having any problems with it. Don't worry about making a mistake. If you don't like the new pill, I'm sure that the doctor will put you back on the one that you were on. Don't be shy. You have to promise you'll let me know if you don't like it or if it makes you feel not right," I said to her.

"Ye know that I'll tell ye," she said.

By the time I got her home it was nearly four in the afternoon so I decided that it wasn't worth going back to the office since it was so late. I also decided that I wasn't going to visit Mom that day. I felt a little guilty for not going to see her, but I just didn't have the motivation in me to drive to Calafort. I tried to allay my guilt by remembering that she had a new hospice nurse who was visiting her on a regular basis, and so I drove directly home.

I made a nice supper that evening for my family, and we spent time talking about the different things that we each wanted to see in Washington, D.C. We were all looking forward to the vacation. I needed time to be physically away from my mother and Delia. That might sound uncaring, but that was the only way that I could recharge and be at the top of my game for them.

A few mornings later I drove Michael to a friend's house to spend the day. It was July 6th.

"Michael, you're going to think that I'm silly but I want you to say a prayer that this is a good day for everyone in our family and that everyone stays safe," I said.

"Mom, your thing about July 6th is really dumb," he said.

"You're probably right but I just don't like this day. It gives me a creepy feeling and I'll be glad when it's over. Just humor me and say a little prayer, okay?" I asked.

"I'll do it for you, but I still think it's dumb," he said.

"Thanks, Honey. I love you and I appreciate it, even though you think it's dumb," I said.

I dropped him off at his friend's house and I went on to a busy day at work.

Midafternoon I received a call from St. Blaise Hospital. Delia was in the emergency room. She had fallen inside her apartment. When her physical therapist arrived, the door was unlocked and she let herself in and found Delia on the floor. She called 911 and an ambulance came and brought her to the hospital.

I quickly told my boss what was going on, and then I rushed to the hospital.

They let me go into the ER when I arrived and I went directly over to Delia's bed.

"I'm so sorry, Sally," she said as she furrowed her brow. "Ye have enough to worry about with your mother in the home."

"Oh my God, Delia, don't worry about me for a minute. You're the only one that we both need to be concerned about. I'm fine and Mom is fine," I said as I tried to take away her concerns.

I found her nurse and asked how she was doing.

"She's broken some ribs and her blood pressure was extremely high when she arrived. It's starting to come down now. She'll be in the hospital for a few days for observation. She told me that she lives on her own, but she's not going to be able to be by herself for a while after she leaves the hospital," she said.

"Do you think that she'll be able to recover fully?" I asked with some trepidation.

"She seems to be in good shape for her age. I think she'll be okay, although, this might be a good time for you to start thinking about alternate living arrangements. She is 94 years old. She may not be this lucky if she falls again," she said.

I thought about the nurse's words as I walked back over to Delia's bed. I must have looked worried because she said, "Sally, am I that bad? What did the nurse say to ye? You're as white as a ghost."

"I'm sorry if I look like that. I just feel bad for you that this happened. The nurse said that you'll be fine because you're in such good shape for your age. You have a few broken ribs and she said that your blood pressure was really high when you got to the hospital."

"No wonder the pressure was high. Those big men lifting me up off the floor and strapping me on the stretcher. I was a nervous wreck. And then the ride to the hospital. Jesus, Mary, and Joseph, help me," she said, almost as if she was talking to herself.

"Do you know why you fell? Did you trip on something? Or turn your head too fast? Do you remember what happened?" I was probably bombarding her with too many questions but I really wanted to know, just like I always wanted to know what caused my mother's fall.

"I just finished eating my breakfast and I put my couple of dishes on the seat of the walker. I was going to bring them into the kitchen to wash them, but when I stood up from the table I was light headed and everything started spinning. I held onto the walker but I pulled it over. Thank God I didn't pull it on top of myself. I'd be in worse shape than the shape I'm in," she said with a sigh.

"Delia, keep in mind that we just saw your doctor. I think that he was sincerely impressed at how good you're doing. He even took you off the nerve pill that you were on," I said.

No sooner had those words come out of my mouth, that I wondered if going off lorazepam and on to alprazolam could have caused her to fall. It was at that point that the nurse came back and told Delia that she'd be staying in the hospital for a few days and that someone was on their way to bring her up to her room.

That's when Delia told me that she would be fine since she'd seen me, and that she knew that I knew what was going on with her. She made it clear that she didn't need me to go up to the room with her.

"Delia, are you in pain?" I had to ask that question before I left.

She looked at me as if I didn't have a clue what was going on. "Well, I don't feel very good, but I'll be alright. They've given me something that's starting to help a little. Now, be a good girl and go on home. God help ye, Sally. Ye already had enough on your shoulders without this happening," she said somberly.

"I'm fine. We just need to get you fine again, too. Try to get some rest when they bring you up to your room. I'll stop by to see you sometime tomorrow. I love you most, Dee Dee," I said as I kissed the top of her head. I was afraid that I might hurt her with a hug.

"Safe home," she said.

I turned back towards her and blew her a kiss, and then I was on my way.

When I left the hospital I did a lot of thinking as I drove to Delia's apartment on my way home. What would have happened if the physical therapist hadn't found her when she did? I knew the answer to that question. I would have called her in the evening and when she didn't answer the phone, I would have driven to her apartment. Would that have been too late to save her? How long could a 94-year-old lie on the floor and survive? I didn't know the answer to those questions.

The nurse in the ER made me think about things that I'd wondered and worried about ever since my mother's fall. Was Delia safe living on her own? She was welcome to live with us, but I didn't think that was ever an option in her mind. Whenever she's stayed with us in the past we always tried to make her feel that our home was also her home, but she always felt that she was in the way and that she was putting us out.

As much as I would have loved for her to move in with us, I knew that wasn't a good long term solution. I decided that I needed to look into assisted living. Maybe that would be something that would work for her. I decided that over the weekend I would check out some of the nearby ones and I'd try to narrow it down to a few that I thought she would like, and that she could afford. Then I'd broach the subject with her. For now, however, we just needed to get her better and out of the hospital.

When I entered Delia's apartment I had a déjà vu of when my mother fell in her house, two years ago that day. I remembered Dave and me walking from room to room in Mom's house trying to figure out what had happened.

When I first walked into the apartment there weren't any obvious signs that anything was out of the ordinary. Her walker had been up-righted and the dishes that she said she was bringing into her kitchen had been washed and standing in the drain board. I assumed the physical therapist took the time to wash the dishes, rather than leaving them scattered on the floor.

I picked up the bottle of alprazolam that was still sitting on her dining room table and wondered again if in some way that could have been the cause of her fall. Those pills were the only thing different in her routine life. I picked up the phone and called her doctor so that I could tell him what had happened, and to ask about the alprazolam.

He was unavailable to speak with me so I talked to his nurse. She pulled Delia's chart and when I asked if she thought that the new medication could have caused the fall, she said that it was a very low dosage, and told me what the dosage was. I had the bottle in my hand and thought that I had misunderstood what she said so I asked her to repeat the dosage. When she repeated what she had just said, my heart pounded as I looked at the bottle.

"The bottle says that it's four times the strength that you're telling me. Could that be why she fell?" I asked.

"Absolutely, that could have caused her to fall," she said, and was then quick to defend herself. "Sally, I know that when I called the pharmacy I gave them the correct prescription. It's right here in the chart, and I read it exactly the way the doctor had written it."

"I'm sure that you called it in correctly. Please be sure to let him know what happened just as soon as you see him in the morning," I said back to her.

"Don't worry, I'll let him know first thing," she assured me.

After we said goodbye I left Delia's apartment and then drove a block to the pharmacy, a pharmacy that both she and my mother had used for more than 30 years. I told them what had happened to Delia and what the nurse said about the prescription. Of course, they were confident that they had filled the prescription precisely the way that it had been called in.

I was upset by what had happened. My 94-year-old aunt was in the hospital with broken ribs through no fault of her own and nobody was going to consider that they may be responsible for her pain. I knew that I shouldn't dwell on who was at fault—it would be wasting my energy on a battle that wouldn't help anyone. My lesson was that I would definitely pay close attention to prescriptions in the future, something that never had occurred to me to do in the past.

Once again it was too late to go back to my office so I headed home. As I drove the short distance home, my mind drifted all over the place. My thoughts were jumping between tours of the White House and Arlington Cemetery and the Smithsonian Museums, to Delia in a hospital bed with broken ribs, to Mom calling my name over and over again in Calafort.

"Dear God, is this what my life has become? Can I do it all? Please give me strength," I prayed.

That's when it hit me that there was a good chance that there wouldn't be a vacation, at least not for me. Dave and the kids could still go without me. It wasn't fair that they should miss a vacation that they were looking forward to.

If necessary, I could stay behind and take care of "the oldsters." Once upon a time we took family vacations and there
was hardly a thought about my mother or aunt. Now, every
time we'd gone away for the last half dozen years, I was always on edge until we returned.

I was totally serious about giving up my vacation and
then it hit me. Resentment. I resented being in a position
where I had to choose between staying home to make sure
that my mother and aunt got the good care that they deserved and were entitled to, and taking a vacation with
my family. There had to be a better way. I should be able
to totally trust that the people who were taking care of my
mother and Delia, would sincerely take care of them. But I
couldn't trust them.

The doctors, the nurses, the CNAs, and now even the
pharmacy all had given me reason to feel this way. They'd
turned me into a snarling watchdog, and I hated being like
that. It wasn't right. It wasn't fair. But it seemed like there
was no choice for me. Those were the cards that I'd been
dealt and I needed to keep doing the best that I could do for
everyone. My plan for the next few days was to visit Mom at
lunchtime and then go to the hospital to see Delia on my way
home from work.

The next day when I visited my mother, I took her for a walk outside. I knew that she enjoyed those few minutes of freedom outside the facility, and aside from the birds singing, it was totally quiet. It was during those quiet times that we could still have a nice chitchat, although some of our talks were a little bizarre.

When I wheeled her back up the sidewalk to the entrance of Calafort, she asked if we could go visit Mom and the others. I squatted down next to her, held her hands that were on her lap, and said, "You're my mom. I'm Michael's and Kathleen's mom. Whose mom do you want to visit?"

"I want to see my mom. Is that okay with ye? Or do ye think they'll be angry if we just dropped in on them?" she asked.

I didn't say anything for a moment. It made me sad to hear her talk like that, but there was no point in correcting her. I decided shortly after she got on the Meadows Unit that if going along with her stories gave her any bit of happiness or satisfaction, I would go along with those stories that she sometimes told me.

"Mom, I think that your mother and father and the rest of the family would be thrilled to see us, but I can't do it today because I need to get back to work. Maybe another day? Is that okay with you?" I asked.

"Sure, Baby. That'll be fine. Where do ye think I should stay tonight?" she innocently asked me.

"I think where we are would be a great place for you to stay. They'll cook you a nice supper and they have a lovely room for you. How does that sound?" I answered.

She seemed totally content for the time being and then added, "Ye must have a lovely boss to let ye off to come see me in the middle of the day. I don't want ye to get in any trouble on account of me."

"I do have a lovely boss, and you never have to worry about me getting into trouble with work," I assured her.

"How's Delia?" she asked as I was wheeling her back to her room.

"Delia is doing just fine. She told me to give you a hug for her." I didn't feel bad telling her the occasional white lie, if it made her feel better.

"Sally, take some money out of my pocketbook to pay for my room for tonight. I don't want ye having to pay for me," she said.

"I think that they'll send a bill, so don't worry about it for now. But promise me that you'll eat the supper that they're making for you. You're getting too skinny," I added.

"Worry about yourself, Baby. I'm okay the way I am." And then she changed the subject. "Wouldn't it be nice to be planning a trip to Ireland? I don't think I've been home for a few years now. I'll treat ye and Dave and the kids to take a trip with me. Wouldn't that be nice?" The corners of her mouth went up slightly when she brought up a trip to Ireland once again. It wasn't much of a smile but it was the best I'd seen for a while.

"Oh my gosh, we'd love to take a trip to Ireland with you," I said. "It's been three years since the last time we went. We'll have a lot of fun planning it, too. Start thinking about who you want to visit and whose house you'd like to stay in, and what side trips you'd like to take," I said with enthusiasm.

I glanced down at my watch and realized that I'd already been gone from the office for nearly an hour.

"Ma, I really hate rushing off now, but I need to get back to work," I said.

"I know that ye do, Baby. I love ye. Thanks for stopping by," she said.

"I love you so much, Mom, that it hurts," I said, and then paused for a moment as I thought about what I had just said. "Do you remember when you used to say that to me?" I asked.

She smiled at me and answered, "I remember. Of course, I remember."

I gave her a hug and off I went, wondering if she really remembered or if she was telling me a white lie, too.

On my drive back to the office, I thought about my mother wanting to go to Ireland. I knew that there would be no more trips to Ireland with her, and that made me sad. I loved being able to visit my cousin and his family in the same house that my mother grew up in, and to look out the window at the same hauntingly beautiful scenery that she saw when she was young.

It was also comforting to stay at my Aunt Mag's or Aunt Kate's or Uncle Pat's house, and listen to the old stories by the blazing peat fire late into the night. I was unhappy that the trips to Ireland with my mother were a thing of the past, but I will be forever grateful for the wonderful memories of Ireland with her and Dave and both kids.

I worked that evening until about 6:00 and then I headed over to the hospital to see how Delia was doing. Right off the bat I wasn't happy with what I saw. It was apparent that she had a catheter and I was immediately concerned that it would cause new problems for her that she didn't have when she was admitted to the hospital the day before.

I asked her nurse why she even had one since she was totally continent. She said that they thought it was best for her to use a catheter so that she wouldn't have to wait for help to take her to the bathroom. And they didn't want to take any chances on her falling if she went to the bathroom unassisted. I told her that I didn't want them to do anything that would cause Delia to become incontinent, and she responded by saying that that shouldn't happen.

I also told her that she'd been getting physical therapy in her home to help her with her walking. I told her that I was worried that if she was confined to her bed in the hospital that she would backslide with the progress that she had made with her physical therapy. I told her that she lived by herself in her own apartment, but if she wasn't able to safely walk when she got released from the hospital that she wouldn't be able to go back to her home, or even to mine.

Maybe she thought that I wasn't looking out for Delia's best interest, and so she answered my concerns to her by saying, "She won't be able to stay on her own when she gets discharged, at least not for a while. A social worker will be talking to you about that, and about her options."

"If you keep her in that bed too much longer, you'll be taking away her options," is what I wanted to say to the nurse, but I wisely bit my tongue and said, "Okay."

She never addressed my concerns about the catheter or about her not getting out of bed. I didn't make an issue out of it because I hoped that this was going to be a short stay and I didn't want to make waves if I didn't have to.

I stayed with Delia until after she finished eating her supper so that she'd have some company. On my way home, I said a prayer, "Dear God, please help me to help Delia and Mom. Give me strength, wisdom, and patience not to explode when dealing with some of these caregivers, be it doctors, nurses, or CNAs. God bless the caregivers and please, God, give them compassion, intelligence, and some common sense. Amen."

Chapter 16

Declining Rapidly

Delia remained in the hospital for a total of four days. By the time she was released, she had a urinary tract infection, probably as a result of the catheter. She was barely able to stand, definitely as a result of being kept in bed for four days.

She went to a rehab/nursing home facility called D.M. Seleerac which had a good reputation. I prayed that Delia's time there would be totally for rehab and that she would be able to return to her own home soon. I said that same prayer for my mother just two years earlier.

There were a couple of key differences between the two sisters. I thought that Delia had an advantage over Mom because Delia was mentally alert. I thought that would make her rehab easier. She was also keenly aware what happened to my mother when she didn't take her rehab seriously. Delia had a huge social network; my mother's social network revolved around Dave, the kids, me, and Delia.

Mom had a few things going for her. She was 88 when she went into rehab; Delia was 94. Could those six years make a difference? Also, my mother was stronger when she fell than Delia was now. She also weighed about 40 pounds more than Delia weighed.

When Delia arrived at Seleerac a stack of papers awaited her initials and her signature. She signed them all herself including a Living Will, and a Durable Power of Attorney. She was already on Medicare, Medicaid, and SSI which meant that I didn't have to jump through the hoops that I jumped through when I got my mother on Medicaid. She had even already made all of her own funeral arrangements.

Over that first weekend that she was in the rehab center, I spent time visiting several assisted living facilities fairly close to my home. I wanted to be proactive so that when she was able to leave the rehab, she would have a back-up plan in case she/we didn't think that she was able to go back to her home. I found some beautiful ones, but sadly there was no way that she could afford any of them.

I found it ironic that her Medicare/Medicaid would pay for long term care in a nursing home but I couldn't find any assisted living facilities in our area that they would pay for. The cost of a nursing home was far more expensive than assisted living. I'm no math wizard but it seemed to me that a ton of people would never have to live in a nursing home, if they could afford to live in assisted living. I firmly believed that Delia wouldn't survive a nursing home environment for the long term.

True to form, she adjusted well to living in the rehab. I'm certain that was because she knew that it was only a temporary arrangement. She believed the harder she worked as a rehab patient, the sooner she'd be back in her own apartment. Ruth was her roommate and they got along well. They became friends in spite of the fact that Delia was 20 years older than she was. They looked out for each other and encouraged each other. Delia's personality was alluring and the staff really liked her. She was having a totally different experience than Mom had when she began her rehab.

In spite of her rehab stay going well, the wound on her left leg had started hurting and was getting larger. I'm sure that the rehab had a doctor who could have looked at her shin, but instead, I decided to take her to her own dermatologist,

Dr. Roundstone. He biopsied her leg and when the results came back days later, I was called and told that she had another skin cancer. He recommended that we once again see Dr. Paul for radiation, because her skin was too thin to surgically remove the cancer, and then to stitch it. Even though she had survived breast cancer and several skin cancers in recent years, this particular diagnosis was the most troublesome of them all and would haunt her for the rest of her life.

****

The summer was going by quickly but neither Dave nor I had made hotel reservations for our Washington D.C. vacation. It wasn't an oversight. I think that we both must have had cold feet about being so far from my mother and Delia. My mother was hardly eating anything and Delia was in the rehab getting physical therapy, as well as I was once again taking her to her radiation treatments. Was this really the time to be several states away? Should we take a staycation this year instead of going away? Should we put off going to D.C. this year, just like we put off the Grand Canyon? It was a tough decision to make because only God knew if the next summer would be one bit better.

There wasn't a lot of time left before Michael and Kathleen would be going back to school; we had to decide one way or the other. Dave and I talked about the pros and cons of going away vs. staying at home. One of the pros was that it might actually be easier with Delia in the rehab because she'd have nurses and CNAs nearby her 24/7. If there was an emergency there would be someone right there to help her. She was also doing well with radiation and I was sure that one or two of her friends would be more than happy to bring her for her treatments while we were away.

I didn't know how to predict how my mother would do without me for a week. I knew, however, that if she didn't start eating significantly better soon, that she would never make it to be Delia's age. It didn't really matter whether I was with her or not, she wasn't consuming much more than thickened liquids and the occasional bite or two of mashed potatoes.

When it was all said and done, we finally decided that we'd go to Washington. I knew that my mother and Delia would be in God's hands and I honestly believed that both of them would have wanted us to take a nice vacation. We had waited so long to make our decision that we wouldn't be returning until the day before the kids would be going back to school.

The night before we left on our vacation, I spent more time with my mother and Delia than I usually did. I wanted to make sure that they were both okay before we started off on our long-awaited getaway. I reminded my mother that we were going to be on vacation and that she wouldn't see me for a few days. I told her so that she wouldn't be worried about me when I wasn't visiting each day; I hoped that she'd remember. She told me to have a good time, to take good care of the kids, and to have a safe journey. Delia, on the other hand, made me feel comfortable that we'd made the right decision and she told me not to worry about her and my mother and to have a great time. She also said, "Safe journey."

I was excited to be getting away on a vacation. I felt like a great burden had been taken off my shoulders, even though I knew it was only for eight days. We planned to leave super early in the morning in hopes of beating some of the traffic. We packed our suitcases the night before and put them in the car before we went to bed.

When our alarms went off early the next morning it wasn't hard for any of us to wake up so that we could get our adventure started. We got dressed quickly and were pulling out of our driveway before 6:00 a.m., with the two kids and their pillows in the back seat where they'd sleep until we stopped for breakfast.

I was incredibly relaxed for the first time in a long time, and had drifted back to sleep, also. That is, until I was startled awake by the sound of my cell phone ringing about three hours into the trip.

"Sally, this is Rosa from D.M. Seleerac," the voice said. "I know that you're on vacation and I'm sorry to bother you. Delia is okay but we're required to call the family whenever there's been an incident."

"What happened to her? Just tell me what happened," I said groggily.

"When she was getting out of bed to use the bathroom she slipped off the bed," she said. "I don't think that there's anything to worry about, but I had to let you know. She didn't want me to call you because she didn't want to ruin your vacation."

"Are you sure that she's okay? Is she in any pain?" I asked.

"I'll keep a close eye on her but I honestly think she's okay," she said.

"She must have been waiting a long time for someone to help her to the bathroom because she knows to use the call light. Rosa, please remind everyone that when she presses the call light, she needs help pretty quickly. She's totally continent but her parts are 94 years old. When she has to go, she has to go." I tried to be diplomatic but I wanted to make sure that everyone knew that Delia wasn't the typical 94-year-old.

"I understand what you're saying about your aunt, and you're right. We don't see too many people her age that are so independent and mentally sharp. I'll remind the CNAs to try to answer her call light quickly. If they're with another resident, sometimes it takes them a little while before they can help the next person. If I notice that she needs help, I'll also try to help her if I'm not busy with someone else," she said.

"Thank you. I appreciate all that you and the others can do to keep her independent. Please tell her I love her. Rosa, please don't hesitate to call me if something is wrong. I know that you don't want to bother me, but I would be upset if I didn't know if she was having a problem," I said.

"Don't worry. She'll be fine. Enjoy your vacation," she said.

We said goodbye and as I hung up my phone I turned to Dave and said sarcastically, "It was a great three-hour vacation until my phone rang. Am I EVER going to be 'off the clock?' I thought that I'd have less to worry about since Delia was in the rehab and she had help."

"I'm sorry, Honey. Is she alright?" he asked.

"I think so. I hope so. Darn, I forgot to ask about x-rays. Hopefully if the nurse thought she needed them, she would have already ordered them, right?" I asked. "I don't need to call her back and ask, do I?"

"I don't think so. She would have said something if she thought that she needed them. I think she probably sees her share of falls in there," Dave said.

The kids had been sound asleep in the back seat with their seat belts on, Kathleen slumped over, with her head on Michael's lap. The phone call woke them both up and they'd been listening to the conversation.

"What happened to Dee Dee?" Michael asked.

"Is Dee Dee okay?" Kathleen asked at the same time.

Both kids loved their great Aunt Delia.

"She slipped off the bed when she was getting up. The nurse said that she's fine. She had to call me and let me know what happened, though. You guys don't worry; Aunt Dee Dee is fine." Then I tried to change the subject.

"Anyone hungry for some breakfast?" I asked.

"I have to go to the bathroom," Kathleen said. "Remember when Dee Dee did the Macarena? That was funny," she added.

"I could go for something to eat now," Dave said.

"How about Waffle House?" Michael asked.

"Yea, Waffle House. I love Waffle House when we're on vacation. It's a tradition," Kathleen added.

So, we found a Waffle House and while we enjoyed a nice breakfast, I tried to erase the worry of the rehab call. When we got back into the car we talked about our plans for the week. Everyone was psyched about all that we were going to be doing. In addition to our days in D.C. we planned a day at Colonial Williamsburg and another day at Busch Gardens.

It took a few more hours of driving before I started to feel relaxed again. I tried hard not to think about Mom and Delia. I figured that there wasn't anything I could do for either of them while I was on vacation, and thinking and worrying about them would only keep me from enjoying this time with my family. There was not a doubt in my mind that my mother wasn't doing well, and I knew that I needed to come back from this vacation in the best mental and emotional shape that I could be in, in order to face what was in store for us both.

By early afternoon we were all starting to think about lunch. That's when my phone rang again. This time I saw "Calafort" on my caller ID. My heart raced as I looked at the phone. I hadn't told them that I was going out of town. Ever since hospice was involved, I occasionally would skip a day of visiting my mother, but I seldom told them when I wasn't coming.

"Sally, this is Mary, from hospice. Your mother hasn't been doing well today. I think that it would be a good idea for you to come on over," said the voice on the other end of the phone.

"Hi Mary. My mother hasn't been doing well for a long time. She's eaten like a bird for months. Actually, she hasn't eaten hardly anything for over a week. What's going on with her?" I asked.

"Well, she has a lot of congestion in her lungs. We've ordered a chest x-ray. Her blood pressure is very low and her heart rate is high. How long till you can get here?" she asked.

"Mary, I'm not able to come. We're on vacation and we're on our way to D.C.," I said.

There was silence on both ends of the phone.

"If we were home, I'd come right now, but we've been driving since early this morning. I'm not coming back at this point," I said.

"Sally, she's very sick," she said.

"I understand what you're saying and I don't like hearing that she's sick, but I've gotten this same call many times already. I promise you that if I need to fly home, I will, but I'm not coming now. Is she talking to you?" I asked.

"Not much," she said.

"Mary, I feel really bad saying this, but I can't come now. Please keep me updated. It doesn't matter how many times you call me, it's important that you keep me updated. Please promise me that you and the other nurses will do that," I said.

"Yea, of course we will," she answered.

I had a feeling that she was a little surprised that we weren't returning.

"Please tell her that I love her," I said.

"No problem. I'm heading back to her room now, and I'll tell her," she said.

"Mary, please call me again later and let me know how she's doing," I said.

"Okay, Sally. I'll let you know if anything changes," she said, and then we both said goodbye.

Dave gave me a funny look and asked, "You didn't tell them that we were going out of town?"

"Honey, I was afraid that if they knew that I wasn't going to be there for a week, that her care would be even worse than it usually is. Isn't it pathetic that I have to play these games?" I asked.

"Do you want to go back home? We can turn around now, if you want to," Dave said.

I knew that Michael and Kathleen were listening from the back seat, although they weren't saying anything.

"No, she'll be okay; she's in God's hands." There was more that I wanted to say to Dave but I didn't want the kids to hear all that was on my mind.

As we continued heading north I thought about other calls that I had received from the nursing home over the last two years telling me to come right away because she was "declining rapidly." Luckily she had rallied all those times before. I hoped that I wasn't becoming cavalier, and that she would rally from whatever this newest problem was.

At that moment I felt deeply immersed in the "Sandwich Generation." I was torn between doing what was best for my children, and what was best for my mother and aunt. At that hour, I really wasn't certain what was best. I prayed that I had made the right decision.

"Thanks for offering to go back home, but let's keep going," I said to Dave.

"Okay, if you're sure," he said as he squeezed my hand.

"I'm sure," I answered quietly.

"Declining rapidly." I came to hate those words. *How far do you have to decline, and how rapidly do you have to go, before you hit bottom?* My mind wandered as I pondered that question.

We arrived in D.C. the following day. Our week together flew by as we did all that we had planned, and then some. I tried to smile often and not let the kids know how nervous I was about what was going on back at home with Grandma. I received more calls during the week from Calafort. One said that she appeared to be improving slightly. The others tried to emphasize that she was "declining rapidly." Three of those calls came while we were inside the Smithsonian museums. I told Dave that I was getting paranoid going to the Smithsonian.

I was sorry when the week came to an end, mostly because I really enjoyed spending the week with Dave and the kids, but also because I feared what lay ahead for my mother and me. Usually I dozed on long car trips, but not on this drive home. I couldn't wait to see my mother, but I was anxious about how I would find her.

When we pulled back into our driveway, I quickly got out of Dave's car and immediately got into mine. I drove faster than I probably should have driven to the nursing home. As soon as I parked my car, I ran from the parking lot, into the building, and down the hallway to Mom's wing of the facility. There were lots of sounds in the background—pots clanging in the kitchen, staff talking, residents hollering for their nurses—but one sound that I didn't hear was my mother calling my name.

I ran to her room but she wasn't there. I didn't see Sandi or Sophia either, her regular nurse and CNA. I asked another nurse where they were and she said that they both were off and that they had agency replacements. She told me that she saw my mother earlier at the other end of the hall by the window.

I quickly went to the hallway where she said my mother was sitting. At the end of that long hallway, where I'd never seen her before, there she sat all by herself facing a wall. I ran to her and then I slowly turned her chair around so that

I wouldn't frighten her. Her head hung down, her tiny chin nearly on her chest. I squatted down next to her and said, "Mom, I'm here with you."

She lifted her head slightly but she said nothing. For the first time ever, I saw drool seeping from the corner of my mother's mouth. She lifted her head up a little more and she looked at me. There was no smile. There was no emotion whatsoever. She didn't ask me how I found her, like she often asked. She didn't ask how I knew where she was. I wasn't sure if she even knew who I was.

"Mom, do you know who I am?" I asked.

She just kept staring at me with those listless, lifeless eyes. I kissed her forehead. I kissed her boney, twisted hands.

"Mom, do you know who I am?" I asked again as we looked into each other's eyes.

She continued staring, and then finally she said, almost in a whisper, "You're my Sally." She spoke so quietly that I barely heard her. But I did hear her. Forever those words will be ingrained in my memory. They will be there just like when I first heard Michael and Kathleen say "Mama" or the first time Dave said, "I love you."

"Yes, Mom, I'm your Sally," I said as tears rolled down my cheeks. I tried not to cry but I couldn't help it.

"Don't cry, Baby. I'll be okay," she said. It was incredibly hard to hear her. I don't think anyone else could have understood her, but I did. At that moment, it only mattered that I heard her. Her words were a déjà vu of when I had to make the feeding tube decision.

She was so weak that I didn't want her to use any of her energy consoling me.

"We'll both be okay, Mom. Whatever happens, we'll both be okay. I'm going to bring you back to your room now," I said, and I gave her a big hug.

I brought her back inside her room and I turned on the TV. I knew that she wasn't going to listen to it, but at least it was some sort of company for her. Then I went to find her nurse.

"I'm Sally, Barbara's daughter," I said to a nurse I'd never seen before. "I just came for a visit and I found my mother all the way at the end of the next hallway, by herself, facing a wall. My mother has been really sick for this past week. She hasn't eaten in over two weeks. Why would she have been left by herself facing a wall? That's mean," I said.

"I think the CNA must have brought her down there so she could look out the window. She must have turned herself around," she said defensively.

"There is no way that my mother turned her chair around by herself. Have you seen her hands? Have you noticed how weak she is? If it was your mother, would you have taken the time to ask if she needed help or if she wanted to be staring at a blank wall?" I asked.

"I'll let her CNA know that she needs to watch her more carefully," she said, trying to appease me so that she could get back to what she was doing.

I wanted everyone to watch her more carefully, but I think that was a pipedream.

I knew that the shift would be changing soon. I wasn't about to leave until I saw who would be replacing the agency nurse and the CNA, so that I would know that my mother would be in better hands. I wanted to know that she would be safe. I spent a few more hours with her but there wasn't anything else that I could do for her right then. They put her into bed for a late afternoon nap. I kissed her goodbye and told her that I'd see her the next day. She just looked at me and slowly nodded.

When I left Calafort, I drove to Delia's rehab before I went home. Since it had been over a week since I'd seen her, I wanted to see with my own eyes how she was doing, rather than calling and asking her nurse.

When I walked into her room I received a totally different greeting from her than the one that I received from my mother. She was getting ready for her supper and was about to wheel herself down to the dining room.

"Welcome back, Stranger. I've missed ye. Did ye have a good trip?" Delia asked with a sparkle in her eyes.

I gave her a hug and said, "It's always great to get away, but it's nice to be home again."

She seemed so happy to see me that I didn't want to burst her bubble by telling her about my mother.

"What's the matter with ye, Sally? Ye don't look very good. Are ye sick?" she asked.

I guess I don't have much of a poker face, and I was too tired to make up a story about why I didn't "look very good."

"Mom isn't doing well and her rehab kept calling me during the week," I explained.

"I told them here not to call ye, but they wouldn't listen at all to me. I told them that ye were on vacation. What's the matter with your mother? Has she eaten anything at all?" she asked.

"The only thing she's doing is drinking the pre-thickened water and pre-thickened cranberry juice. That's pretty much what's keeping her alive," I told her.

"Jesus, Mary, and Joseph, she's going to die if she doesn't eat something. Sally, make her eat. Ye can do it. She'll do it for ye," she said.

It was hard to know how to respond.

"Dee Dee, I've come to the conclusion that there are two things you can't make a person do, and that's to make them walk or to make them eat. My mother has proven that to me. I know that she needs to eat something. I don't know how much longer she can keep going on otherwise. When my mother turns down potatoes you know that she doesn't want to eat. They've been giving her fortified shakes, but they're only a couple hundred calories. Plus, she doesn't like the taste of them so she doesn't drink much. What good is that?"

"Keep trying. Coax her, Sally. She'll do it for ye," she repeated.

"I didn't think that there was anything in the world that my mother wouldn't do for me. I'm afraid that I was wrong," I said as I pictured her little body slouching in her wheelchair.

"Dee Dee, I know that I just got here, but I'm not going to stay long this evening. The kids go back to school in the morning and I'll be busy tonight with laundry, and lunches, and just hanging out with them. You and I will catch up during the week," I said as I pushed her wheelchair towards the dining room.

"Ye didn't need to see me tonight at all. Seeing your mother was plenty for ye to do after your long drive home," she said.

"I wanted to see you. I still have a few more days of vacation left before I go back to work. I'm planning on spending as much time as I can at the nursing home and I'll try to do all that I can do to get my mother to eat. Delia, is there anything that I can do for you?" I asked.

"Don't be silly. Ye do enough for everyone. Get your mother to eat and then start worrying about yourself. We'd all be lost without ye, Sally." And then, almost as an afterthought, she added, "I feel bad that your vacation didn't do ye one bit of good when ye have to come back to these problems."

"Are you kidding me? I had a great vacation. I'm rested and relaxed and ready for whatever comes my way," I tried to say convincingly.

I wondered if I really was ready for whatever came my way.

"Dee Dee, I'm going to make you a cup of tea that you can sip on while you wait for your supper," I said as I pushed her wheelchair into the dining room table.

As I looked through one of the drawers in the dining room for a tea bag, I came across several packets of thickener for drinks. One of the nurses confirmed my hunch that they were used to thicken drinks for the residents who aspirated. I asked if they had pre-thickened water and juice in Seleerac and she said that they didn't. She said that the nurses and CNAs thickened all the drinks themselves. I didn't know what I would do with them, but I asked if I could take some of the packets with me and she said it was okay.

I sat at Delia's table for a few minutes and asked how her rehab was going. She said that it was slow going but thought that she was doing okay. I told her that I'd bring her to her radiation treatments during the week, and I asked how they went while I was gone.

"It's a piece of cake," she said. "Karen picked me up here and took good care of me. Ye don't have to worry about me, Sally. I'll be fine," she said.

Radiation is a piece of cake? Delia was absolutely amazing. She looked so frail but she was actually one of the strongest people that I knew. Why was she so strong?

"Sally, I hate chasing ye home, but go on home. Ye need to get some rest," she said as she reached up to hug me. "Safe home, Honey."

I knew that she would've liked a long visit with me, but she could see the stress that I was under with my mother.

On my way home I stopped at the grocery store to pick up some milk and a few other things that I knew that we needed. As I hurried through the store I walked down the aisle with the instant breakfast drinks. For some unknown reason, they caught my attention so I stopped and read the labels. When I saw that they were full of vitamins and minerals, a light bulb turned on in my head. Since my mother wasn't drinking much of the fortified shakes that she was being served, I thought that these instant breakfast drinks might be a good alternative. Maybe she'd like them better. I didn't see any reason why they couldn't be mixed with milk and the thickener that was used in Delia's rehab.

I bought a few packages with different flavors. I thought that if she would at least try it, and if she liked it, that just maybe it would help her get some nourishment. At that point anything was worth a try. I thought that we were running out of time to turn things around.

The next morning, after taking the "first day of the school year picture" of the kids, I drove to the nursing home. Mom was already dressed and sitting in her wheelchair when I walked into her room. I wasn't sure why, but she actually looked a little better than when I saw her the day before, even though she still looked dreadfully bad. *Could seeing me yesterday have been enough to bolster her?*

I brought her to the dining room and tried to get her to eat a little oatmeal. No luck. I tried some egg. No luck. I tried some grits. No luck. The only thing that she would drink was the pre-thickened cranberry juice.

"Mom, I love you with all my heart and all my soul, but you have to start eating or you'll be going to Heaven soon," I said. "Is that what you want? Do you want to die?"

She looked at me for a moment, and then answered, barely loud enough for me to hear, "I'm not hungry."

Was she upset that she hadn't seen me for a week? Had she forgotten that we were on vacation? Or was she angry because of where she was living, even though she wasn't sure where she was? Was it possible that she had gone so long without eating that she really wasn't hungry? How could she not be hungry? Did she want to die? Was she trying to starve herself to death? Too many questions, but no answers.

"Mom, just eat a little something. I promise you'll feel better if you eat. Tell me what you'd like and I'll get it for you," I pled.

"Not hungry," was all she said.

"Ok, we'll try again later. Maybe you'll feel more like eating later," I said. I tried to smile at her, but I had to fight back the tears.

"We sat silently for a while longer. The CNAs had started bringing the other residents back to their rooms. I tried another approach.

"Mom, would it be easier for you to eat if you hold the spoon, or would you like me to help you eat?" I asked as I put a little oatmeal on her spoon and brought it to her mouth.

She tightly closed her lips and shook her head.

I didn't want her to get upset. That wouldn't help at all. "It's okay, Mom," I said. "We'll try again at lunch time. Maybe you'll be hungry then."

I gave up trying to get her to eat her breakfast and decided to take her outside. It was a beautiful summer morning.

"Mom, it's a gorgeous day, isn't it?" I asked. I got no response as I squatted down in front of the chair.

"Do you hear the birds singing? They're talking to each other. Can you hear them?"

She slowly nodded yes.

I wished that I knew what she was thinking.

"I love you, Mom," I said.

Once again, another nod was all that I got.

As I pushed her wheelchair around the grounds, I saw a pretty plumbago bush full of bright blue flowers. I broke off a couple small branches and put them in one of her hands that was resting on her lap.

"God help ye," she said quietly as she slowly turned her head back and forth.

I cocked my head a little and looked at her and wondered what she meant by those words. I didn't know what anything meant anymore.

We didn't stay outside too terribly long because she literally looked sick and tired.

"Mom, you look sleepy. Do you want to go back inside and lie down for a little while?" I asked.

"Okay," she answered.

As I wheeled her towards her room, I saw her CNA. I asked her to please help my mother into bed for a nap. I asked her to check on her every now and then to make sure that she was okay. She said that she would do that.

Since I had told Delia that I would take her to her radiation treatment which was at Noon, I asked Sandi if she would please work with my mother at lunchtime. I gave her a few packets of the instant breakfast drink, and asked her to please mix it with milk and the thickener from Delia's rehab. She was the only person working at that time that I trusted with that request.

"Sally, you know that I'm happy to help. We have to figure out something to get your mother to start eating again," she said.

As I listened to her tell me that she'd help me, I had a flashback of when I was told that my mother was going to be moved to the Meadows Unit. I was told that I would like her new nurse, Sandi. They were right.

Later that afternoon Sandi called me and for once it wasn't bad news from Calafort. I could almost hear the smile in her voice as she told me that my mother drank most of the instant breakfast at lunch, and that she liked it. I thanked her sincerely for calling me and letting me know the good news. She said that she was working a double shift and that she would try it again at supper.

That evening I called the nursing home as soon as I thought supper would have been over. I could hardly wait to ask Sandi if she had any luck getting my mother to drink the instant breakfast twice in one day. She sounded almost as relieved as I was when she gave me another happy update. She said my mother liked it and drank it all up. I was being cautiously optimistic and thought that if we could get her to keep it up, that maybe there might be a chance that she would try some pureed food.

She did keep it up and most days she was drinking it two or three times a day. However, she still refused to eat food, and so she continued to lose weight. That didn't make sense to me because she seemed stronger and she was definitely more "with it" mentally.

I was happy that we were once again able to have conversations that had some substance to them. She even surprised me one evening when she asked me to bring her the Sunday newspaper so that she could help me cut out grocery coupons. Things were far from being good with my mother, but she was definitely doing better—at least that's what I wanted to think. In reality, I knew that if she didn't start eating food soon, that she was going to die.

Chapter 17

Totally Unresponsive

This was an extremely busy time for me. I was back at work, I was trying to visit my mother and aunt daily, and the kids were back in school. Michael was on the cross country running team and Kathleen was in Girl Scouts. Saturdays were particularly busy. I never missed any of Michael's meets that took up most of the morning. I always wanted to be there to cheer for him and his teammates. Girl Scouts often had events that involved us moms, and I would never consider not being there with Kathleen. I waited a long time to become a mother and I didn't want to miss out on anything.

Saturdays were also when I still stopped by Mom's house and Delia's apartment to water their plants, and to pick up

Delia's mail. The old African violet plants on Delia's window sill were blooming so beautifully that they almost looked artificial. Mom's plants, however, looked like they were on their last leg and barely alive. The similarity between the plants and my mother and aunt was not lost on me.

It was on a Saturday while I was still at Mom's house that I received a call from Esther, the Director of Nursing at Calafort. I always felt like she thought of me as an annoyance. I always thought of her as a deaf ear who humored me when I would voice my concerns. She had just found out about the instant breakfast drink and she was calling to let me know that we could no longer give it to my mother.

"What do you mean we can't give it to her? We finally came up with a plan that's getting extra calories into her. She's not having any problems drinking it. She's not coughing when she's drinking it. She's finally—"

She interrupted me. "It's against our company's policy for the staff to thicken liquids. That's why we have the drinks that come into the facility pre-thickened."

"Please tell me why the nurses or dietary people can't thicken it for her?" I asked, as calmly as I could be.

"Because the consistency of the drinks will always be different when you have different people thickening it. Each person will add slightly different amounts of the thickener to the drink. It's a liability issue," she said.

"Tell me that you're kidding me. Please tell me that you're kidding me. My mother hasn't eaten in nearly two months. We have finally found something that may help her, and you're telling me that we can't do it. How much longer do you think that she's going to live if she doesn't start getting some nutrition?" I asked in desperation.

"I'm sorry, but, it can't be done here," she said.

"Esther, I don't want to have this conversation with you on the phone. Are you going to be there for a while?" I asked.

"I'll be here for a few more hours," she said.

"I'm on my way over there now," I said as I hung up. I think that she was starting to say something else, but whatever it was would have to wait for her to tell me in person.

As I drove to Calafort, I remembered a form that I was asked to sign a few weeks earlier. I knew that my signature on the form would be protection for them for liability issues. It stated that I was aware that if my mother didn't start eating on her own, or unless she had a feeding tube, that she would die. I'm sure that I was asked to sign the form so that the facility wouldn't be sued if she died from starvation. I signed it because I knew that the statement was correct. I also knew that there would be no feeding tube and that's why I was working so hard to get her nourishment the way the vast majority of us get our nourishment—through the mouth.

When I got to the nursing home I went directly to Esther's office. I always knew that I had to pick my battles. I was ready for this battle. I was fighting for my mother.

"What in the name of God are you talking about? You had me sign a form saying that I knew that my mother will die if she doesn't start getting nutrition. I am doing everything in my power that when she dies, that it won't be because she starved to death. She's finally making progress and you say that she has to stop taking the only thing that seems to be working. What is wrong with you?" I asked slowly. I could see my chest rising and falling.

"I told you, it's the company's policy that we can't thicken liquids. It's not that we don't want to do everything that we can do to help your mother. We could be liable if she was to aspirate on a drink that we thickened. I'm not going to lose my job by allowing something that I know we're not supposed to be doing," she said.

"Esther, your nurses are dispensing psychotropic drugs and narcotics. Are you telling me that they don't have the ability to follow the directions on the back of a packet of thickener? The Seleerac nursing home is just a few miles from here. Why are they able to do it?" I asked.

The more that was said, the more exasperated I got. I could not believe the words that came out of her mouth next.

"Since we all seem to be frustrated about your mother's condition, and you not being satisfied with the care that she's getting here, maybe you should move your mother," she said.

I was flabbergasted. Did she say what I thought she said? How do I even respond to such a callous and asinine comment?

We both just stood there for a few moments and stared at the other.

"What did you just say to me? Please repeat what you just said."

I think she quickly realized that what she said wasn't appropriate, but once words are spoken you can never take them back.

"Sally, I know you want what's best for your mother but I don't think you're happy with the care that we're giving her. Maybe if she was where your aunt—"

I interrupted her. "Esther, listen carefully to what I'm going to tell you because I mean it," I said as we locked eyes.

"My mother may not remember the names of all the CNAs and nurses who help her each day, but she knows their faces. She depends on them and I think that some of them who have worked with her for a long time love her. She has spent the last of her money to live here in your facility. She's almost 92 years old and this has been her home for over two years now.

"You, on the other hand, have been here for five months. You're the third Director of Nursing who's been here since my mother moved in. Let me make it clear. If one of you will be leaving this facility, it won't be my mother. How dare you even suggest that I move her?"

I turned around and left her office without giving her a chance to respond. I really didn't want to hear anything else that woman had to say to me. I walked down to Mom's room but she was asleep in her bed and I didn't want to wake her. I noticed that she had a dry washcloth rolled in each of her hands.

I found her nurse and I was happy that it was Sandi who was working that day.

"Hi, Sandi. I just went into my mother's room. She's sleeping. Will you let her know that I came by to see her and tell her I love her?"

"Of course, I will. Did Esther talk to you about the thickener?" she asked.

"She did. She also suggested that I should move my mother to another nursing home," I said.

"She said that? Are you thinking about moving her?" she asked.

"I'm not moving my mother anywhere," I answered.

"Good," Sandi said.

Since I didn't want to put her in the middle of what had just happened in her boss' office, I changed the subject.

"What's up with the washcloths in my mother's hands?" I asked.

"Since they cut her physical therapy back to two days a week, we're supposed to get her to squeeze rolled up washcloths. That'll be good for her hands," she said.

I closed my eyes and counted to 10, and then said, "Nobody ever said anything to me about her PT being cut back, and you know that my mother doesn't tell me about that sort of thing. She's probably not even aware. I really think the therapy is helping, but she's still not as flexible as she used to be."

"You'll need to talk to Physical Therapy, but usually when someone gets to a point that their progress has plateaued, the number of PT days are cut back, until finally they're put on some sort of a maintenance program. Give them a call and see what they have to say," she said.

I was quiet for a moment, but then said, "The reason this news bothers me so much is because there's a part of me that thinks that Calafort could have proactively kept her from getting into this position to begin with. I'll talk to the person in charge of PT and see if I can talk him into keeping her on the three times a week schedule. It's obvious that she's made progress, but I think that she can still be much better than she is."

That's when one of the residents started hollering, "Nurse."

"Sandi, I'm going to leave now. When my mother wakes up, please remember to tell her that I stopped by to see her but that I didn't want to wake her. I'm bummed by that bizarre conversation with Esther, and I think that it's best that I leave now. I have to figure out something, anything to get her to eat," I said.

"I'll let your mom know that you were here. I'll try to encourage her to eat some mashed potatoes at supper. Take it easy, Sally," she said.

I was worn out and I didn't have any more fight left in me for the day. I had to leave. As I was walking out the front doors of the facility I noticed a posting on the door that said that the State Survey would be starting on Monday. I didn't know exactly what that entailed but I knew that everyone seemed to be getting prepared for something over the last few days and that it probably was a big deal. I figured that I would know more next week about what was going on.

Dave and I and Kathleen went out for dinner that night with three other families. As difficult as it was to do, I had to put Calafort out of my mind. As I've said before, that was my way of coping.

When I went to the nursing home on Monday evening, the staff all seemed to be on their best behavior. My mother was already in the dining room and she looked much better than usual. Her clothes matched and her hair was nicely brushed. I noticed a couple people who had teeth in their mouths that I never saw with teeth before. The tables were all set with the appropriate utensils, and the CNAs weren't talking across the room to each other. They even seemed to be paying more attention to the residents than they normally did.

The food didn't stay long on the carts before it was served to the residents. When Mom was given her plate, the pureed food was still hot. The administrator of the nursing home stuck his head into the room and asked if everything was okay. That was a first. I found out that the "Survey" was some sort of inspection and the facility didn't want to receive any "deficiencies."

That evening at supper I tried my best to coax my mother to eat the food on her plate, but she pursed her lips and said, "No." The only things that were of any interest to her were her pre-thickened cranberry juice and pre-thickened water. I tried to get her to drink her fortified shake but she only took a couple of sips. It was absolutely ridiculous that we were now back to where we were weeks ago before she started drinking the instant breakfast drink. As much as I didn't want to talk with Esther ever again, I knew that I had to speak with her and convince her that my mother needed to drink the instant breakfast, and that it needed to be thickened.

I left my mother sitting at the table and told her that I would be back in a few minutes. I went in search of Esther but when I spotted her, it was apparent that she was hurrying down the hall to do something. Unless someone was about to die, there wasn't anything more important than what I had to say.

I caught up to her and said, "Listen, Esther. This is beyond absurd. My mother is exactly like she was weeks ago before she started getting nourishment. She is going to starve to death. She looks like a skeleton. She looks like she's been in a concentration camp. Tell me whom I need to speak to in your corporate office about using the thickener."

"Sally, I can't talk to you about this now. I'm really busy. Can I call you in a little while?" she asked.

Good manners and politeness had left me, which was apparent in my answer to her. "I'm sorry that you're busy. I'm busy too, but this is important. I want to talk to you this evening."

I could see her looking over my shoulder down the hallway behind me. I turned around and saw two men whom I'd never seen before and they looked a little out of place. They were gazing in our direction.

"I'll meet you in my office in 20 minutes," she said, and walked in the direction of the two men, without waiting for an answer from me.

I was at my wits' end and I was feeling the same emotions I felt when my mother was in the hospital and I couldn't find a doctor who would take over her care. After Esther walked off, I stayed where I was but leaned against the wall with my eyes closed. I was totally frustrated. What was I supposed to do to help my mother? I couldn't let her starve.

I was deep in thought when I heard someone say, "Excuse me. Is everything okay?"

The two men that were standing down the hallway were now standing in front of me. They introduced themselves and said that they were at the facility for the Survey. They asked me a few questions and I told them why I was upset. I had absolutely no reason to keep my mother's terrible situation a secret. If these two men were in a position to help her, then I was happy to tell them anything that they wanted to know.

I decided not to go to Esther's office because I knew that I would just be wasting my time. I decided to go directly to Tom, the administrator. I wanted him to know what was going on with my mother, from my perspective. I felt sure that Esther had already filled him in from her perspective.

I went to his office but he had already left for the day, so I called him early the next morning. He was in a meeting when I called so I left a detailed message asking for the phone numbers and email addresses for the president and CEO of

Calafort. If the corporation had a policy against using a thickener, I naïvely thought that I could get them to make an exception for my mother. She was running out of time and I needed their help. In this case, naïveté paid off.

Tom returned my call in less than 10 minutes. He told me that we should be able to work it out ourselves because it would reflect poorly on him and the facility if I brought this to Corporate's attention.

When I told him that his Director of Nursing had suggested that I find another nursing home for my mother, he apologized profusely. He said that she'd been on call, as well as she was under a lot of pressure this past week because of the Survey. I could have said that I'd been on call for years and I, too, had been under a lot of pressure, but some things are better left unsaid.

Later in the afternoon Tom called me back and said that he had a meeting with Pamela, Calafort's nutritionist, and that they had come up with a plan. I had been the one buying the instant breakfast drink up until the day that Esther said that they would no longer use the thickener. Tom said that they would now order the instant breakfast for my mother, and would mix it with the pre-thickened milk which would take away the need for the thickener.

That was such an incredibly good and simple solution that in retrospect I will never know why NONE of us had thought about it until I threatened to call the head of the corporation. I'm surprised that none of her nurses, the nutritionist, the Director of Nursing, or any of the CNAs ever thought about such an easy fix. It's myself, however, that I'm most disappointed. Why didn't I think of it?

It was the proverbial "not seeing the forest for the trees." I was fixated on using the thickener, and Calafort was hooked on their fortified shakes. When my mother was brought to the facility two years earlier, she was a robust 140 pounds; now she only weighed 79 pounds. I prayed that it wasn't too late to help her, but at the same time I didn't understand how she was doing as well as she was.

On a happier note, Delia would soon be finished with her radiation treatment. She had also been working hard during her physical therapy and the hard work paid off. Seleerac told her that it wouldn't be much longer before she would be well enough to go back home to her own apartment.

For me, Delia going home was bittersweet news. Of course, that was always the ultimate goal, but with everything that was going on with my mother, I knew that when Delia went back to her apartment there would be far more stress on me to make sure that she was safe. At least in the rehab, I felt that there were additional people keeping an eye on her around the clock.

When they told us the target date that she would be going home, I made sure that her refrigerator was stocked with food that I thought would be easy for her to prepare during the day. I knew that for a while I would be stopping by each day to check on her and to fix either her breakfast or supper, or maybe both. I also called several of her friends so that they would know that she'd soon be back in her own home. I knew that they would be checking on her, also. God blessed her not only with a long life, but He also blessed her with a lot of friends who loved her and helped her in her old age.

It was a Friday evening that she got to go home. As she was getting ready to leave the rehab, she and her roommate, Ruth, hugged goodbye. They had encouraged each other and had become good friends during the six weeks that they had shared a room together. I knew that they were going to miss each other. Many of the nurses and CNAs who took care of her also made a point of stopping by her room to say goodbye and to wish her good luck. I was happy that Delia was going home. I wished that Mom had had the same happy ending to her rehab.

One thing that I meant to do before she went home to her apartment, but didn't get around to actually doing, was to get her some sort of a medical alert button to wear when she was alone. Since it was already Friday evening, I figured that I wouldn't be able to do anything about it until Monday morning. If my mother had worn one of those buttons, she wouldn't have lain on her floor all night and the following day, by herself, with a shattered hip.

****

Delia was happy to be in her own home again. She was looking forward to getting back to her own bed, and friends, and routine. One thing that she wasn't thrilled about, however, was when I told her that I was going to spend the night sleeping on her couch, at least for her first night home. I told her that if I slept at my house, I'd be worrying about her all night and that I wouldn't get any sleep.

"I thank ye, Sally, but I'm fine and I'd like it if ye went home now. Ye can call me in the morning, if ye would like," she said.

By that time, she had already put on her nightgown, had one last hot cup of tea for the night, and had brushed her teeth. She seemed to be maneuvering well with her walker around her apartment, but I still insisted that I was going to stay. I needed to know that she was able to safely get to the bathroom by herself, which I knew she did several times each night.

"Sorry, Dee Dee, but I'm staying with you tonight," I said.

"Ye don't bend, Sally, do ye? Once you've made up your mind to do something, there's no stopping ye. There's an extra pillow and blanket in the closet. Make yourself comfortable. Will David be upset if ye stay here for the night?" she asked.

"Dee Dee, we all want to make sure that you're okay. We want you to be safe. There's no way on earth that I'm leaving you by yourself tonight. If everything goes well tonight, I won't stay tomorrow night. Okay?" I asked.

"Thank ye, Sally," she said.

I wasn't sure if she was thanking me for spending the night with her or for not staying the following night.

I did little to help her during that night because I wanted to make sure that she could do everything she needed to do by herself. I was there only if she had an emergency. My main concern was when she went to the bathroom. I guess that her physical therapy did her a lot of good because she appeared much stronger and better able to walk than she did before her fall.

She did well during the night and I told her that I was proud of her. I told her that if she really wanted to be on her own, that I wouldn't sleep on her couch anymore. She told me that she appreciated my help for the first night, but that she was ready to solo.

We spent a lot of time with her on Saturday and Sunday. I was there to fix all her meals, and to wash her dishes afterwards. As hard as she worked to get strong while she was in the rehab, I wasn't taking any chances on her backsliding now that she was finally back in her apartment. I figured that when I went to work on Monday, she'd be able to start fixing at least one meal a day for herself.

It definitely was not a relaxing weekend. Both days I was either at Delia's apartment or at Calafort with my mother. I thought that both of them were on the upswing which I was happy about. I knew that Mom was doing better because when I visited her, I could hear her calling my name as I got closer to her room. It broke my heart to hear her do that, but on the other hand, when she was "declining rapidly" she didn't call my name, at least not loud enough for anyone to hear.

Delia was in good spirits all weekend and I knew that she was happy to be back home again. After my visits with Mom, Delia wanted detailed updates. Even though we were both happy about my mother drinking the instant breakfast again at each meal, we knew that she needed to be eating "real" food. We both knew that it wasn't going to be long before the inevitable would happen, if she didn't start eating.

I said an early goodnight to Delia on Sunday. I needed to go home and have a few hours to unwind, and to put my worries concerning the oldsters on the backburner. It was going to be a busy week for me at the office and I needed to relax, whatever "relax" meant, before going to bed. I told Delia that I would call her in the morning and that I would stop by for a visit on my way home from work.

"Sally, thank ye for everything. Don't worry about me. I'm fine. God bless ye," she said as she reached up from her chair to hug me. "I'm not walking ye to the door tonight. I'll start doing that again tomorrow. Safe home."

"I love you, too, Delia. I'm only a few minutes away. Call me if you need anything," I said before I left.

****

The evening flew by and before I knew it, my alarm was going off signaling the start of another week. As I got ready for work, I called Delia to say good morning and to see how her night was. She wasn't answering her phone. The first few times I wasn't concerned because I knew that if she was in the bathroom, or if she was fixing something to eat in the kitchen, she wouldn't answer the phone.

When she still hadn't answered it by the time I was ready to leave for work, I started to worry. I knew that I needed to stop by her apartment to make sure that she was okay. As I drove to her apartment, the rational side of my mind reminded me how well she had done over the weekend. The other side of my brain reminded me that she was 94 years old and had been in a rehab for the last six weeks.

When I got to her apartment the door was still locked. I let myself in and then called her name, but there was no answer. She wasn't in her kitchen. As I rushed through her dining and living rooms, I felt like I was in the middle of a bad dream. I wasn't prepared for what I saw when I reached her bedroom. She was lying on the floor.

"Oh my God, Delia, are you okay?" I asked as I knelt down next to her. What I really meant was "Are you alive?" For a moment I didn't know the answer.

She had no color in her face. Her eyes were open, but she didn't answer me.

"Delia, I'm going to call the ambulance. Please hold on. You'll be fine once a doctor sees you. I promise. Please hold on. You'll feel much better in a little while. Please hold on," I said as I quickly called 911.

After I made the call, she turned her eyes towards me and whispered slowly, "So sorry, Sally," and then she closed her eyes. I kept calling her name but there was no response.

"Dee Dee, you have no reason to say you're sorry," I said as I held back my tears. "I'm the sorry one. I should have been with you. I'm so, so sorry."

I didn't know what to do while we waited for the ambulance. *Do I put a blanket over her to keep her warm? Do I put a pillow under her head to make her more comfortable? If I move her at all will I hurt her? Does she have broken bones? Did she have a heart attack? A stroke?*

A few minutes later, her house phone rang and when I answered it, the lady at the front desk said that she was calling to say that the ambulance had arrived and the paramedics were on their way up to the apartment. She wanted to make sure that the door was unlocked.

When they arrived at her fifth-floor apartment, they knocked but came in without waiting for me to open the door. They asked me some questions, and then took her vitals. They called her name a few times but there was no response. Delia was unconscious.

I followed the ambulance to the hospital. I prayed this wasn't how it was going to end for her. She had worked so hard to get out of the hospital after her alprazolam fall, to finish her radiation, and to make it successfully through physical therapy. Now that she finally made it back to her own home again, it seemed so not right that she wasn't able to enjoy more than two days of independence.

When she arrived at the hospital, all sorts of tests were done on her—chest and pelvic x-rays, head and brain scans, an EKG, as well as blood work. The results were good in that she hadn't broken any bones or had a stroke. However, she was extremely dehydrated and her sodium level was exceptionally low. She was on an IV to help with both those issues.

She was assigned a hospitalist that turned out to be Dr. Cathedra. Even though I wasn't thrilled at the way he treated my mother in the nursing home, I still attributed his help two years earlier, to having saved her life. I thought that if any doctor could pull Delia through this nightmare, that it would be Dr. Cathedra.

Things looked pretty grim. For the remainder of Monday, she was totally unresponsive. All day Tuesday she was totally unresponsive. She looked like she was in a very deep sleep. Throughout both days, I continued to have one-sided conversations with her as if she could understand everything that I was saying.

I fibbed and told her that Mom was doing better. I thought that if I gave her some good news, it might be the spark that would wake her. It didn't. Since she was such an extremely religious person I thought that it might help her if I prayed out loud. Sadly, that didn't make any difference either.

I wanted her to get better and I pictured her back in her apartment again. In my mind's eye, I saw her a few years earlier in her apartment doing the Macarena with Michael and Kathleen. I could see their happy faces. I prayed that God would let her rally and give her more quality time before her days were over. During my long vigil I also thought that if God took her then, while she appeared to be sleeping, that that might be a peaceful end to her long life. I never wanted her to suffer. It was then that I said another prayer —"God's will be done."

I went to work on Wednesday not knowing that somewhere between late Tuesday night and Wednesday morning she had turned the corner and came out of her deep sleep. When I walked into her room on Wednesday evening, I was happy to see her sitting up in the bed. She was weak, but was able to speak. I knew that things were looking up when she told me that she was hungry and then asked me to get her something to eat.

I knew that it would be a while before supper would be served. I didn't want her to have to wait so I decided to go downstairs to the hospital cafeteria and buy her something to eat. I ran into Dr. Cathedra on my way to the cafeteria, and we had a short conversation. He told me that he was pleased to see that she was improving, but that he was also concerned because she appeared to be aspirating.

I was worn out from the last few days, and I probably didn't hear everything that he was telling me, and it's even possible that I took things out of context. However, the words "pureed food" and "feeding tube" were amplified in my brain as I listened to what he had to say.

"Doctor, she was eating regular food four days ago. She told me that she's hungry now and is actually asking me to get her something to eat. I don't understand how she's suddenly aspirating," I said.

"Your aunt has had a lot of birthdays. Aspiration pneumonia is a major cause of death in the elderly. It may be that she's been aspirating for a while but it wasn't detected. Now that we suspect it, we need to be careful with her diet," he answered.

I took a deep breath, and said, "Dr. Cathedra, I'm going to get this conversation behind me right now since you're saying that Delia might be aspirating. There will never be a feeding tube for her, not now, not two years from now. It's not something that I need to give any additional thought to for all the same reasons that I didn't want one for my mother. I'm sure that Delia will tell you the same thing herself."

He stood quietly and listened as I continued, "I'm sorry, but when I hear Delia asking me to get her something to eat, I can't say, 'No'."

I thought that he was going to chastise me, but he didn't. He carefully chose his words which reminded me why I liked him so much to begin with.

"Sally, you've been taking care of your mother, and now your aunt, for years. It's a lot for one person to do and I know that you've had to make some pretty big decisions for them. I admire you for always looking out for their best interest and doing what you think is best for them. It's important that you understand that aspiration pneumonia is a painful way to die. I've already written orders for your aunt's food to be pureed while she's here in the hospital and her drinks will be thickened," he said.

"Doctor, I totally get what you're saying, but let me share something with you. My mother is still living in the nursing home, and it's been nearly two months since she's eaten solid food. Can you even imagine not eating for that long? I'm doing everything that I can do to get her to eat, but she refuses. At the same time my mother is starving to death, Delia is telling me that she's hungry and wants to eat. I'm going to give her food.

"I think that it's still going to be a while before the kitchen sends any food to her room and that's why I was on my way to the cafeteria. All I was going to get her was some mashed potatoes. You think that'll be safe for her to eat?" I asked.

"Add some extra milk to it and make sure she eats it very slowly. She hasn't eaten anything in days. Take it easy on her. When I discharge her, I'm going to send her back to Seleerac recommending a pureed diet," he said.

"Thanks, Doctor. I hate to cut our conversation short, but I'm going to go to the cafeteria now since I know that she's hungry." As an afterthought I added, "Did you know that she'd been in the rehab for about six weeks and then went back to her own home for literally two days before she ended up back in the hospital? Two days was all she had at home."

"I saw that in the chart. That's too bad. It's really too bad," he said.

On my way to the cafeteria, I called David. "Sorry to bother you, but can you come to the hospital for a while? I need you. I don't want to be here by myself."

"Is Delia worse? What's the matter?" he asked with concern.

"She's actually better, Dave. She's awake and she's talking and she wants to eat," I said.

"That's great news. I don't understand why you sound upset," he said.

"I saw Dr. Cathedra and I think that he's drunk the aspiration cocktail. At one point he even mentioned a feeding tube. Then he started talking—" I was telling Dave as he interrupted.

"Is he nuts? I hope you said that there's no way for a feeding tube. I'll be there with you in about 10-15 minutes and you can tell me the whole story," he said.

"Thanks, I really appreciate it," I said. "Please drive carefully."

I bought a couple servings of mashed potatoes and a small carton of milk. I added some of the milk to the potatoes and mixed it well. Then I heated it in the microwave and rushed it back to Delia's room so that it would still be hot.

"Why did this have to happen now?" she asked. "We were doing so good, I thought."

"You were doing good, and you'll be doing good again soon. What happened? Do you remember what happened?" I asked.

"I was going into the room to go to bed and then I thought that I'd like a slice of toast before I got into bed. I guess I turned around too fast and lost my balance and fell. Thanks be to God that I didn't pull the walker over on myself. I don't think that I'd be here to talk about it, if I did that to myself," she said.

Good grief, I thought. That was the second time, in as many months, that she said those same words about falling and about her walker.

"Delia, you're looking good tonight," Dave said as he walked into the room. "I'm glad to see you're eating after your long sleep." He came over and kissed the top of Delia's head and then gave me a hug.

"What are ye doing here, David? Don't ye have anything better to do?" she asked.

"There's no place I'd rather be right now than here with ye," he said, always joking about her "ye."

"Well, I'm always glad to see ye. They said that I slept for over two days," she said.

"I can vouch that that's the truth. I was here with you most of that time," I answered.

"Sally, if I was sleeping, ye didn't need to be here, did ye?" she said. I couldn't tell if she was making a joke or if she was serious.

"One thing that I know is that you're a million times better than you were. You scared the heck out of me for a few days," I said as I gave her a little pat on her legs. "I feel bad, Dee Dee, that you'll have to go back into the rehab for a while, but, you'll be back home again before you know it."

"We'll see, Sally. We'll have to wait and see," she said pensively.

Even though she had slept for two days, she looked tired. I was worn out, too, and wanted to go home. I had visited my mother the day before and she seemed okay, although "okay" was a relative word when it applied to Mom. I was too pooped to see her that night.

We visited with Delia for a little while longer but then I told her that I was really tired and was going to call it a day. I told her that I'd see her tomorrow. As I watched Dave hug her goodnight, I could tell that she was happy that he came.

While we walked to our respective cars, I filled Dave in on Dr. Cathedra's conversation.

"It was like he had become one of 'them'. The words that came out of his mouth sounded just like those other doctors sounded two years ago with my mother. How could he have changed so much in just a couple of years?" I asked.

"Don't worry about him. You did the right thing. Let's just put our energy into getting her out of the hospital as quickly as possible, getting her through some rehab, and back to her apartment," he said.

He walked me to my car and we talked a few more minutes. "Do you really think that she'll be able to go back to her apartment again?" I wanted to know what he thought. I needed to hear some words of encouragement.

"I think that we'll have to wait and see, but I don't see any reason why she wouldn't be able to. She did just fine living on her own until that doctor or pharmacy overdosed her on alprazolam. If that didn't happen to begin with, she wouldn't be in the situation that she's in now. Aren't I right?" he asked, but didn't wait for an answer. "Wasn't she doing just fine living on her own? Wasn't she? Those careless idiots..."

I could tell he was getting angry just thinking about what had happened to my little aunt all because someone wasn't paying attention.

"I hope that you're right. I don't think that she would do well if she had to live permanently in long term care," I said as I slowly leaned in to him. "Thanks for coming to the hospital. I needed some moral support."

He hugged me and said, "You're welcome. Let's go home now. When you get home, go take a nice long bath or a shower and I'll cook us some supper. The kids have already eaten. Then let's plan on getting to bed early tonight."

"Sounds good to me," I answered, and then gave him a hug before getting into my car.

Chapter 18

Give Up a Little Independence to Stay Independent

The following morning was the start of the day that I told you about at the beginning of my story. It was the day that I went to work in the morning, visited Mom at lunchtime in the nursing home, and then stopped by my house to get an umbrella, but then I couldn't remember where Delia was. I think that I've pretty much have gotten you up to speed. But my story is far from being over...

I always thought that I was a strong person but by now I was getting to the end of my tether. I was always waiting for the other shoe to drop, or for the next crisis to begin, which wasn't a happy or healthy way to live.

When I got home from work the day that I "lost" Delia, I told Dave, "I don't know how much longer I can keep doing this. Something has got to give. I want to take care of them. I worry about them. I love them both so much, but I'm about to have a breakdown. If I wasn't working, it might be easier. If there weren't two of them, it might be easier. I'm not complaining, I'm just venting." In reality, I was having another meltdown.

He hugged me and said, "Honey, it can't keep going on. Enjoy spending time with them both. Your mom can't live much longer if she doesn't eat, and it doesn't look like that's ever going to happen. Delia is 94 years old. She's had a good life, too, but she can't live forever. Think of all you've done for both of them. They'd be sad if they knew how hard it is on you."

I knew he was right, but knowing that he was right didn't make me feel any better. Actually, I felt a little guilty for saying anything at all. They both were always so good to me; how could I not reciprocate now when they both needed me? The answer to that question was easy—I couldn't. I knew that I would always take care of them; I would always be there for them.

Delia got released from the hospital on Friday evening and returned to Seleerac. I knew that it must have been a huge disappointment for her to be back to square one again on her road to recovery. She may have been visibly frail, but her constitution was one of the strongest that I had ever known. If anyone had the inner strength and stamina to overcome this type of challenge, it would be Delia.

Since it had only been a week since she had been in the rehab, her bed had not yet been assigned to another person. She went back to the same room that she had shared with Ruth.

When Ruth first spotted Delia that evening, she had a look of astonishment which quickly turned to tears. The two of them awkwardly hugged the other from their respective wheelchairs. I think that Ruth's tears were for sadness that Delia was back in the rehab, but in a way, they were also tears of happiness that she and Delia would once again share a room.

Delia wasn't given the volume of admission papers and brochures that she received a few months earlier, the first time that she was admitted. There was a form, however, that she hadn't seen before. It was a DNR—Do Not Resuscitate form. She read it over carefully and said that she was inclined to sign it, but wanted to know if I agreed with her.

Basically, the form said that in the event that she was to have cardiac or respiratory arrest, that CPR, intubation, and defibrillation would not be used on her. Even though it wasn't pleasant to make a decision that said not to do everything possible to keep her alive, I viewed it the same way that I viewed a feeding tube. I didn't want to put her through what could be a violent event for the sake of keeping her alive.

I told her that I agreed with her decision to sign the DNR, and so began another six weeks of planned physical therapy in hopes of getting her back to her own home sweet home again.

One of the things that I put on my "to do" list for Monday morning was to absolutely, positively figure out what needed to be done to have a medical alert bracelet or necklace waiting for her when she hopefully arrived home again. If she had been wearing one earlier that week when she fell, she wouldn't have spent the night lying on her bedroom floor. And I thought once again that if my mother had one, she too, might have had a totally different outcome than the one she had.

What a roller coaster ride of a week we just had! And now we were literally back to where she was seven weeks earlier. Like most evenings at that time, I was getting ready to wheel Delia to the dining room for her supper. Last week around that same time I was getting ready to wheel her out to my car and to take her to her apartment. Unless someone had told you about her week, you would never know that she had had the thrill of going back to her own home or the agonizing defeat of falling and spending five days in the hospital. I felt like I was waking from a bad dream.

One thing that was different from a week earlier was that when the CNA brought Delia her supper, there were three colorful scoops of pureed food on her plate. During her first six weeks in Seleerac she was served mechanical soft food. I was sitting next to her when her "lovely" dinner arrived. We both looked at the plate and then looked at each other.

"Don't worry, Dee Dee, I'll start bringing supper to you again each day, but for now, eat this tonight. Dr. Cathedra was concerned that you were aspirating so he told me that he was sending orders for pureed food for you. I'm pretty sure that they'll soon be doing a swallowing test, and that it won't be long before they're serving you mechanical soft food again," I explained.

I didn't wait for her to finish eating. I was ready to call it a day. I was happy that it was the weekend and that everything ended on a happy note for the week. After our goodbyes, and our hugs, and our "I love yous" I left Seleerac with a sigh of happy relief.

During the next few weeks there was no new crisis with either my mother or Delia. Delia was doing well, if not better, than the first time she was in the rehab. If the therapist asked her to do 10 repetitions of an exercise, she would do 12. If she was supposed to walk once a day, she would ask her CNA to take her a second time. She went to arts and crafts; she played Bingo and would happily tell me when she won; and she had a lot of visits from her friends. I was proud of how hard she was working and I told her often.

My mother seemed more alert and more "with it." I didn't know what to attribute that improvement. Perhaps it was because she was more hydrated and drank the instant breakfast three times a day. I know that when elderly people are not properly hydrated, they tend to become confused.

Sadly, she still wasn't eating and was down to 76 pounds. At that point it had been nearly two and a half months since she had eaten anything. I am not exaggerating. If I hadn't been with her almost daily, I wouldn't have believed it. My mother was literally starving to death. I was at the point that whenever the phone would ring at odd hours, my heart would drop because I thought that the nursing home was calling to say that she had passed away.

On Saturday morning I woke up early and decided to visit her while the rest of my family was still sleeping. When I walked through the doors of Calafort, I was a little surprised at how good it smelled. Breakfast was definitely being cooked. Usually I visited during my lunch hour or at suppertime but those meals didn't smell as inviting as breakfast did on that day.

As I walked down the hallway towards her room, I didn't hear her calling my name. I knew that there would soon come a day that I'd never hear her doing it ever again. I went first to her little dining room. I walked in there but immediately walked out when I saw that she wasn't there. Then I walked faster to get to her room. There she was sitting, waiting patiently for someone to bring her to the dining room.

"Hi Baby. I'm glad to see ye. Where're the kids?" she asked. There was something different about her. It took me a few seconds to figure it out. She looked content. Her brow wasn't furrowed; she didn't look like she was about to start crying. She actually looked somewhat relaxed.

"It's Saturday morning, Ma. They're still sleeping," I said.

"Ye should be sleeping, too. Ye need your rest," she said.

I gave her a hug and pulled up a chair to have a little chitchat before I brought her to the dining room, where I'd try to coax her once again to eat something.

"Sally, I don't know what in the name of God is the matter with me but I'm as hungry as hell. Do ye think we can get something to eat?" she asked.

"Huh?" I grunted. "What did you say, Ma?" I thought that I was hallucinating. I thought that she said that she was hungry. I wanted to hear those words for such a long time. I prayed that I would hear those words. My imagination was playing a cruel trick on me.

"I'm hungry, Baby. Let's see what they have to eat down there," she said.

I jumped up and I hugged her. "Mom, I love you! I love you! Don't go anywhere; I'll be right back," I said as I headed to the door of her room. I needed to find her nurse and tell her that my mother wanted to eat.

I turned around and went back over to her, and then I hugged her again. "Oh my gosh, Mom. I'm so happy. I love you! I really love you. Oh my gosh."

Did I just ask her not to go anywhere? Where did I think she would possibly go? She always stayed exactly where she was put.

"Are ye okay, Baby?" she asked as she looked at me as if I had lost my mind.

"I'm fine, Ma. Oh my gosh. I'm so happy. Oh my gosh. I'll be right back," I said as I hugged her again.

I quickly found Sandi and told her what my mother had just said. She, too, was happy to hear the news. She was in the middle of grinding Lillian's pills and mixing them with applesauce. She said that she'd come to my mother's room just as soon as she finished giving Lillian her meds.

A few minutes later she was in my mother's room.

"Barbara, Sally told me that you're hungry. I'm happy to hear that you've gotten your appetite back. We were all getting a little worried about you. What would you like to eat?" she calmly asked, but I knew that she was as excited as I was.

"Don't go to any trouble. Whatever is easy for ye to make," she said, as if she had only missed a meal or two.

"Okay, we'll fix something for you right now and we'll bring you down to the dining room. Sophia was actually on her way to get you," Sandi told her.

Then she gave me some instructions so that she wouldn't get sick to her stomach since it had been such a long time since she'd consumed anything other than liquids. She told me to try some oatmeal first and to feed her small bites and to make sure that she ate slowly.

She acknowledged that my mother used to be able to feed herself, but she cautioned me not to let her do that now. She said that since it had been so long since she'd eaten, that it was important that we take it easy for a little while. She told me that I could also mash a banana and see if she would eat that.

I wheeled her to the dining room, and gave her a cup of thickened cranberry juice to sip on while I got her "real" food. I was thrilled that she ate the oatmeal, and the banana, and probably would have eaten more if I gave it to her. There was a part of me that wanted to give her more, but instead, I carefully followed Sandi's advice. I didn't want to take a chance on her getting sick, if she ate too much, too soon.

I had almost given up hope that my mother would ever eat again. I'll never know why she had stopped eating two and a half months earlier. Nor will I ever know why she decided to start eating again when she did, but when I said my prayers that night, I thanked God with all my heart for what had happened that morning in that crowded little dining room in Calafort.

****

It seemed like the tide had turned because for a while things continued to go well for both my mother and for my aunt.

After several more weeks of physical therapy, Delia once again was able to go back to her apartment, hopefully to live out her days. Things were different this time for her, different in a good way. I had gotten her a medic alert necklace before she went back to her apartment and she wore it faithfully. Because her income was low, she paid virtually nothing for it.

Her friends continued to visit often which made her happy, and in turn gave me a little reassurance that other people were also checking on her. She still had all the same services that she had before she ever went into the rehab— home health care, housekeeping, and frozen prepared meals delivered to her home.

I'd say that at 94 years old, Delia had most of her bases covered. She didn't have all those services because she was lucky. Nor did she have them because she was wealthy or because she was poor. She had those services because she mostly, and me a little, looked for them. Delia wanted to be able to stay in her own home, and she knew that the only way that she could do that, would be to accept help to do the everyday things that she no longer thought was safe for her to do on her own. In order to remain independent in her own home, she had to give up a little independence and accept help.

Over the course of the next several weeks my mother continued to eat well. She remained on a pureed diet and ate pretty much everything that was put in front of her. When I was there at lunch or supper she would finish everything on her plate and would often ask for more. It wasn't unusual that I would go to the kitchen to get her seconds and sometimes even thirds of the food that she liked.

I was happy that she continued to gain weight and by Thanksgiving she weighed 95 pounds. That was a long way from the 140 plus pounds she weighed before her woeful fall, but it was a heck of a lot better than the 76 pounds she weighed, just six weeks earlier.

The weather was getting refreshingly cooler but since she was always cold, I needed to bundle her up whenever I took her outside for a walk. I tried to do that as often as I was able to fit it into my schedule. I've said it before and I'll continue to emphasize how medicinal our walks were for my mother.

She made me laugh one day when we were outside and I pointed out a squirrel gathering nuts.

She looked at me and said, "Baby, those aren't the only nuts around this place."

Sometimes, however, her comments weren't funny at all. She still occasionally asked me with an innocent look on her face, "Would ye like to go visit Mom?"

"Whose mom do you want to see?" I always asked.

"Our mom, Sally," she'd say. "Maybe she'll fix us a cup of tea. That would be nice, wouldn't it?"

Even though we had had many similar conversations about her mother, they still threw me for a loop. Had her mind just travelled 50 or more years back in time? Her sister, Sally, died many decades earlier during childbirth in Ireland. Is that who she thought I was at that moment? Her sister Sally? And both her parents had passed away in Ireland long before I was ever born. We had had this same conversation so many times, that it almost sounded scripted.

"Mom, she would be thrilled to see us and I'm sure that she'd fix us something good to eat. But, do you mind if we visit on another day though, because I really have to get back to work pretty soon?"

"Of course, Baby, we'll visit them when you have more time. Where do ye think I should stay tonight?" she asked.

"This is a fine place to stay. You've stayed here before and you told me how much you liked it. Is that okay with you?" I asked.

"Baby, I'll leave it up to ye. Ye know what's best," she said, totally relying on my judgment, and then added, "I hate to see ye go but if ye think it's okay for me to stay here, bring me back inside and to my room."

"That's where we're heading now," I said as I wheeled her towards the entrance of the facility.

"Will I see ye tomorrow?" she asked.

"Of course you will, Mom. You're stuck with me," I said as we walked back into the building.

When we went back inside, Midge was sitting in her wheelchair near the front door and was giving me a goofy look. She didn't respond to my friendly, "Hello, Midge."

"Stuck with ye? Ah, Baby, don't say that. I'd be lost without ye," she said.

"I love you, Mom. You know what?" I asked.

"Tell me," she answered.

"God knew what He was doing when He gave you to me," I said as I bent over the back of her wheelchair and gave her a kiss.

She reached for one of my hands and gave it a little squeeze.

We were almost at her room but rather than bringing her inside her room, I left her sitting in front of the nurses' station. That way she'd have a little company, as well as the nurses could keep an eye on her. We said goodbye and I told her that I would see her tomorrow.

As I neared the front door Midge motioned for me to come over to her. It appeared that she was looking at my head.

"Is it real?" she asked.

"Is what real, Midge?" I asked back.

"That hair. Are you going to keep it?" she asked.

I laughed to myself and said, "Yep, I'm planning on keeping it."

"I wouldn't have it," she answered back.

"That's just fine, Midge, because I'm not gonna give it to you," I said to her. "I'll see you tomorrow, Midge."

"Maybe you will. Maybe you won't," she said.

"Well, Midge, I really hope that I do," I said.

On my drive back to my office I thought about the conversation that I just had with my mother about visiting her mother. That's when I remembered that for several months before she went into the rehab, she was on donepezil. That was the medication that Dr. Diarmuid prescribed for her to slow down the progression of her dementia.

I never saw any great improvement in her memory when she was on it when she was living at home. I always thought, though, that if she didn't take it that she might have been a lot worse. That's the sort of thing we never really know, do we? When she went into Calafort, the donepezil was discontinued. It always seemed like there were bigger fish to fry with the nursing home, so I never made an issue about getting her back on the medication.

I also thought about conversations that I had with some of my friends who had mothers and fathers in the same situation as my mother. One of them insisted that he needed to correct his mother, who lived in an assisted living facility, whenever his mother got confused. I asked if correcting her brought her back to reality and he said that it didn't always help, and that sometimes it even frustrated her. My friend thought that if he continued correcting his mother enough times, that it would eventually sink in.

I chose not to put my mother through the frustration. If, for a few minutes, she thought that she'd be seeing her mother and father for a visit, and that made her happy, I thought it was best to go along with it. I knew that in a short while, she'd have forgotten the conversation, whether or not I corrected her.

While my mother's memory was definitely not good, her appetite had become incredibly good! It gave me great satisfaction to make those extra trips to the kitchen to get her second and third helpings of the food that she liked. The kitchen staff was equally happy to give me the additional food. Sandi told me that my mother was feeding herself again, even when I wasn't there. That may not sound like much of an accomplishment, but from my perspective, it was huge.

One day at lunch Mom asked me if she could have a slice of bread with a little bit of jam on it. She was always a lover of good bread. I pointed to a little circle of white mush on her plate and told her that that was bread. It was next to another circle of white mush that I told her was rice.

"Baby, have ye been drinking?" she asked.

Her question made me laugh out loud, partially because I didn't know if she was joking with me or if she meant it.

There was no question in my mind, however, that she wanted a slice of bread, so before I went back to work I asked Sandi if maybe that was something that she could start eating again. She told me that she had been giving her an occasional graham cracker and she seemed to be doing fine with it. She suggested that I speak with someone in speech therapy and request another swallowing test to see if she was still aspirating. She said that if she wasn't aspirating that she'd be able to eat a mechanical soft diet rather than a pureed diet. She surprised me when she said, "You usually get what you ask for here."

Mom was eating so much food that Dave joked and asked me if she could be dietetically bipolar. Her mind was sharper than it had been for quite some time, and I attributed that achievement to her drinking enough fluids and eating a healthy diet. I remember one Saturday I had a lot of things that I needed to do, and so after a short visit I used the excuse that I needed to leave because I had to do the grocery shopping. That wasn't a problem. The next day, however, I used the same excuse not to stay long, but that time I got caught in my little white lie.

"Baby, did ye forget something when ye went to the store yesterday?" she asked.

"Uh, yea. I forgot to buy milk," I fibbed again, which wasn't a nice thing to do, but I didn't want to hurt her feelings. Even though I had gotten caught, it did my heart good to know that occasionally her memory seemed totally normal.

I was happy that she was improving mentally, and that she was eating well, but at the same time I was sad to see what had become of her body. Her once strong and meaty arms had gotten so skinny that they looked like they belonged to an anorexic teenager. I was happy that she still was getting physical therapy, but her arms and hands were still nowhere as nimble as they were when she first moved into Calafort.

In my mind's eye, I thought back to two and a half years earlier and pictured her standing at my kitchen counter, teaching Kathleen how to knead dough to make Irish soda bread. Then I pictured her standing on a step stool and easily washing my windows. That's how my mother got physical therapy when she was in her late 80s and still living at home.

Now, in spite of getting "real" physical therapy, the CNAs still had difficulty dressing her because her arms weren't as flexible as they should've been. Don't get me wrong, I was sincerely grateful that she was getting the therapy, but there was also a part of me that thought that if I hadn't been such a pain in the neck that it would have already been discontinued. When it came to picking my battles, however, I knew that physical therapy would be one of the things that I would continue fighting for her to get.

Another issue that I thought had long ago been resolved had to do with the pharmacy bills. You might recall that for a while Calafort wasn't sending the Cifdano's Pharmacy bills to my mother's Blue Cross insurance. Eventually that problem was resolved. A new problem surfaced when she was approved for Medicaid and was no longer covered by Blue Cross.

At that point, Cifdano's Pharmacy was supposed to bill Medicaid directly. Instead, they continued billing Blue Cross. For months, I received statements from Blue Cross stating that they would not pay because my mother wasn't covered by Blue Cross. Cifdano's Pharmacy received that same statement, and would then send the bill to me.

The first couple times that happened I called the insurance lady at Cifdano's and patiently explained that my mother no longer had Blue Cross insurance and that the bill needed to be sent to Medicaid. By the time that the conversation was over, I'd think that the problem was resolved. Unfortunately, it was only resolved in my mind.

That process happened enough times that pharmacy lady and I were losing patience with each other. I didn't want to be receiving those bills anymore, and she wanted payment. Pharmacy lady won. Once again she made me believe that they would stop delivering my mother's medication to the nursing home if the bill wasn't paid. I couldn't risk that she wouldn't get her meds, so I paid the bill myself for a few months, expecting that pharmacy lady would figure out how to get payment from Medicaid in the future.

She apparently didn't figure it out because I continued receiving and paying their bills. Eventually I gave up in my ability to resolve the problem, and brought the next bill to Tom, Calafort's administrator. I told him that I wasn't going to pay it. Since Cifdano's Pharmacy was the pharmacy that Calafort ordered all their medication, I told him that I was turning the problem over to him.

To his credit, he deducted from my mother's nursing home bill, the amount that I had paid out of my own pocket to Cifdano's. He told me that he would work out the problem directly with the pharmacy. I told him that I hoped that the pharmacists at Cifdano's Pharmacy were better than the woman who did their billing.

The day after I turned over my Cifdano's Pharmacy problems to Tom, I spent my lunch break at a meeting with Medicaid so that Mom's eligibility would be granted for another year. The meeting was easy compared to the preceding year, considering all the documentation that was needed and all the work that had to be done to get her on the program initially. Thankfully, this year's approval letter was mailed to me the same day as the meeting.

While my mother's Medicaid re-certification gave me reason to smile, right around the corner were things that made me wince.

The dermatologist and radiologist both were in agreement that Delia's left shin needed additional radiation treatment. One of the main side effects of radiation therapy is fatigue. Delia, however, never complained that she was getting worn out, nor did she ever say, "Why me?" Like in the past, I took her for her treatment whenever I was able to take a long lunch break; on the days when I couldn't take her, the cancer center picked her up at her apartment and brought her back home when she was finished.

On one of Delia's radiation days when I wasn't able to take her, I called her to wish her luck and to have a little chitchat before she was picked up. Just as I had said goodbye to her and hung up the phone, the phone rang. "Calafort" was on my caller ID. Oh, how I dreaded seeing that word.

I quickly answered and heard Sandi's voice. She said that my mother had just fallen out of her wheelchair. Sandi sounded annoyed that the CNA hadn't secured the seatbelt, and that my mother had been left alone in her room. She said that my mother seemed fine and that there wasn't any need for me to come see her, but that she had to let me know.

Most of the calls from the nursing home fell into one of two categories, and I never knew which of the two to expect when their name appeared on my caller ID. The first category was the "she's declining rapidly, you need to come right away." I hated those calls. The second category was to tell me about some sort of an accident that she had had. Those included falls, or bruises because she was bumped into a wall when she was being wheeled somewhere, or skin tears, which usually happened while she was being dressed or bathed or put into bed. Calafort calls seldom put a smile on my face.

Chapter 19

'Tis the Season

W e were once again into December and the staff at Calafort, as well as the small staff who worked at Delia's apartment building, went all out in decorating for Christmas. They wanted their respective residents to be happy during the holidays and to feel the good tidings of the season. As a means to that end, they put up beautiful Christmas trees, and they decked their halls with boughs of holly. They even had a few well-placed menorahs. The merry atmosphere was bittersweet for me, however, because I knew that for a handful of the Calafort residents, this would be their last Christmas.

There were as many lights and decorations on the outside of Calafort, as there were on the inside. I sincerely appreciated the efforts of the person or persons from the maintenance department who must have spent hours on a ladder decorating the exterior. They outlined the building with colorful Christmas lights; they put a giant Santa, along with his reindeer and sleigh, on the roof; and then they carefully placed a huge wreath at the entrance to the facility.

This was my mother's third Christmas in long term care. I knew how much she had always enjoyed the Christmas season, and I was thankful that she'd once again get to experience some holiday traditions that we sometimes take for granted. I took her on several walks at night when the Christmas lights were turned on and the building looked particularly festive. The weather was nippy so each time we went outside I put a warm scarf on her head and a blanket over her clothes. I didn't share my thoughts with her, but I thought that she looked like she was going on an Iditarod in Alaska rather than a wheelchair walk in Florida.

I think that these holiday walks were good for both of us. One night in particular stands out in my mind. I remember that while I was pushing her wheelchair, she was pointing out Santa on the roof. That's when an old photograph popped into my mind. It was a picture of my mother with a big smile on her face pushing me in my baby carriage, and I was pointing at something. That image really hit home "the circle of life."

Since my mother never learned to drive, as a child I did a lot of walking with her. In my mind's eye I pictured me as a little girl with her holding my hand to keep me safe, as we walked along roads without sidewalks. I also pictured her carrying me on her back when I got too tired to walk. But the walk of all walks with my mother and me was our walk on Christmas night, just four years earlier, when we walked hand in hand up my street. That walk taught me the true meaning of carpe diem (seize the day) and that we don't know where we'll be next year at this time.

****

Thank God that Delia was doing great and was enjoying the Christmas season in her own apartment. She sent Christmas cards to her family and to her many friends, and she even did a little Christmas decorating. She put a tabletop Christmas tree on her coffee table and placed big holiday snow globes around her apartment. She also hung a festive wreath on the outside of her door and taped the many Christmas cards that she received to the inside of it. When she and I went for walks in her apartment building's hallways, she wanted to take the elevator to a different floor each time, so that she could see how her neighbors had decorated their doors.

The residents of her six story apartment building had a holiday tradition that she and I had always enjoyed. At the beginning of December, the management gave each of the residents electric candles to place on their window sills. Each evening through New Year's Day, when night fell, the candles were supposed to be turned on. It was common practice that if you weren't going to be at home, that you asked a friend to turn on your candles for you. It was a pretty sight to see this large six story building with candles lit in all of the windows. That subtle tradition signaled the start of the holiday season in Delia's neighborhood.

Calafort also had a nice tradition that I appreciated. A few weeks before Christmas, they hosted a dinner party in the big dining room for the residents and the families of the residents. I was impressed to see how pretty the room was decorated when Kathleen and I arrived. I was also happy to see that my mother, as well as the other residents, were dressed much nicer than usual. So were Kathleen and I.

"Kathleen, ye look gorgeous tonight, Baby," Mom said as soon as she saw her granddaughter. Because of the therapy that she'd been getting, she was able to raise her arms up high enough to give Kathleen a hug, and the two of them embraced.

"Thanks, Grandma. You look pretty, too," Kathleen said with a smile.

The staff had prepared a Christmas feast for the residents and their families. I have to say that they really made it a special night for everyone, and it was heartwarming to see the residents interacting with their families.

We had our own table with a white linen tablecloth, napkins, and a festive centerpiece. Kathleen and I enjoyed a traditional Christmas dinner with all the trimmings. Mom had the same meal, just in a pureed form. Christmas music played throughout the evening and at times we were encouraged to sing along. I loved seeing most of the residents singing along to the familiar music. There were even a few residents that I had seldom seen speak before, singing along to Jingle Bells.

I tried to take a mental snapshot of as much of this special night as possible. It was special because I was able to see the love between my mother and my daughter. I could hear how they spoke to each other, as only a grandmother and a grandchild speak. I could see their smiles to each other. I tried to soak in and savor as much of this interaction as possible because there was a part of me that knew that we wouldn't have many more of them.

On our drive home that evening Kathleen and I were both deep in our own thoughts. I'm not sure what she was thinking about but I was thinking about a Christmas present for my mother. Even though she was 92 years old and even though she had dementia, I knew that she still liked looking nice. It only took me a few minutes before I decided that a good present for her would be pretty sweaters and slacks. I knew that she would like getting new outfits, and I was already anticipating what she would say when she opened her presents on Christmas morning.

She'd look at each of us and then she'd say, "I love the clothes, but ye shouldn't have gotten me anything." Then she'd pause for a moment, and then smile and say, "But I'm glad that ye did."

I wasn't being clairvoyant; it was just something that she had said the last few years that she lived at home. I hoped that I'd get to hear her say it again.

****

Long after this happy evening was over and I was snuggled into my warm bed on this cold December night, the house phone rang and woke me. It was 1:00 a.m.

"Hello?" I said.

Nobody was talking on the other end of the phone but I could hear a stern voice saying the rosary.

"Hello. Hello," I said again, this time louder. "Delia, can you hear me? Are you okay?"

"What's up?" Dave asked, now sitting up in bed.

"Delia, can you hear me?" I asked again.

All I could hear was a recording of the rosary that she often listened to after she turned the TV off for the night.

"Dave, she must have pushed the button for the medic alarm, but she's not answering me. I need to go down there and see what's going on," I said as I got out of bed and headed to the bathroom to change my clothes.

I heard him say that he was coming, too, but I told him that I didn't know how long I would be there and to please stay home and get the kids ready for school in the morning. I told him that I'd call and let him know what was going on.

A few minutes later I was in my car heading to Delia's apartment. I had already made this apprehensive drive way too many times in the past when I was concerned that there was something wrong with my mother or with Delia. Each of those times I was scared of what I was going to find when I walked through their door.

There was virtually no traffic that time of the night so it didn't take long to get to her apartment building. It goes without saying that I was nervous as I parked my car and walked to the front door of the building. The door was locked, so I had to ring the doorbell and wait for a man working in the office to let me in. I explained why I was there and he told me to let him know if he could do anything to help.

When I got to Delia's apartment, unlocked the door and went inside, I had a déjà vu of just a few months earlier when I found her on the floor. Once again she was on the floor, only this time she was lucid and was able to talk to me. I knelt on the floor next to her.

"I'm okay, Sally. I just can't get up. I'm so sorry that I had to wake ye up in the middle of the night. Did I wake up David?" she asked.

"Delia, don't worry about us. We're both fine. Dave wanted to come with me but I told him to stay home with the kids and that I would let him know if we needed him. Do you want to try to get up with my help?" I asked.

"I don't think that you're strong enough to get me up. I don't want ye to hurt your back. Who's working in the office?" she asked.

"Some man. I don't know his name. Delia, where do you hurt?" I asked.

She looked tired. She looked discouraged that she was once again on the floor and wasn't able to get up. She looked like a fish out of water.

"I don't hurt now. I'll feel it tomorrow. Yea, I'll be feeling it for the next week," she said.

"Dee Dee, I'm going to the lobby and ask the man at the desk to help us. You're probably right about me trying to do it by myself; I don't want either of us to get hurt," I said.

When I went back downstairs I explained to this nameless man who worked the midnight shift what had happened. He asked if Delia needed an ambulance and I told him that she seemed to be okay but that I needed his help to get her up off the floor. I told him that I would drive her to the hospital if she or I thought that she needed to go.

He immediately got into the elevator with me and walked quickly to her apartment. He got her up all by himself and stayed for a few minutes just to make sure that she was okay. After he left, she slowly drank a glass of water, and then walked to the bathroom. I walked next to her to give her confidence.

We talked for a while longer and she told me that she had turned too quickly and that's why she fell. I told her that she needed to be more careful about trying to do anything quickly. We both agreed that having the medic alert button may have saved her life.

"How do you feel?" I asked.

"I'm okay. Thank ye for helping me, Sally. I'm sorry to be such a pain in your backside. I ruined your good night's sleep," she said.

"Don't worry about it. I know that you'd do the same for me," I said, and then I gave her a hug.

"You're full of macaroni. Now go on home and get some sleep before ye have to get up in the morning. Maybe ye can stay home tomorrow," she said.

"There's no staying home tomorrow for me, but…" I hesitated for a moment. "Dee Dee, I know that you're not going to like what I'm going to say to you but I've been thinking about it since you got up off the floor. I know that you said that you feel okay, but please just humor me and let me take you to the hospital and be checked out. There's no way that I'll be able to sleep well, whether it's tonight or even tomorrow night, until I know that you're okay. I'll drive you there and if we're lucky, you'll be back home in a few hours. Will you do that for me?" I asked.

"Ye don't think it would be silly to take me?" she asked.

I was a little surprised that she didn't give me a decisive "No" and say that she wasn't going.

"I think that it would be silly if you didn't go, especially after all you've been through. You've worked so hard to get back here. Let's keep working to keep you here in your own home." That was all it took to convince her to go to the hospital.

"Okay, I guess I better change my clothes. What should I put on?" she asked.

"It doesn't matter as long as it's warm. It's really cold outside," I answered. I was relieved that it was so easy to convince her to be checked out.

Thankfully, it didn't take long at the hospital before she was taken into the emergency room and examined. Several tests were ordered including blood work, a chest x-ray, an EKG, and a CT of her brain/head. Even though we were lucky enough to get into the ER quickly, I had a feeling that we were going to be there for quite a while. That concerned me because I had an important meeting that I had to attend at 10:30.

I knew that she and I both would have preferred that I stayed with her until she could leave, but I felt like she was stable and would do okay if I wasn't there. I found her nurse and asked what she thought. She didn't make me feel guilty in the least and said that she thought that it would be okay if I left. She made sure that she had my cell phone number. Next I needed to tell Delia that I wasn't going to stay.

"Dee Dee, I know that it was my idea that you came to the hospital, but there are still a handful of tests that they want to do. It's gonna be a while before they'll be discharging you. Would you mind if I left you here, and then went to work this morning? I'll come back just as soon as my morning meeting is over, and then I'll bring you home."

She wasn't jumping for joy but said, "Ye know I'll be alright. Can ye get a little sleep before ye go in to the job?"

"Nah, I'll be fine without going back to bed. I'll catch up on the beauty sleep tonight," I joked. "The nurse has my number and she'll let me know what's going on. You'll be back in your own bed tonight."

I gave her a hug and told her to behave and that I'd see her later.

It was nearly 6:30 before I got back to my house. I had just enough time to take a shower and to get ready for work. My life had truly become a balancing act with Dave, Michael, Kathleen, Mom, Delia, and work. I didn't seem to be able to fit myself into the equation.

That was okay, though, because I knew that this topsy-turvy time in my life wouldn't go on forever. There would come a time when those hectic days and nights would all be behind me. At 92 and almost 95, Mom and Delia were at the end of their worldly journey and I knew that the day wasn't far off when they'd no longer be a part of the equation either.

One of my co-workers once said to me, "Your mother and aunt have lived long lives. Why are you spending all the time with them that you spend? That's not fair to you and to your family, is it?"

I was surprised that a friend could ask me that sort of a question, but then I realized that a lot of people must have that same philosophy. That was probably the reason why only a handful of residents in Mom's nursing home or in Delia's rehab had family that visited them as often as I visited my mother and my aunt.

I meant it sincerely when I told my friend, "I do it because I love them with my heart and my soul. I do it because

I know that they would do the same for me, probably even more."

I went to work and stayed until my meeting was over. I had been awake since 1:00 a.m. and I was really tired so I requested to take the afternoon off as vacation time.

By the time I got to the hospital, Delia's tests were all over. Everything seemed fine except that her blood work showed that her sodium level was too low, which was a diagnosis that she had had before, and which she would continue to have in the future. For now, the simple fix for that problem was for her to use more salt on her food. Throughout her life she seldom used salt on her food, so using any salt at all would be an improvement.

After I arrived at the hospital it didn't take long for her nurse to complete the discharge papers. By the time I finally got her back to her apartment, I'm not sure if we were more hungry or more tired. I fixed us each a sandwich and a cup of soup. After we were done eating, I walked with her to the bathroom for the second time since she had arrived back home.

Then I announced, "Dee Dee, I'm sure that you must be more tired than I am, and I know that I'm about to drop. Do you mind if I take a nap on your couch?"

"Ye know that ye don't have to ask such a question. Stretch out on the couch for a while. Ye know where the pillow and blanket are in the closet," she said, and then added, "I think that maybe I'll try to get a few winks, too. There was too much commotion going on at the hospital to get any sleep."

Great, my plan worked, I thought.

I really was exhausted and a nap would be nice, but my ultimate goal was for her to get some sleep, and for me to keep an eye on her throughout the afternoon.

She stayed in bed most of the next few hours, although she got up a few times to go to the bathroom. After she got up for good, I heard her talking on the phone to a friend. I also heard her opening and closing the refrigerator a few times, as well as I heard the kettle whistling, probably for a hot cup of tea. If I didn't know better, I wouldn't have thought that I was in the apartment of a 94-year-old. When I would open my eyes to watch her walk, she seemed steady on her feet. Still, I didn't feel comfortable with her staying by herself through the night, not after what happened the night before. Later in the afternoon I told her that I was going to spend the night with her.

As I mentioned to you before, Delia was incredibly strong-willed and independent and never wanted to put anyone out of their way in order to help her. She really didn't want me to stay the night with her.

I, too, am strong-willed, and while she put up some argument about me spending the night, in the end I won. I think we were both tired, and it was easier just to humor me by letting me stay with her, than for her to stand her ground.

My evening was a bit fragmented. First I fixed her supper and did the dishes. Then I went home and fixed and ate supper with Dave and the kids. The dishes were their problem that night. I spent a few hours at my house and then I drove back to Delia's apartment.

She and I chitchatted for a while, and I told her all about the Christmas dinner the night before at Calafort. I knew that it made her feel good to hear how well Mom was doing. It would have been great to stay up late and talk some more, but the previous 24 hours showed in both of our faces. We were equally beat and so we called it a night fairly early. I stayed up until I knew that she had gotten into her bed and then I went in to her bedroom to say goodnight.

I looked at the large foam wedge in her bed that enabled her to sleep in a position that was halfway between a horizontal and a sitting position.

"Delia, that looks so awkward. Are you at all comfortable?" I asked.

"It helps me to breathe. If I lie flat on my back, I think that I would smother during the night. Thank God they make this contraption. When I think of the people in the old country, I wonder how did they live without having the things that we have today," she said.

"I don't know, Dee Dee. We've come a long way, haven't we?" I added.

We talked for a few more minutes and then we said goodnight. I made myself comfortable on her couch. My plan was to wake up early, fix her something in the morning to eat, and then go back to my house to shower and to go to work.

She must have gotten up four or five times during the night to use the bathroom. The first time I heard her get out of bed, I rushed to her bedroom to help her to the bathroom. I was afraid that she would fall again. She insisted that I didn't get up anymore with her during the night. Once again she reminded me that if I did too much for her, that she wouldn't be able to do anything for herself.

In the morning as I watched her start her day, without her noticing that I was watching, I could see that that was probably the toughest part of her day. Her breathing was labored and she moved exceptionally slow as she walked from her bedroom to her dining room. That is where she took her "puffer" (her inhaler) and used her "breather" (her nebulizer). After taking her medicine, it was obvious that she was able to breathe more easily.

I knew that she was going to have a home health care worker with her in the morning so I didn't feel too concerned when I told her that I needed to leave. She thanked me for all the help since yesterday and asked, "Will I see ye this weekend?"

I was about to go out her front door when I answered, "Dee Dee, I'm sorry to give you this news, but I plan on staying with you again tonight, and maybe even tomorrow night."

I gave her a quick hug, and said, "See ya later, Gator," and then I closed the door behind me before she had a chance to argue with me about my plans.

I did spend that night, as well as the next one with her. When it was all said and done, I think that spending those three nights with her gave us both the confidence to know that she would be okay. While I was a little nervous to leave her on her own, she seemed to be as ready as she would ever be to stay by herself throughout the night.

During the next few weeks things were pretty quiet with Mom and Delia. On Christmas day we visited each of them in their humble abodes, and gave them their presents. They both were really happy to see all four of us together, because it was highly unusual when we all visited at the same time. We tried to get Delia to come back to our house to spend the rest of Christmas with us, but she was coming down with a cold and wanted to stay home.

Christmas evening Dave said to me, "Honey, Joe just called and asked if we wanted to go camping with them later in the week. Your mom was so sick in July when we were in D.C. that I know that it wasn't much of a vacation for you. It's only for four days and we'll be less than an hour away if anything were to happen with them. I think it's something that all of us would enjoy. We'll be back home on the 31st. What do you think?" he asked.

I thought about it for just a few seconds and then said, "Other than Delia having a little head cold, this probably would be a good time to have a mini vacation. I am so ready to go away for a little while, and this may be the calm before the next storm. I'm on vacation from work until after the first of the year. Let's do it."

"Great! I'll let Joe know," he said.

Chapter 20

My Cheerleader

As you may have predicted, Delia's cold got worse. When I talked to her on the phone the morning that we were supposed to go away, it sounded like it may have moved into her chest. I knew that wasn't a good sign for someone her age.

I told Dave that I was going to go to her apartment and see in person how she was. I told him that I might need to take her to the doctor. I told him that if that happened that he and the kids could go by themselves and that I'd meet them at the campground later in the day. That's what my plans were. Delia wasn't going along with my plans, however. She was determined that she wasn't going to ruin our getaway.

"Sally, I want ye to go camping with your family and your friends. I'm just fine here without ye. There're a lot of other people that I can call if I get sick enough. I have your number, too, and I promise I'll call ye, if I need to," she said.

I didn't know what to say so I just sat quietly.

"Honey, it would make me very sad if I thought that I kept ye from these few days with Dave and the kids. Don't worry about me," she said through a few coughs. "Ye can bring me the cough syrup that's in the kitchen and then go on home before they leave without ye."

"Dee Dee, are you sure you'll call me if you feel any worse?" I asked.

"I promise. Now stop worrying. You're as bad as your mother worrying about everyone," she said.

"All right, I won't nag you anymore today; but if you're not better when I get back then I'm going to take you to your doctor," I said.

She didn't argue with me and agreed with what I wanted. Then she walked me out to the hallway to say goodbye, and safe journey.

As I was getting ready to leave I told her that I was going to go over to see Mom for a few minutes before we headed out. I think that she was happy to hear that I'd be checking on her, since there was nobody else for my mother.

****

On my drive from Delia's apartment to the nursing home, I had an uneasy feeling leaving her the way she sounded. The rational side of me knew that there would always be something brewing with either Delia or my mother and that I still needed to live my life. Thank God that Dave and the kids were healthy. Oh yea, me too. Knock on wood, I seldom got sick.

When I got to Calafort, I was happy to see my mother sitting out by the nurses' station. She was wearing one of the new sweaters that I had bought for her Christmas present. I just stood there for a minute and watched her as she talked to the lady in the chair next to her. That lady was totally oblivious to whatever my mother was saying.

As I stood there watching, I wondered what her life would have been like if she had aborted me like her doctor suggested. I wondered what her life would have been like if she didn't have a child to raise. I also thought about how much happiness Michael and Kathleen had brought to her, late in her life.

I walked over to her and her eyes lit up when she saw me. I bent over and gave her a hug.

"What are ye doing here now? Is everyone okay?" she asked.

"Everything and everybody is great. I just wanted to let you know that Dave and I and the kids are going camping for a few days. The campground is less than an hour away, so I won't be far away from you. Ma, before we left I wanted to stop by and see you, and tell you how much I love you and how happy I am that you're my mother," I said.

I was feeling extremely emotional as I said those words to her and for some reason I had to hold back my tears. My goodness, I was getting to go away for a few days. I should've been jumping for joy, but I wasn't. I felt so bad for my mother sitting there in front of me in a wheelchair, in a nursing home. For years I prayed that would never happen, but I had learned that sometimes we don't get what we pray for.

Before I got any more emotional I told her that we were going to go look at the Christmas decorations again. I knew that in less than a week, they'd all be neatly boxed away for another year and to paraphrase my mother, "Only God knew where we'd be next year at this time."

I wheeled her all around the inside of the building and then we sat for a few minutes near a Christmas tree by the front entrance. We chitchatted about unimportant things but she looked like she had something on her mind.

"Mom, is there something that you want to tell me?" I asked.

She took my hand and caressed it. Then she looked deep into my eyes and said, "Don't forget to pray for me."

"Mom, I pray for you every day," I said.

"I know that ye do, Baby. I don't know what made me say that," she said.

At that moment I would have been just fine foregoing the camping trip and spending the entire day with my mother, but I knew that I couldn't do that. I needed to be with my husband and my kids.

"Mom, I'd love to stay longer today, but I know that the kids want to get going. Do you want to go back to your room and watch TV?" I asked.

"Whatever ye want to do is fine, Doll." When I was younger she used to call me Doll all the time. I hadn't heard her call me that in a long time.

I brought her back into her room and we hugged and said goodbye. I told her that I would see her in just a few days.

"Safe journey, Baby," she answered.

As I walked down the hallway I heard her calling my name, "Sally, I'll love ye forever. Do ye hear me? I'll love ye forever. Forever."

I stopped walking for a moment and tried to decide whether to go back and give her another hug. I decided instead to stop at the nurses' station to let Sandi know that I wouldn't be there for a few days and to call me if anything came up.

"Have a great time. You need to get away," she said. As an afterthought, she added, "I heard what she just said to you. That was beautiful."

"I love her so much. Please take good care of her," I said.

I knew that I had spent more time with Delia and my mother than what I had planned and I knew that my family was probably chomping at the bit to get out to the campground. I was right. By the time that I pulled into our driveway, Dave's car was packed with everything that we would need. The only thing missing was me. Minutes after I got home, I was in Dave's car and we were on our way.

****

The next few days should have been a time to relax with my family and friends. I tried my best not to think about Mom and Delia but I couldn't get them out of my mind. Even though we were doing fun things, and I totally enjoyed watching my family having a good time, my thoughts kept wandering back to my mother and aunt.

I didn't call Calafort to see how my mother was doing because I knew that they'd tell me that she was fine, unless, of course, she was declining rapidly. I was tempted to call Delia, however. I wanted to hear her voice to see if she sounded better than when I left her. I knew that if she sounded better, that I would stop worrying, and be able to enjoy my few days away. That's all that I wanted—to be carefree for just a few days.

I reminded myself that she said that she'd call me if she wasn't doing well, but knowing Delia as well as I knew Delia, she'd have to be on the brink of death before she'd "bother" me. When I couldn't resist any longer, I foolishly gave in and I called her. Much to my disappointment, she sounded worse than she did just the day before.

I told her that as soon as she and I hung up that I was going to call her doctor and make an appointment for New

Year's Eve, in the afternoon. She didn't try to talk me out of it. Before our short phone call ended, she promised me that she would call me, if she felt worse. For some reason, I believed her this time.

Our little vacation was only for four days, but it did me a world of good to get away. I was re-charged and ready to get back to helping my mother and aunt. An hour after we pulled into our driveway, I had already picked up Delia and was sitting with her at her doctor's appointment. The doctor examined her and said that she definitely had bronchitis and gave her a prescription for an antibiotic. He also wanted to rule out pneumonia so he told us that she needed to have an x-ray. He asked his nurse to call and make an appointment to ensure that she would be seen that afternoon, and that she wouldn't have a long wait.

I was happy for the appointment, but in spite of it, she sat in the waiting room for more than an hour before she was seen. It was packed with other people also needing x-rays before the office closed for the New Year's holiday. While Delia waited patiently for her name to be called and for x-rays to be taken, I left her long enough to get her antibiotic prescription filled, and to buy another bottle of cough syrup. By the time I returned, her x-rays had been taken and she was ready to leave.

Not too long after we were back in her apartment, her doctor called to say that she didn't have pneumonia. I thanked him for letting us know the results so quickly. If Delia hadn't been 94 years old, I wouldn't have worried so much about something that started out as just a little cold, but at her age I knew that pneumonia could easily be the end of her.

Even though she didn't feel well, after spending the afternoon with her, I felt comfortable leaving her alone in her apartment. I fixed her a light supper, and I told her that I'd see her tomorrow. I told her that the New Year was going to be a better one for her, and that I wished her good health and much happiness.

"You're the best aunt in the world, Dee Dee, and I love you most," I said as I hugged her goodbye and said, "Happy New Year!"

"Happy New Year to ye, too, Sally. I won't be such a bother to ye next year. Tell Dave and Michael and Kathleen that I love them all," she said.

"I'll tell them, and I want you to know that you're never a bother to me. You're my role model," I said.

"Ye are full of macaroni, now go on home with ye," and then added, "I love ye, too. Be careful driving. The drunks will be out on the road."

When we had left the campground earlier in the day, my plan was to take Delia to the doctor and then to go visit my mother. Since Delia had to have x-rays, I spent more time with her than I thought I'd be spending. By the time that I was leaving her apartment and thought about driving to Calafort, I changed my mind. I decided that I would wait until the morning to see my mother and give her a huge Happy New Year hug.

Dave and I had no plans to go out to celebrate on New Year's Eve which was fine with me. I was totally content just staying home with my family. Dave made a great dinner for us, and then we spent the rest of the evening relaxing and watching a few DVDs.

Every now and then my mind would wander to my mother and Delia and I wondered what they were doing. I also thought about past New Year's when Mom, Delia, and Dave's Dad would often spend the evening with us. My dad passed away while we were still newlyweds.

As midnight approached we turned the TV on and watched the big Waterford Crystal ball slowly fall in Times

Square. I thought about the hope and new beginnings that a New Year brings to us all. I also wondered if my mother even knew that it was New Year's Eve. Probably not. I thought about what she said to me earlier in the week when I left her room, "I'll love ye forever." That thought of my mother made me smile.

"Ten, nine, eight, seven," Dave and the kids were counting down the seconds left before the New Year greeted us.

I joined in, "Three, two, one. Happy New Year!" We all hugged each other and wished each other a Happy New Year. Dave and I toasted each other. The kids did their part and made lots of noise as we welcomed the New Year. Fire crackers went off in the neighborhood and fireworks lit up the sky, and the phone rang a handful of times as friends and relatives called to wish us a Happy New Year. A fresh start, a new beginning. It felt good.

The kids each went back to their rooms to call and text their friends. Dave and I went outside with our arms around the other's waist as we continued to watch the fireworks decorate the dark sky. While we were outside we heard the phone ring again and we quickly went inside to see who was calling to wish us a Happy New Year.

Dave answered the phone, not with a "hello" but with a "Happy New Year." His smile immediately disappeared as he handed me the phone. He didn't budge, however, from where he stood.

"Sally, it's Sandi from Calafort. I'm sorry to be calling now, but your mother isn't doing well. You need to get over here right away," she said, with a tone that I hadn't heard from her before. It was even more somber than her "your mother is declining rapidly" calls that she had made to me over the last two and a half years. I didn't ask any questions and quickly said, "Okay" as I hung up the phone.

"We have to go to the nursing home right now and I don't have a good feeling about it. I need you to come with me," I said.

I was hoping that everything would be okay when we got there, but I had an ominous feeling that something was terribly wrong. Kathleen had already fallen asleep. We told Michael that we needed to go see Grandma and that we'd be back soon.

Thankfully there wasn't much traffic. I guessed that most of the revelers were still inside partying. That being said, the 10-minute drive to the nursing home seemed to take forever. I silently prayed that whatever the problem was, that she would rally one more time.

"I'm scared, Dave," I said as we pulled into a parking space at Calafort. I quickly opened the car door and ran to the front entrance.

Sandi was standing right inside the door. That was a first, and I knew that something terrible had happened.

She said to me, "I'm sorry, Sally. Your mom is gone."

"No. No," I cried as I ran as fast as I could to her room.

There she lay, forever silent, forever still. I sat on the bed next to her and held her warm hand. I cried quietly as the tears ran down my cheeks. I felt Dave's hands on my shoulders and I heard him say, "I'm sorry, Honey. She really is in a better place. Your mother wouldn't have wanted to live like this. And she wouldn't have wanted to put you through what you've been through the last few years."

I knew that he was right, but it didn't make it one bit easier to say goodbye to her. He stayed with me in the room for a while longer. He then bent over and touched her cheek with his hand and told her that he loved her. Then he left me alone with her. I needed that time with her.

I looked at the details on her hands, all the features on her face, her hair, even the bunions on her feet. I wanted to remember the minutia of my mom. I wanted to hear her voice, her lovely Irish brogue, but that was not to be.

I thought of the different phases of our relationship. She was Mommy, Mom, Mother, and then Ma. She was always my number one cheerleader. She loved me and her grandchildren more than life itself. And now she was gone. And then I remembered what she said earlier in the week, "I'll love ye forever."

Those words will always be with me. I believe that her love will never die. How could it?

I didn't want to leave her but I knew that it was time to say goodbye. I was still sitting on her bed as I kissed her forehead one last time and told her that she was the best mother in the world, and that I loved her most. I stood up slowly and took a few steps towards the door. Before I left her room, I turned around and told her, "God knew what He was doing when He gave you to me. Safe home, Mom."

Dave was waiting for me down the hall. He walked over to me and held me close, as I cried some more. We slowly walked down the hallway and out the front doors of Calafort for the last time. I thought it was ironic that the facility was so happily decorated on a night that was so sad for me.

When we got home, Michael was still awake and worried about his grandma. We told him the unhappy news. He was in high school and I hadn't seen him cry in a long time; the look of sorrow on his face broke my heart. He wanted to wake Kathleen and tell her, but we convinced him that it was best to let her sleep through the night and that we would tell her in the morning.

Kathleen wasn't the only person that I needed to tell in the morning. Along with Mom's friends, close relatives in the U.S. and in Ireland, I also had to tell Delia. I dreaded having to tell her. She and my mother were as different as night and day, but they were extremely close.

This wasn't the first time that I had to break the news of a sibling's death to Delia. When her brother, Coleman, died in New York, I told her. When her brother, Pat, and her sister, Kate, died in Ireland, I told her. None of those deaths caused her to cry, at least not in front of me. Instead she stoically comforted me.

Breaking the news this time was going to be tougher than those other times that I brought bad news. As close as Delia was to her brothers and other sisters, the bond between her and my mother was the strongest. Delia was my mother's maid of honor, and my mother chose Delia to be the god-mother of her only baby.

When I knocked on her door the next morning and then let myself into her apartment, I found her drinking a cup of tea and eating a bowl of oatmeal.

"Happy New Year to ye. Ye must have stayed up all night celebrating. Ye look warn out," she said.

"I'm just a little sleepy. I was up pretty late last night," I answered. "Delia, that antibiotic must be potent stuff be-cause you look and sound better than you did yesterday. How do you feel?"

"I feel a little bit better. Ye can't kill a bad thing; ye know that," she joked.

I was trying to be strong and not to cry, but it was tough to hold back the tears. I was trying to find the right words to tell her that Mom was gone.

"Sally, what's the trouble with ye? Are the children and David okay? It's your mother, isn't it? Is she dead?" she asked.

Oh my God. Did she have to be so blunt?

"I'm sorry, Dee Dee, she died right after the New Year. They called me right after midnight. Delia, I wanted to be with her. I always wanted to be with her when she died. I didn't want her to die alone. I wasn't with her. How could I not have been with her?" I asked as I cried my heart out in front of my 94-year-old aunt.

I knew that she was upset because her eyebrows were going up and down. I seldom saw her do that, only when she was really upset about something. However, her eyes were dry, not a tear was shed. As she had done many times in the past, she comforted me; first, with a long loving hug, and then with her words of wisdom.

"Your mother loved ye and the children more than anything else in the world. Maybe she couldn't bear for ye to see her die. That was no place for your mother. She was never happy there. She was lonely for her home. She was lonely to have people around her that she knew well. I feel very, very bad that I didn't go over there to see her. I should have done that," she said.

I had already come to the conclusion that no matter how much we do for a person, the moment that they die, we regret the things we didn't say or do—all the would haves, should haves, could haves. But then it's too late.

"Delia, you did the most important thing that you were able to do. You prayed for her every day. I was seeing her all the time, so honestly you have no reason to feel bad that you weren't able to get over there. You asked about her every day, and she asked about you. And remember she had a roommate for a while that she thought was you. See, it was almost like you did visit her. Dee Dee, please don't ever feel bad about not going over there much," I said as I tried to find the words to make her feel better.

I stayed with her for a while longer, but I still had a lot of phone calls to make, and a funeral to plan. I told her that I would come back later to check on her, and thankfully she didn't tell me not to come.

When I got home I finished making phone calls to tell everyone. Without exception each person I spoke with made me feel a bit better, as they not only shared my grief, but talked about their memories of how my mother touched their lives.

The next few days were busy which was good because it didn't give me much time to dwell on my sadness. I was glad that the unpleasant task of picking out a casket had already been done when I was getting her Medicaid ready.

The entire family helped to plan the funeral. Kathleen went with me to Mom's house and she picked out the dress that her grandmother would be buried in. Michael went to the church with me and helped to pick out the readings for the funeral Mass. He, Kathleen, and Dave would all do a reading. I knew that I wouldn't be able to get through a reading without breaking down. Both of the kids wrote letters to their grandma that were placed in her casket.

Two of my cousins, Bobbie and Maureen, who were close to my mother, came all the way from New York. They helped me tremendously in an unexpected way. They spent a lot of time with Delia and made her feel special during this sad time for her.

The night before the funeral was the viewing. It lessened my sadness to see that many people came. My close friend Amy's Mom and Dad were there. Normally that wouldn't be a big deal, but it touched my heart when I saw them walk into the room. Charlie had been diagnosed with cancer a year earlier and was very sick. Coming to the viewing was a brave thing for him to do because his immune system was virtually non-existent because of his chemo treatment. However, he put on a facemask and told Katie that if she wouldn't drive him to the viewing that he would call a taxi. It's kindness like Charlie's that let you know just how much you're loved. A few months later, we attended Charlie's funeral.

I thought it was a little odd to call this a viewing since the casket remained closed during most of the evening. It wasn't until the last of the guests had left that the casket was opened for the family to see Mom for the very last time. Only my cousins and I decided to go back into the room where she was, but after a little while, they left me alone with her.

As I stood over her body, I told her that I loved her and that I was going to miss her. That's when I felt Dave's hands on my shoulders giving me the strength to say one last good-bye. After a few minutes of knowing that he was there with me, I turned around to give him a hug. That's when I saw that it wasn't Dave. It was Michael.

I hugged him tightly and through tears said, "Thank you, Michael. You know Grandma loved you very, very much. You and Kathleen were her world."

"I know, Mom," he said, with tears in his eyes.

****

The next day was the day that I had dreaded for many years.

I don't know if there is such a thing as a lovely funeral, but if there is such a thing, this was it. I know that my mother would have been "tickled pink" to be the object of so much attention from so many people.

Some of the songs that were sung were Irish songs. My dear friend, Bob, sang Danny Boy so beautifully that I had chills. Father Henry's sermon during the funeral Mass was all the more meaningful because he was from Ireland.

Kathleen, at only 10 years old, did a great job when she read Ecclesiastes 3:1 which talks about there being a time for every purpose under Heaven, including there being a time to be born and a time to die.

When it was Michael's turn to do a reading, he leaned over to me and tearfully said, "Mom, I can't do it. I'm sorry, I can't."

I turned to Dave sitting on the other side of me and said, "Dave, Michael is too upset, you'll need to do his reading, too."

If I could have done it for him, I would have, but I knew that I, too, would have broken down.

Then I turned back to Michael and said, "That's okay, Honey. Don't feel bad." I put my arm around him and pulled him close as Dave went to the front of the church and read the Second Reading.

I don't remember too much more about the actual funeral, although I do remember some of my friends telling me afterwards that it was a beautiful ceremony.

After the funeral and the burial were behind us, Dave, the kids, Delia, my cousins, and I went back home, along with a handful of our closest friends. I remember that my friends had brought a lot of food that was already on the kitchen counter by the time we got to the house. It was emotionally uplifting for me to spend the day with the people that I was closest to and to hear their different remembrances of my mother.

As we all sat in the family room together, three of my best friends told Delia that their mothers had passed away and asked if she would be their "adopted" mother. Of course she said, "Yes."

Michael mournfully told her that he was sad that he didn't have a grandma anymore and asked if she could take over. Michael was close to his grandmother so it meant a lot to Delia for him to say that to her. Once again, of course she said, "Yes."

We all spent the rest of the day reminiscing, laughing, crying, and eating, but as the sun began to set, I was happy to see the end of that sorrowful day.

When everyone but Delia had gone home, she said to me over a cup of tea, "Sally, ye did a beautiful job with the funeral. Your mother would have been very happy. The flowers were pretty, the priest's sermon couldn't have been one bit nicer, and there were a lot of people there to send her off. She would have been surprised that even your boss' boss was there. Before today I'd only seen him on the television. Plan it the same way when ye do mine," she added.

"Delia, please, I don't want to plan any more funerals for a very long time. You better stay healthy. Please stay healthy," I half way pleaded.

"How long do ye want to keep me around? Till I'm a hundred?" she asked, with her dry humor.

"Dee Dee, a hundred would be good. Let's plan on at least a hundred," I said as I gave her a hug.

Afterword

I hope that you enjoyed reading *I'll Love Ye Forever*. It was a difficult story for me to write, but it was a story that needed to be told. Across our country, at this very moment, thousands and thousands of people are experiencing the same angst that my mother and I felt during her nursing home years. The specific details of my story were unique to my mother and my family. The overall frustration that I felt with elder care, however, is being felt from coast to coast.

Few people aspire to live in a nursing home, nor do we look forward to the day that our parents or loved ones will need that type of care. It's a topic that is rarely discussed, until we have to discuss it. However, if our loved ones, or ourselves, for that matter, are lucky enough to live to a ripe old age, long term care may very well be in our future.

The struggle in America to find compassionate elder care has become epidemic as the baby boomer generation ages. My story is far more than a personal reflection. It is a call to advocacy for our senior citizens. Each of our seniors deserve to have a happy, healthy, and loving environment to spend their twilight years, no matter if they are rich, or they are poor. We must be vigilant in taking care of the people who once took care of us.

I hope that my story will be the spark that gets people talking about this "taboo" subject. I hope that my story will be a catalyst to improve "God's Waiting Rooms" around our country, because there may be a chair there waiting for someone that we love.

For those of you who may be wondering what happened to Delia after my mother passed away...

She continued to be a big part of my life until the day God called her home when she was nearly 102 years old. Her mind was still as sharp as a tack, and she never lost her great Irish wit. She always knew how to make me laugh, but there were times during her final year when she had reason to dry my tears.

After reading *I'll Love Ye Forever* you know a little bit about Delia's personality as an old lady, but you know little about her youth. I'd like to share with you a side of her that few people are aware. She was brave. It may be a little difficult visualizing someone over 100 years old as having been brave, but that was one of her many attributes. Let me share a few scenes from her life.

During Ireland's War of Independence from England, the notorious Black and Tans (former British soldiers) terrorized the Irish. Delia's village was sometimes the target of that terror, mostly because her uncle was an important IRA rebel. One day the "Tans" entered the village and started torching homes, including her uncle's home and the schoolmaster's home. Her parents and most of her siblings fled to a nearby mountain to escape the raid. Somehow Delia and her little brother were left behind. Delia made sure that she and Coleman stayed safe until her parents returned the following day. I'd say that was pretty brave.

She often told me that Ireland's Civil War, which followed the War of Independence, was even scarier. That was because you never knew whom you could trust. Your neighbor could be an informant, just as easily as the stranger passing through the village. It wasn't unusual that her uncle and his band of men would seek refuge for a night in Delia's home. Delia, along with her brothers and sisters, were warned by their parents, "Not to tell our business to anyone. I don't care who is asking ye." Since she was one of the oldest of her siblings, she had to be mindful of what the younger ones said when they were with her. These were indeed troubling times for Delia, but she remained brave even though she wasn't much more than a child herself.

I think one of the bravest things that she did in her youth was when she emigrated from Ireland. The day she hugged her parents, her brothers, and her sisters goodbye, she did not know when, or if, she'd ever see them again. Her father, along with a neighbor who owned one of the few cars in the village at the time, brought her to the train station. From there she took the train to Cobh, which was the Titanic's last port of call. She was only 17 years old that day when she boarded the ship all by herself. She carried a trunk of clothes on to the ship with her, but she had little English, as Gaelic was her native language. In my mind's eye, I can picture her on the deck of the ship watching the outline of her country getting smaller and smaller as the boat sailed away. I know that I could never have done such a brave thing all by myself when I was only 17 years old.

In the years to come Delia lived in Boston, and then Chicago, but eventually settled in New York City. Somehow, she always seemed to find interesting jobs. One of them was in the Museum of Modern Art in New York City. It was in the museum that a typical day at work ended with her standing outside a window on a ledge high above the ground, waiting to be rescued by firemen.

The cause of her precarious perch on a ledge outside the museum was a fire that had started in the second-floor gallery. In addition to the people who inched their way onto ledges, there were others who somehow ended up on the roof and waited for firemen to help them. She told me that a handful of people jumped from one rooftop to another in an attempt to expedite their escape. As thick smoke floated through the building, firemen broke out windows to help people get out. Tragically, one person died as a result of the fire, and dozens more were injured including several firemen.

I think that I would have panicked if I was in Delia's shoes (or on her ledge) that day. When I asked her what kept her calm she said that she prayed that God would help her. I think that throughout her life she often asked for God's help at the scariest of times when she needed to have courage.

Yes, my aunt was a brave lady in her younger years, but I think it was during the last few years of her life that she was the bravest. That's because she, too, ended up living in long term care. Her journey, however, was a totally different experience than the one that my mother had. I'm not saying that it was smooth sailing, but it was better in some ways.

One of the reasons that it was better for Delia was because her mind was sharp and she was able to tell me about issues that I probably would not have been aware of. Additionally, I had learned volumes from my mother's experience in Calafort that I was able to use to help Delia. Plus, I never stopped learning. It wasn't surprising that Delia also faced challenges in long term care, challenges that easily could have compromised (and sometimes did) her well-being. With each new issue, I worked hard to figure out the best way to overcome the problem, and I used that solution to help with future crises.

My ultimate goal was to keep her safe, and to make her life as easy and happy as it possibly could be at that time in her life. I worked hard to achieve that same goal with my father, my father-in-law, and of course, my mother. I learned much from each of their journeys, and the next person in line always reaped the benefits of my "education." This wasn't an education that I sought to have, but it's one that's now on my life's resume.

They say that experience is the best teacher, and for more than two decades I definitely was given a lot of experience taking care of my elders. From the bottom of my heart, I would like to share with you what I learned from my loved ones' journeys so that you, too, can help someone that you love.

I used a quote from Delia as the title of my next book...

I'D BE DEAD IF IT WEREN'T FOR YE

COMING SOON

By Sally K. Browne

Proof

Made in the USA
Columbia, SC
29 June 2018